WORKS ISSUED BY

The Hakluyt Society.

———×———

SELECT

LETTERS OF

CHRISTOPHER COLUMBUS,

ETC.

M.DCCC.XLVII.

I0225212

SELECT

LETTERS

OF

CHRISTOPHER COLUMBUS,

WITH OTHER ORIGINAL DOCUMENTS,

RELATING TO HIS

FOUR VOYAGES

TO

THE NEW WORLD.

TRANSLATED AND EDITED BY

R. H. MAJOR, Esq.

OF THE BRITISH MUSEUM.

" Tu spiegherai, Colombo, a un novo polo
Lontane sì le fortunate antenne,
Ch'a pena seguirà con gli occhi il volo
La Fama c'ha mille occhi e mille penne.
Canti ella Alcide e Bacco, e di te solo
Basti ai posteri tuoi ch'alquanto accenne ;
Chè quel poco darà lunga memoria
Di poema degnissima e d'istoria.
            Tasso.—Gerusalemme Liberata.

LONDON:

PRINTED FOR THE HAKLUYT SOCIETY.

M.DCCC.XLVII.

RICHARDS, 100, ST. MARTIN'S LANE.

THE HAKLUYT SOCIETY.

Council.

SIR RODERICK IMPEY MURCHISON, G.C.St.S , F.R.S.,.Corr. Mem. Inst. Fr.;
Hon. Mem. Imp. Acad. Sc. St. Petersburg, &c. &c., President.

Vice-Admiral SIR CHARLES MALCOLM, Kt. ⎫
The Rev. H. H. MILMAN, M.A.   ⎬ Vice Presidents.
                                    ⎭

CHARLES T. BEKE, ESQ., PHIL. D., F.S.A.
CAPTAIN C. R. DRINKWATER BETHUNE, R.N., C.B.
MAJOR-GENERAL J. BRIGGS, F.R.S.
CAPTAIN F. BULLOCK, R.N.
BOLTON CORNEY, ESQ. M.R.S.L.
CHARLES DARWIN, ESQ., F.R.S.
SIR HENRY ELLIS, K.H., F.R.S.
JOHN FORSTER, ESQ.
J. E. GRAY, ESQ., F.R.S.
W. R. HAMILTON, ESQ., F.R.S.
T. HODGKIN, ESQ., M.D.
SIR JAMES M'GRIGOR, BARONET, M.D., F.R.S.
R. H. MAJOR, ESQ.
R. MONCKTON MILNES, ESQ., M.P.
SIR J. RICHARDSON, M.D., F.R.S.
ANDREW SMITH, ESQ., M.D.
SIR GEORGE T. STAUNTON, BARONET, M P., F.R.S.

WILLIAM DESBOROUGH COOLEY, Esq., F.R.G.S., Secretary.

EDITOR'S PREFACE.

———

SHOULD the reader of the following highly interesting letters meet with some passages deficient in that ease of expression, or that connectedness of construction to which his ear and his taste are accustomed, he is requested to bear in mind that the originals are the compositions of men, who, though intelligent observers of the facts they describe, and strongly actuated by the feelings to which they give expression, were yet far from being accomplished masters of the use of the pen.

The Spanish scholar will readily perceive that the inaccuracies of the original, both in spelling and grammar, the frequent use of obsolete words, and the disjointed character of the sentences, must have rendered it a matter of no inconsiderable difficulty to avoid a certain harshness of style, in the endeavour to give a correct version of the author's meaning. In the execution of his task, however, the Editor has never hesitated to sacrifice ease to accuracy, where the two were incompatible with each other.

Since writing the following introduction to these letters, the Editor has seen those passages in *Kosmos* which refer to Columbus and to the antecedent voyages to the New World, and is happy to find the remarks of the illustrious Humboldt in this latter work in no way contradictory to the statements in the *Géographie du nouveau Continent*, to which the Editor has been indebted in the progress of the following pages.

R. H. M.

INTRODUCTION.

In introducing these letters for the first time to the English reader, it will perhaps be necessary to forewarn him that he is not to expect to find in them a detailed history of all the events that occurred in the four important voyages to which they refer. The inducement to translate them has been, that though falling far short of a complete history, they are yet filled with a most interesting series of incidents, described by the pens of those to whom these incidents occurred; while at the same time they present us, from Columbus's own mouth as it were, with a clear view of his opinions and conjectures upon many remarkable and important subjects; and of the magnanimity with which he endured an accumulated burthen of unmerited affliction.

The translated documents are seven in number. Five of them are letters from the hand of Columbus himself, describing respectively his first, third, and fourth voyages. Another, descriptive of the second voyage, is by Dr. Chanca, the physician to the fleet during that expedition; and the seventh document is an extract from the will of Diego Mendez, one of Columbus's officers during the fourth voyage, who gives a detailed account of many most interesting adventures undertaken by himself, but left undescribed by Columbus.

It will be requisite, however, for the satisfaction of the reader, to enter more minutely into the history of each of these documents individually.

The first and by far the most interesting of the letters is that addressed by Columbus from Lisbon, under date of the 14th of March, 1493, to Raphael Sanchez, treasurer to Ferdinand and Isabella, and describes the occurrences of his first great discovery. This letter, the only one of the number now published that has hitherto appeared in the English language, was translated very loosely and without comment in the *Edinburgh Review* for 1816.

It is not known whether the original, written by Columbus, in Spanish, be now in existence or not, but it is possible that it may still lie, like a diamond in the mine, in some unexplored Archivo in Spain.

On its first appearance, in 1493, the astonishing narrative it contained caused so much excitement as to occasion numerous editions to be issued in the same year from the various great printing cities of Europe. Those at present known are the following :—

"Epistola Christofori Colom : cui etas nostra multum debet : de insulis Indie supra Gangem nuper invētis. Ad quas perquirendas octavo antea mense auspiciis et

ere invictissimorum Fernandi ac Helisabet Hispaniā
Regū missus fuerat; ad magnificum dñm Gabrielem
Sanches; eorundem Serenissimorum Regum Tesaura-
riū missa: Qua' generosus ac litteratus vir Leander
de Cosco ab Hispana idiomate in Latinū cōvertit;
tertio Kaleñ Maii M.C.C.C.C.XC.III. Pontificatus Alex-
andri Sexti anno primo. Impressit Romæ Eucharius
Argenteus anno dñi M.C.C.C.C.XC.III." There are
copies of this edition in the Grenville Library, British
Museum; and in the libraries of Mr. James Lenox of
New York and Mr. John Carter Brown, of Providence,
Rhode Island.

"Epistola Christofori Colom : cui etas nostra multum
debet : de Insulis Indie supra Gangem nuper invñtis.
Ad quas perqrendas octavo antea mense auspiciis et
ære invictissimorum Fernandi et Helisabet Hispaniæ
Regū missus fuerat, ad magnificum dñm Gabrielem
Sanchis eorundē Serenissimorum Regum Tesaurariū
missa: quā nobilis ac litteratus vir Leander de Cosco
ab Hispano idiomate in Latinum cōvertit tertio kal's
Maii. M.CCCC.XCIII. Pontificatus Alexandri Sexti Anno
primo. Sine loco et anno." Four leaves and thirty-
three lines in a full page.

Copies of this edition exist in the Grenville Library,
British Museum; in the Royal Library, Munich; and
in the libraries of Mr. James Lenox of New York, and
Mr. John Carter Brown of Providence.

" Epistola Christofori Colum : cui etas nostra multū
debet : de Insulis Indie supra Gangem nuper inventis.
Ad quas perquirendas octavo antea mense auspiciis et
ere invictissimi Fernandi Hispaniarum Regis missus

fuerat: ad Magnificum dñm Raphaelem Sanxis: ejusdem serenissimi Regis Tesaurariū missa: quam nobilis ac litteratus vir Aliander de Cosco ab Hispano ideomate in latinum convertit : tertio kal's Maii. M.CCCC.XCIII. Pontificatus Alexandri Sexti anno Primo. Sine loco et anno et typ. n." Four leaves, thirty-four lines in a full page.

Copies of this edition are in the Grenville Library, British Museum; the Royal Library of Munich; and in the libraries of Colonel Thomas Aspinwall, United States, Consul-General at London, and Mr. John Carter of Providence.

" De Insulis nuper inventis. Epistola Cristoferi Colom (cui etas nostra multū debet: de Insulis in Mari Indico nup'invētis. Ad quas perquirendas octavo antea mense: auspiciis et ere Invictissimi Fernandi Hispaniarum Regis missus fuerat) ad Magnificum dñm Raphalez Sanxis: ejusdē seremissimi Regis Thesaurariū missa. Quam nobilis ac litterat' vir Aliander d' Cosco: ab Hispano Ydeomate in latinū convertit: tercio kl's Maii. M.CCCC.XCIII. Pontificatus Alexandri Sexti anno primo. 8vo. s. l. 1493." Six wood-cuts, one of them (the Oceanica Classis) repeated; nine leaves, twenty-seven words in a full page.

Copies of this edition are in the Grenville Library, British Museum; and in the library of Professor Libri.

Another edition, 4to., was printed at Paris (1493), the only known copy of which is in the library of Mr. J. C. Brown of Providence.

There was likewise another edition printed in Paris

(1493), with a wood-cut on the title, one copy of which is in the Bodleian Library, and another in the University Library of Göttingen.

"Eyn schön hübsch lesen von etlichen insslen die do in kurtzen zyten funden synd durch de' künig von Hispania, und sagt vō grossen wunderlichen dingen die in dē selbē insslen synd. Getruckt zu Strassburg uff gruneek vō meister Bartlomess Füstler ym jar M.CCCC.XCVII. uff sant Jeronymus tag." 4to. Seven leaves, thirty lines in a full page.

The only known copy is in the Grenville Library, British Museum.

"De insulis nuper inventis. Epistola Christoferi Colom (cui etas nostra multum debet: de insulis in mari Indico nuper inventis ad quas perquirendas octavo antea mense: auspiciis et ere invictissimi Fernandi Hispaniarū Regis missus fuerat) ad magnificū dominu' Raphaelem Sanxis: ejusdem serenissimi Regis Thesaurarium missa: quam nobilis ac litteratus vir Aliander de Cosco: ab Hispano ideomate: in latinum convertit: tercio Kalendas Maii. M.CCCC.XCIII. Pontificatus Alexandri Sexti anno primo." Seven leaves, twenty-eight lines in a full page. Four wood-cuts.

This book forms the sequel to "Verardus in laudem Ferdinandi Regis."

There are copies of this edition in the Grenville library, British Museum; and in the libraries of Mr. John Carter Brown, Mr. James Lenox, Mr. Henry Stevens, and Mr. O. Rich. It is less rare than the others.

Copies of another edition of the letter forming a sequel to *Verardus*, folio, printed in Basle, 1533, are in the British Museum, and in the libraries of Messrs. Brown and Lenox; but are of no remarkable rarity.

No sooner did this letter make its appearance in print, in the year 1493, than the narrative it contained was put forth in Italian ottava rima by Giuliano Dati, one of the most popular poets of the day, and there is reason to believe that it was sung about the streets to announce to the Italians the astounding news of the discovery of a new world. The only known copy of this curious and valuable poem has recently come into the possession of the British Museum. Whether regarded with reference to the bibliography of early works relating to America, or of the early poetry of Italy, this little work must be acknowledged to possess the highest interest.

It consists of four leaves, comprising a title page and sixty-eight stanzas. The title runs thus: "La lettera, dell' isole che ha trovato nuovamente il re dispagna." End of the volume.—" Finita la Storia della inventione delle nuove isole dicanaria indiane tracte duna pistola di Christofano Colombo et per...Giuliano Dati tradocta. A di 26 doctubre 1493. Florentie." On the title-page is an engraving representing the arrival of Columbus with his fleet at one of the newly discovered islands in the West Indies, with the king of Spain sitting enthroned in the foreground.

A copy of the poem is given as an appendix to this introduction.

All the remaining documents are taken from Navarrete's "Coleccion de los viages y descubrimientos que hicieron por mar los Españoles desde fines del siglo 15." The second letter, which is written by Dr. Chanca, was copied by Navarrete (as he himself says at the end of the letter in his work) from a manuscript, in the possession of the Royal Academy of History at Madrid, written in the middle of the sixteenth century, and was amongst the collection of papers referring to the West Indies, collected by Father Antonio de Aspa, a monk of the order of St. Jerome, of the monastery of the Mejorada, near Olmedo.—This document was unpublished previous to Navarrete's compilation. A copy was taken from the original by Don Manuel Avella, and deposited in the collection of Don Juan Bautista Muñoz, and from that copy, after collation with the original manuscript, the transfer was made by Navarrete into his valuable work. This letter is followed by a Memorial respecting the second voyage, addressed to the sovereigns by Columbus, through the intervention of Antonio de Torres, governor of the city of Isabella. At the close of each chapter or item is affixed their highnesses' reply. The document was taken by Navarrete from the Archives of Seville.

The two letters next in order in the present translation, are from the hand of Columbus himself, and are descriptive of the events of the third voyage. The first, addressed to the sovereigns, was taken by Navarrete, under careful collation by himself and Muñoz, from a manuscript in the handwriting of the bishop Bartholomew de las Casas, found in the archives of the duke del Infantado. The second, addressed to the nurse of Prince John, is taken from a collection of manuscripts, relating to the West Indies, made by Muñoz, and deposited in the Real Academia de la Historia at Madrid. The text was collated by Navarrete, with a copy inserted in the Codice Colombo Americano, said to have been taken in the monastery of Santa Maria de las Cuevas in Seville.

The letter by Columbus, descriptive of his fourth voyage, was taken by Navarrete, from a manuscript in the king's private library at Madrid, written in the handwriting of the middle of the sixteenth century, and probably the same copy as that which Pinelo, at page 61 of his *Biblioteca Occidental*, 4to., 1629, describes as having been made by Don Lorenzo Ramirez de Prado, from an edition in 4to., which does not appear to be now in existence. It was translated into Italian, by Constanzo Baymera of Brescia, and published at Venice, in 1505, and had become extremely scarce, until republished, with some learned comments, by Morelli, the librarian of St. Mark's at Venice, in 1810.

That it had been printed in Spanish is asserted both by Pinelo and by Fernando Columbus.

It is presumed that the manuscript from which Navarrete made his copy was that made by Ramirez de Prado, because it had been removed to the king's library, from the Colegio Mayor de Cuenca, in Salamanca, where the papers of Ramirez had been deposited.

It is impossible to read, without the deepest sympathy, the occasional murmurings and half suppressed complaints which are uttered in the course of this touching letter. These murmurings and complaints were wrung from the manly spirit of Columbus by sickness and sorrow, and though reduced almost to the brink of despair by the injustice of the king, yet do we find nothing harsh or disrespectful in his language to the sovereign. A curious contrast is presented to us. The gift of a world could not move the monarch to gratitude; the infliction of chains, as a recompense for that gift, could not provoke the subject to disloyalty. The same great heart which through more than twenty wearisome years of disappointment and chagrin, gave him strength to beg and to buffet his way to glory, still taught him to bear with majestic meekness the conversion of that glory into unmerited shame.

Our list of translated documents concludes with an extract from the will of the brave and faithful Diego Mendez, without the aid of whose devoted and unflinching fidelity, Columbus must have inevitably perished, under the overwhelming disasters of his fourth voyage.

The will itself is deposited in the archives of the Duke of Veragua, the lineal descendant of Columbus; and the extract was made for Navarrete, by the canonigo Tómas Gonzalez, on the 25th March, 1825.

A series of documents so highly interesting both for originality and importance as those that have been here enumerated, might appear to need but few words either of introduction or recommendation, since the entire history of civilization presents us with no event, with the exception perhaps of the art of printing, so momentous as the discovery of the western world; and, independently of the lustre which the intrinsic importance of that event confers upon the discoverer, there is no individual who has rendered himself, on the score of personal character and conduct, more illustrious than Christopher Columbus. There have, nevertheless, not been wanting those, who, from various motives, and on grounds of various trustworthiness, have endeavoured to lessen his glory, by impeaching his claim to the priority of discovery, or by arguing that the discovery itself has proved a misfortune rather than advantage to the world at large. In order, therefore, to vindicate the value of the original documents here translated, it will not perhaps be deemed superfluous that allusion be made as briefly as possible to such pretensions to prior discovery as have been at different times put forth, that thus a fair estimate may be formed of the relative merits of each.

Various have been the absurdities set forth by speculative writers respecting the original colonization of the western hemisphere. Athanasius Kircher, in his *Prodromus Coptus and Œdipus Ægyptiacus*, gives the Egyptians the credit of colonizing America, as well as India, China, and Japan, grounding his argument upon the religious worship of the sun, moon, stars, and animals. Edward Brerewood, at pages 96 and 97 of his *Enquiries touching the Diversity of Languages*, contends that the Americans are the progeny of the Tartars. Marc Lescarbot, in his

Histoire de la Nouvelle France, maintains that the Canaanites, when routed by Joshua, were driven into America by storms, and that Noah was born in America, and after the flood showed his descendants the way into their paternal country, and assigned to some of them their places of abode there. But Hornius, in his treatise *De originibus Americanis*, after touching upon the various conjectures here quoted, conceives that Paracelsus has reached the height of presumption and folly, when he states, that a second Adam and Eve were created for the peopling of the western world.

The first specific statement, however, of a supposed migration from the shores of the old world to those of the new, is that which the learned De Guignes presumes to be demonstrable, from the relation given by a Chinese historian, Li-Yen, who lived at the commencement of the seventh century. The said historian speaks of a country, named Fou-sang, more than forty thousand *li** to the east of China. He says that they who went thither started from the province of Lea-tong, situated to the north of Peking; that after having made twelve thousand li, they came to Japan; that travelling seven thousand li northward from that place, they arrived at the country of Ven-chin, and at five thousand li eastward of the latter, they found the country of Tahan, whence they journeyed to Fou-sang, which was twenty thousand li distant from Tahan. From this account De Guignes endeavours, by a long chain of argument, to prove that the Chinese

* The *li* is about one-tenth of the common league.

had pushed their investigations into Jeso, Kamtschatka, and into that part of America which is situated opposite the most eastern coast of Asia.

This surmise of De Guignes has been answered by Klaproth, in a paper which appeared in the *Nouvelles Annales des Voyages*. His arguments go to show that the country named Fousang is Japan; and that the country of Tahan, situated to the west of Asiatic Vinland, can only be the island of Saghalian. Humboldt observes upon this subject that the number of horses, the practice of writing, and the manufacture of paper from the Fousang tree, mentioned in the account given by the Chinese historian, ought to have shown De Guignes that the country of which he spoke was not America.

The presumed discovery of America, which comes next in chronological rotation, is that by the Scandinavians, the earliest *printed allusion* to which occurs in Adam of Bremen's *Historia Ecclesiastica Ecclesiarum Hamburgensis et Bremensis*, published at Copenhagen, 1579, 4to. The Baron von Humboldt has asserted that the merit of first recognizing the discovery of America, by the northmen, *belongs indisputably* to Ortelius, who, in his *Theatrum Orbis Terrarum*, with unjust severity says, that Christopher Columbus had done nothing more than to place the new world in a permanently useful and commercial relationship with Europe. The ground upon which the priority is claimed for Ortelius, is that the first edition of his work came out in 1570, although the reference which Humboldt himself gives is to an edition of 1601, which was after the death of Ortelius, and the earlier editions do not contain the chapter on the Pacific Ocean, in which the passage occurs. It is true that in the *Bibliotheca Hulthemiana* the edition of 1601 is said to have been revised and augmented by Ortelius before his death in 1598, but, even if the assertion were made by Ortelius, and not by the editor of his work after his death, it still leaves perfectly unimpeached the claim of Adam of Bremen to having first mentioned the discovery in ~~1579~~. Abraham Mylius, in his *Treatise de Antiquitate Linguæ Belgicæ*, Leyden, 1611, makes all Americans to be sprung from Celts; stating that many Celtic words were to be found in use there; and with more reasonable showing affirms that the coast of Labrador was visited by wanderers from Iceland. Hugo Grotius, in his *Dissertatio de Origine Gentium Americanarum*, (Paris, 1642, 8vo.), follows Mylius, and states that America was colonized by a Norwegian race, who came thither from Iceland, through Greenland, and passed through North America down to the Isthmus.

The earliest *printed detail* of these discoveries is given by the Norwegian historian, Thormodus Torfæus, in a work entitled *Historia Vinlandiæ Antiquæ, ex Antiquitatibus Islandicis in lucem producta,* (Hanniæ, 1705, 12mo.) But in the invaluable work by Professor Rafn, published in 1837 by the Danish Royal Society of Antiquaries, under the title of *Antiquitates Americanæ*, the manuscripts which record these discoveries are given at length in the original, accompanied by a Latin translation, and careful and learned geographical illustrations. The following is a summary of the principal events recorded, in this highly interesting volume, and the geographical inferences are those supplied by the professor himself.

⸌ One Eric Rauda, or Eric the Red, son of Thorwald, a Norwegian noble, having been condemned to a banishment of three years, for killing Eyolf his neighbour, emigrated in the spring of the year 986, to a country to the west of Iceland, which had been discovered a short time previously by a man named Gunbjorn. After two years absence, he returned to Iceland, and in order to hold out an inducement to colonization, named the newly discovered country, Greenland, intending by that name to express the richness of the woods and meadows with which it abounded. Amongst those who had accompanied Eric was a man named Heriulf Bardson, who established himself at Heriulfsnes. Biarne, the son of the latter, finding, on his return home from a trading voyage to Norway, that his father had quitted Iceland, resolved upon following him, though he, as well as those who had accompanied him, were quite unacquainted with the Greenland sea. Soon after leaving Iceland they met with northerly winds and fogs, and were carried they knew not whither: the weather clearing they found themselves near a flat woody country, which, not corresponding with the descriptions of Greenland, they left to larboard. After five days sailing with a south-west wind, they came to a mountainous country, covered with glaciers, which they found to be an island; but as its appearance was not inviting, they bore away from the island, and standing out to sea with the same wind, after four days sailing with fresh gales, they reached Heriulfsnes in Greenland.

Some time after this, in the year 1000, Lief, son of Eric the Red, equipped a ship with thirty-five men to make a voyage of discovery, with the view of examining the new found lands more accurately. They came to a land where no grass was to be seen, but everywhere there were vast glaciers, while the space intervening between these ice mountains and the shore appeared as one uninterrupted plain of slate. This country they named Helluland (*i. e.* Slate-land.) Thence they stood out to sea again, and reached a level wooded country, with cliffs of white sand. They called this country Markland (*i. e.* Woodland.) Again they put to sea, and after two days sail reached an island, to the eastward of the mainland, and passed through the strait between this island and the mainland. They sailed westward, and landed at a place where a river, issuing from a lake, fell into the sea. Here they wintered and built houses, which were afterwards called Leifsbuder (Leifsbooths.) During their stay, one of their number, named Tyrker, a German, happened to wander some distance from the settlement, and on his return reported that he had found vines and grapes. These proving to be plentiful, Lief named the country Vinland (Vineland), and in the ensuing spring returned to Greenland. In the year 1002, Thorwald, Lief's brother, being of opinion that the country had been too little explored, borrowed his brother's ship, and with the assistance of his advice and instructions, set out on a new voyage. They arrived at Leifsbooths, in Vinland, remained there for the winter, and, in the spring of 1003, Thorwald sent a party in the ship's long-boat on a voyage of discovery southwards. They found a beautiful and well-wooded country, with extensive ranges of white sand; but no traces of men, except a wooden shed which they found on an island lying to the westward. They returned to Leifsbooths in the autumn. In the summer of 1004, Thorwald sailed eastward and then northward, past a remarkable headland enclosing a bay, and which was opposite to another headland. They called it Kialarnes (Keel-Cape.) Continuing along the east coast, they reached a beautiful promontory, where they landed. Thorwald was so pleased with the place that he exclaimed, " Here is a beautiful spot, and here I should like well to fix my dwelling." He had scarcely spoken before they encountered some Skrellings (Esquimaux) with whom they fell to blows, and a sharp conflict ensuing, Thorwald received a mortal wound in his arm from an arrow. He died and was buried by his own instructions on the spot which had excited his admiring remark, the language of which appeared prophetic of a longer stay there than he had at first contemplated.

In the summer of 1006 two ships arrived in Greenland from Iceland, one commanded by Thorfinn Karlsfore and Snorre Thorbrandson, both men of illustrious lineage; the other by Biarne Grimolfson of Breidefiord, and Thorhall Gamlason of Austfiord; and in the spring of 1007 these two ships, together with a third (in which Thorbiorn, a relative of Eric's family, had formerly come to Greenland) set sail for Vinland.

They had in all one hundred and sixty men, and as they went with the intention of colonizing, they took with them a great variety and quantity of live stock. They sailed, first, to the Tresterbygd, and afterwards to Biarney (Disco); then to Helluland, where they found an abundance of foxes; and thence to Markland, which was overgrown with wood, and plentifully stocked with a variety of animals. Proceeding still in a south-westerly direction, with the land on the right, they came to a place where a frith penetrated far into the country; off the mouth of it was an island, on which they found an immense number of eyder-ducks, so that it was scarcely possible to walk without treading on their eggs. They called the island Straumey (Stream-Isle) from the strong current which ran past it, and the frith they called Straumfiordr (Stream-Firth). Here Thorhall and eight others left the party in quest of Vinland, but were driven by westerly gales to the coast of Iceland, where some say that they were beaten, and put into servitude. Karlsefne, however, with the remaining one hundred and fifty men, sailed southwards, and reached a place where a river falls into the sea from a lake; large islands were situated opposite the mouth of the river; passing these, they steered into the lake, and called the place Hóp. The low grounds were covered with wheat growing wild; and the rising ground with vines. Here they stayed till the beginning of the year 1008, when finding

d

their lives in constant jeopardy from the hostile attacks of the natives, they quitted the place, and returned to Eric's fiord. In 1011 a ship arrived in Greenland, from Norway, commanded by two Icelandic brothers named Helge and Finnboge; to these men, Freydisa, a natural daughter of Eric the Red, proposed a voyage to Vinland, stipulating that they should share equally with her the profits of the voyage. To this they assented, and it was agreed that each party should have thirty able-bodied men on board the ship, besides women; but Freydisa secretly took with her five men in addition to that number. They reached Liefsbooths in 1012, and wintered there; when a discussion arising, Freydisa had the subtlety to prevail on her husband to massacre the brothers and their followers; after the perpetration of which base deed they returned to Greenland in the spring of 1013.

A numerous and illustrious race descended from Karlsefne, among whom may be mentioned the learned Bishop Thorlak Runolfson, to whom we are principally indebted for the oldest ecclesiastical code of Iceland, written in the year 1123. It is also probable that the accounts of the voyages were originally compiled by him.

It is fortunate that in these ancient accounts they have preserved the statement of the course steered and the distance sailed in a day. From various ancient Icelandic geographical works, it may be gathered that the distance of a day's sailing was estimated at from twenty-seven to thirty geographical

miles—German or Danish—of which fifteen are equal
to a degree, and are consequently equivalent to four
English miles. From the island of Helluland, afterwards called Little Helluland, Biarne sailed to Herjul-
fones (Ikigeit), in Greenland, with strong south-
westerly winds, in four days. The distance between
that cape and *Newfoundland* is about one hundred and
fifty miles, which, if we allow for the strong south-
westerly gales, will correspond with Biarne's voyage;
while the well-known barrenness of the flats of Newfoundland corresponds with the Hellur, or slates which
suggested the name the northmen gave to the island.

Markland being described as three days sail south-
west of Helluland, appears to be Nova Scotia; and the
low and level character of the country, covered with
woods, tallies precisely with the descriptions of later
writers.

Vinland was stated to be two days sail to the
south-west of Markland, which would be from fifty-
four to sixty miles. The distance from Cape Sable to
Cape Cod is reckoned at about two hundred and ten
English miles, which answers to about fifty-two Danish
miles; and in the account given by Biarne of their
finding many shallows off the island to the eastward,
we recognize an accurate description of Nantucket,
and Kialarnes must consequently be Cape Cod. The
Straumfiördr of the northmen is supposed to be Buz-
zard's Bay, and Straumey, Martha's Vineyard, though
the account of the many eggs found there, would
seem to correspond more correctly with Egg Island,
which lies off the entrance of Vineyard Sound.

Krossanes is probably Gurnet Point. The Hóp answers to Mount Hope's Bay, through which the Taunton river flows, and it was here that the Leifs-booths were situated.

The ancient documents likewise make mention of a country called Huitramannaland (Whiteman's Land), otherwise Irland it Mikla (Great Ireland) supposed to be that part of the coast of North America, including North and South Carolina, Georgia and Florida. There is a tradition among the Shawanese Indians, who emigrated some years ago from Florida, and settled in Ohio, that Florida was once inhabited by white people, who possessed iron instruments. The powerful chieftain, Are Marson of Reykianes, in Iceland,—according to the account given by his contemporary Rafn, surnamed the Limerick-trader,—was driven to Huitramannaland by storms in 983, and was baptized there. Are Frode likewise (the first compiler of the Landnama, and a descendant in the fourth degree from Are Marson), states that his uncle, Thorkell Gellerson, had been informed by Icelanders that Are Marson had been recognized in Huitramannaland, and was held in high respect there. This statement therefore shows that there was an occasional intercourse in those days between the Orkneys and Iceland, and this part of America.

It is further recorded in the ancient MSS. that the Greenland bishop Eric went over to Vinland in the year 1121; but nothing more than the fact is stated, and it simply corroborates the supposition of intercourse between the countries. Again, in the year

1266, a voyage of discovery to the Arctic regions of America, is said to have been performed, under the auspices of some clergymen of the bishopric of Gardar in Greenland; and from the recorded observations made by the explorers, would seem to have been carried to regions whose geographical position has been more accurately determined by our own navigators, Parry and the two Rosses. The next recorded discovery was made by Adalbrand and Thorwald Helgason, two Icelandic clergymen, in the year 1285. Contemporaneous accounts state that they discovered a new land to the westward of Iceland, supposed to have been Newfoundland. The last record preserved in the ancient Icelandic MSS. relates a voyage from Greenland to Markland, performed by a crew of seventeen men, in the year 1347. The account written by a contemporary, nine years after the event, induces the belief that intercourse between Greenland and America had been maintained as late as the period here mentioned, for it speaks of Markland as a country still known and visited in those days.

The obscurity of many portions of these narratives leaves much to be cleared up, with reference to this interesting subject; but their general truthfulness being corroborated by the traces of the residence and settlement of the ancient northmen exhibited in the inscriptions discovered in Kinkigtorsoak, Greenland, and Massachusetts, no room is left for disputing the main fact of the discovery.

Between this period and the date of the first voyage of Columbus, the coast of America is reported to have been visited by the Arabians of the Spanish Peninsula, the Welsh, the Venetians, the Portuguese, and also by a Pole in the service of Denmark.

The Arabian expedition is described both by Edrisi and by Ebn-al-ouardi. It appears to have been undertaken by eight persons of the same family, called the Almagrurins or the Wandering Brothers, who having provided themselves with everything requisite for a long voyage, swore they would not return till they had penetrated to the extreme limits of the Dark Sea. They sailed from the port of Aschbona or Lisbon, and steered towards the south-west, and at the end of thirty-five days arrived at the island of Gana or Sheep Island. The flesh of the sheep of this island being too bitter for them to eat, they put to sea again, and after sailing twelve days in a southerly direction, reached an island inhabited by people of a red skin, lofty stature, and with hair of thin growth, but long and flowing over their shoulders. The inhabitants of this island told them that persons had sailed twenty days to the west without discovering land, and the Arabian brothers, diverted from the pursuit of their hardy enterprise by this discouraging account, retraced their course, and returned safely to Lisbon. From this description the elder de Guignes inferred that the Arabs had either reached the eastern coast of America, or at least one of the American islands; an opinion, however, which appears to have as little to sanction it, as his above mentioned conjecture that the Chinese had discovered the west coast of America in the fifth century. The Baron von Humboldt concurs with the opinion expressed by the learned orientalist Tychsen, in his *Neue oriental und exegetische Bibliothek*, and repeated by Malte Brun, that the island reached by the Arab wanderers was one of the African islands. This conclusion is drawn from the circumstance that the Guanches, the original people of the Canary group, were a pastoral race, and also possessed the same external characteristics as the islanders here described. Moreover, the fact that the king of the island had an interpreter who spoke Arabic, together with the circumstance that the red men had sailed westward for a month without seeing land, strongly corroborates the opinion advanced. The precise date of this voyage is unknown, but Humboldt presumes that it must have been considerably anterior to the expulsion of the Arabs from Lisbon in 1147; because Edrisi, whose work was finished in 1153, speaks of the occurrence as if it were by no means recent.

It is but upon a slight foundation, that the Welsh have pretended to raise a claim to the discovery; but slight as it is, there is certainly enough to render a decidedly negative assertion on the subject, to the full as presumptuous, as one decidedly affirmative would be. But as we have no concern with mere conjectures, we must in candour narrate, as succinctly as possible, the grounds upon which these pretensions have been founded.

The first account of this discovery is found in Humphrey Llwyd's translation of the *History of Wales*, by Caradoc of Llancarvan, published by Dr. Powell in

1584. According to him the occurrence took place as follows:—On the death of Owen Gwynedd, prince of North Wales, in 1169, a contention arose amongst his numerous sons, respecting the succession to the crown, when Madawe, or Madoc, one of their number, seeing his native country was likely to be embroiled in a civil war, deemed it more prudent to try his fortune abroad. In pursuance of this object, he sailed with a small fleet of ships to the westward, and leaving Iceland on the north, came at length to an unknown country, where everything appeared new and uncommon, and the manner of the natives different from all that he had ever seen. The country appearing to him, from its fertility and beauty, to be very desirable for a settlement, he left most of his own men behind him, (amounting, according to Sir Thomas Herbert, to a hundred and twenty), and returning to Wales, persuaded a considerable number of the Welsh to go out with him to the newly discovered country, and so with ten ships he again departed, and bade a final adieu to his native soil. This account of the historian Caradoc of Llancarvan is the only affirmative written document the story has upon which to ground its claim to authenticity, with the exception of an ode, written by a Welsh bard, Meredyth ab Rhys, who died in 1477, fifteen years before Columbus's first expedition, in which an allusion is made to the event.*

* The most strenuous advocate for the truth of the tradition, that America was discovered by Prince Madoc, was Dr. John Williams, of Sydenham, who wrote two tracts on the subject, in the year 1791 and 1792, which, if betraying a little of the bias of prejudice, yet manifest a degree of research that does great credit to his industry and zeal.

A circumstance which would appear to confirm the truth of Madoc's voyages, is a peculiar resemblance that has been found between some of the American dialects and the Welsh language; but, as Dr. Robertson reasonably remarks, the affinity has been observed in so few instances, and in some of these is so obscure or so fanciful, that no conclusion can be drawn from the casual resemblance of a small number of words. Dr. Williams adduces in confirmation of his favourite idea the authorities of Lopez de Gomera, Hornius, and Peter Martyr, pretending that they assert that traces of Christianity were found among the Americans by the Spaniards, as well as that there was a tradition among the Mexicans, that many years before a strange nation came amongst them, and taught them the knowledge of God. His references however appear entirely incorrect.

Another pretension to an early discovery of America has been founded upon an account given in a work published at Venice, in 1558, entitled *Dello scoprimento dell' Isole Frislanda, Eslanda Engrovelanda, Estotilanda, ed Icaria, fatto sotto il Polo Arctico da due fratelli Zeni, M. Nicolo il K. e M. Antonio.*" The substance of the account is, that in 1380, Nicolo Zeno, a Venetian noble, fitted out a vessel at his own cost, and made a voyage to the north, with the intention of visiting England and Flanders, but was driven by a storm to Friseland, supposed to be the Fœroe Archipelago. Being rescued from an attack of the natives, by Zichmni, a neighbouring prince, Zeno entered into the service of the latter, and assisted him in conquering Friseland, and other northern islands. He shortly after dispatched a letter to his brother Antonio, requesting him to find means to join him; whereupon the latter purchased a vessel, and succeeded in reaching Friseland, where he remained fourteen years. During his residence there he wrote to his brother Carlo, in Venice, and gave an account of a report brought by a certain fisherman, about a land to the westward. This account stated, that about twenty-six years before, the fisherman was overtaken at sea, when out with four fishing boats, by a tempest, which drove them about for many days, and at length cast them on an island, called Estotiland, about a thousand miles from Friseland. The inhabitants conveyed them to a fair and populous city, where the king sent for many interpreters to converse with them, but none that they could understand, until a man was found, who had likewise been cast away upon the coast, and who spoke Latin. They remained several days upon the island, which was rich and fruitful, abounding with all kinds of metals, and especially gold. Though much given to navigation, they were ignorant of the use of the compass, and finding the Friselanders acquainted with it, the king of the place sent them with twelve barques to visit a country to the south, called Drogeo. They had nearly perished in a storm, but were cast away upon the coast of Drogeo. The fisherman described this Drogeo as a country of vast extent, and that the inhabitants were naked and eaters of human flesh. He remained many years in the country, and became rich with trafficking between

Estoliland and the main land, and subsequently fitted out a vessel of his own, and made his way back to Friseland. His narrative induced Zichmni to undertake a voyage thither, in which he was accompanied by Antonio Zeno. It was unsuccessful: landing on an island called Icaria, they were roughly treated by the inhabitants, and a storm afterwards drove them on the coast of Greenland.

This account is stated by its compiler, Francisco Marcolini, a descendant of the Zeni, to have been compiled from the fragments of letters written by Antonio Zeno to Carlo, his brother.

Malte Brun supposes the island of Estotiland to be Newfoundland, and Drogeo to be Nova Scotia and New England. In the library of St. Mark there is a map,* by Andrea Bianco, bearing the date of 1436, on which is laid down a large extent of land, five or six hundred leagues west of Gibraltar, above which is written the word "Antillia." With reference to this subject, Malte Brun says, " M. Pinkerton croit que cette Antillia, qui se trouve aussi sur d'anciennes cartes Vénitiennes, n'est qu'une création systematique des géographes, qui s'imaginaient qu'il devait y avoir un continent opposé à celui de l'ancien monde, et destiné à contra-balancer celui-ci. Mais je ne vois pas que M. Pinkerton donne aucune raison de son opinion."

The following passage occurs in Sir John Barrow's *Chronological History of Voyages in the Arctic Regions*, which, if it stated a defensible truth, would

* A copy of this map is given in the second vol. of Sastre's *Mercurio Italico*, Lond. 1789, 8vo.

present another claim, anterior to that of Colombus, to the discovery of America. The passage is headed "Cortereals, 1500":—

"The Portuguese, not content with having discovered a route to India, by sailing round the tempestuous extremity of Africa, soon after engaged in an equally dangerous enterprise: that of finding a route to India and the Spice Islands, by sailing westward round the northern extremity of America.

"This bold undertaking was reserved for the CORTEREALS, the enlightened disciples of the school of Sagres. The first navigator of the name of Cortereal, who engaged in this enterprise, was John Vaz Costa Cortereal, a gentleman of the household of the infanta Don Fernando, who, accompanied by Alvaro Marteus Homem, explored the northern seas, by order of king Alfonso the Fifth, and discovered the *Terra de Baccalhaos* (the land of cod fish), afterwards called Newfoundland.

"This voyage is mentioned by Cordeiro,* but he does not state the exact date, which however is ascertained to have been in 1463 or 1464; for, in their return from the discovery of Newfoundland, or Terra Nova, they touched at the island of Terceira, the captaincy of which island having become vacant, by the death of Jacomo Bruges, they solicited the appointment, and in reward for their services the request was granted, their patent commission being dated in Evora, 2nd April, 1464."

* The work quoted is Cordeyro's *Historia Insulana das Ilhas a Portugal sugeytas no Oceano Occidental*, Lisbon, 1717.

It will be seen by the wording of this passage, that Sir John Barrow has fallen into the inaccuracy of asserting, that in 1463 or 1464, Cortereal was engaged in the enterprise of finding a route to India and the Spice Islands, by sailing westward round the northern extremities of America. We must presume that the Portuguese were aware of the existence of the American continent, before they could conceive the idea of sailing westward round its northern extremity. Mr. Biddle (in his *Memoir of Sebastian Cabot*, London, 1831, folio 288), charges Sir John Barrow with not having even looked into the work which he professes to cite as his authority. It is just possible, from Sir John's doubtful expression, "*if the patent should specify, &c.*", that he had not consulted Cordeiro; but should that be the case, he is nevertheless to be vindicated from the imputation of having made any statement not borne out by the work itself. Mr. Biddle is, however, correct in saying the patent commission of the appointment of Cortereal and Homem to the government of Terceira, does not specify that the service for which it was granted, was the discovery of Newfoundland; and, moreover, at the end of Faria y Sousa's *Asia Portuguesa*, there is a list of all the armadas which sailed from Lisbon, on voyages of discovery, between 1412 and 1640, and this expedition is passed by in silence; so that the validity of the whole statement hangs on the authority of Cordeiro. Barbosa makes honourable mention of this writer, but the account is altogether so extremely improbable, from the very silence of the Portuguese, at the time, on so important a subject, as to leave Cortereal but small chance of a successful rivalry with Sebastian Cabot.

The last on the list of those who have been said to precede Columbus, in the discovery of America, is a Polish pilot, named John Szkolny, whose name has been erroneously Latinized by Hornius, Zurla, Malte Brun, Wytfliet, and Pontanus, " Scolvus," or " Sciolvus."   He was in the service of Christian II of Denmark, in the year 1476. He is said to have landed on the coast of Labrador, after having passed along Norway, Greenland, and the Friseland of the Zeni. Upon this subject the great Humboldt thus expresses himself: " I cannot hazard any opinion upon the statement made to this effect by Wytfliet, Pontanus, and Horn. A country seen *after* Greenland may, from the direction indicated, have been Labrador. I am, however, surprised to find that Gomara, who published his *Historia de las Indias* at Saragossa, in 1553, was cognizant even at that time of this Polish pilot. It is possible that when the codfishery began to bring the seamen of southern Europe into more frequent connexion with those of the north, a suspicion may have arisen, that the land seen by Szkolny must have been the same as that visited by John Sebastian Cabot in 1497, and by Gaspar Cortereal in 1500. Gomara says what is in other respects not quite correct, *that the English took much pleasure in frequenting the coast of Labrador, for they found the latitude and climate the same as that of their native land, and the men of Norway have been there with the pilot, John Scolvo, as well as the English with Sebastian Cabot.*

Let us not forget that Gomara makes no mention of the Polish pilot, with reference to the question of the predecessors of Colombus, though he is malignant enough to assert, that it is in fact impossible to say to whom the discovery of the New Indies is due."*

In the American Philosophical Transactions for 1786, is a letter addressed to Dr. Franklin, by Mr. Otto of New York, in which he not only asserts that the illustrious cosmographer Martin Behaim discovered the Azores, but quotes a passage, from what he calls an authentic record, preserved in the archives of Nuremberg, the tenor of which is as follows:—" Martin Behem, traversing the Atlantic Ocean for several years, examined the American Islands, and discovered the strait which bears the name of Magellan, before either Christopher Columbus or Magellan navigated those seas ; and even mathematically delineated, on a geographical chart for the king of Lusitania, the situation of the coast around every part of that famous and renowned strait." He also quotes passages from Hartman Schedl, and from Cellarius, in confirmation of this statement. Don Christobal Cladera, in his *Investigaciones Historicas*, says that, in order to refute these statements, he procured from Nuremberg a description of Behaim's globe, together with historical notes on the life and family of that geographer,

* Humboldt has fallen into an error in saying that Joachim Lelewel, in his *Pisma pomniejsze geogr. historyczné*, 1814, has recently called up fresh attention to this Polish pilot. The editor has examined the work carefully from beginning to end, and does not find the name even once mentioned, although the page to which reference is made contains allusions to early discoveries.

and upon examining these, and the unpublished works of the Academia de las Ciencias de Lisboa, he became convinced that the observations of Mr. Otto were totally unfounded; and De Murr, who has well investigated the question, assures us that the passage quoted by Mr. Otto from Schedl was not to be found in the German translation of that work by George Alt, in 1493. Moreover, the real globe of Behaim, made in 1492, does not contain any of the islands or shores of the New World; a fact which sets at rest the two questions of Behaim's earlier discovery, or of Colombus gaining his information from Behaim.*

From the series of evidences contained in the preceding accounts, the fact that America had been visited by European adventurers before the time of Columbus, is rendered too probable to admit of contradiction, even from the most sanguine advocate of the glory of the great discoverer. But, on the other side, it cannot be denied that the discovery of Columbus, however much later in date, deserves the meed of highest honour, as being the result of sagacity and judgment, and as having been carried on with an energetic endeavour to bring into active operation the incalculable advantages which it opened up to the world at large. To vindicate the correctness of this statement, it will be well to give a brief sketch of his eventful life, and to pourtray as briefly as we may the high qualities to which, far more than to accidental circumstances, the glory of this great

* A copy of part of this globe is given in Cladera's *Investigaciones.*

discovery is due. The retrospect of his history will at the same time shew, that while every previous discovery was attributable to accident, the greater portion of the accidental or uncontrollable circumstances in the life of Columbus were such as, instead of assisting him, tended to thwart him at every step of his painful career.

It is generally agreed that his father was a wool weaver or carder. There is reason, however, to presume that though his parentage was humble, he was descended from a family of consideration. On this subject his son, Don Ferdinand, denies* with great indignation an assertion which occurs in a curious life of the admiral, inserted in the *Psalterium Octuplex Augustini Justiniani*, Genoa, 1516, folio, under the comments on the nineteenth psalm, that he was "vilibus ortus parentibus," and complains that he is falsely called a mechanic.

The date of his birth is a " vexata quæstio," which it would be out of our power in the limits of this introduction to discuss. Washington Irving, relying upon the evidence given by Bernaldez, the "Cura de los Palacios," states it to be about 1435 or 1436. This inference he draws from the remark of Bernaldez, that he died in 1506, at the age of seventy, a little more or less. Juan Bautista Muñoz† concludes that he was born in 1446. Don Ferdinand, the admiral's son, relates, that in a letter addressed by his father to the king and queen, dated 1501, he states that he had

---

* *Historie del S. D. Fernando Colombo,* cap. iv. † *Historie del Nuevo Mundo,* lib. ii, sec. 12.

f

then been forty years at sea, and in another letter
that he was fourteen years old when he went to sea;
so that allowing a year either way for probable inat-
tention to minuteness in these statements, we get the
date of his birth, fixed by his own hand,. at about
1447. Navarrete, who recognizes these two passages,
translates the former, as if the forty years were only
to include the time passed by Columbus on the ocean,
and accordingly adds to this period the eight years
spent in Spain, between 1484 and 1492. Whether he
is justified in this rendering of the passage, the reader
may judge. The sentence runs thus: " *Di età molto
tenera io entrai in mare navigando, ed vi ho contin-
uato fin' hoggi : ed l'istessa arti inclina a chi la segue
a desiderar di sapere i secreti di questo mondo : ed
hoggimai passano quaranta anni, che io uso per tutte
quelle parti, che fin' hoggi si navigano.*" The conclusion to be drawn from the right reading of this, and
the subsequent statement, that the admiral went to
sea at fourteen years of age, agrees with the inference
of the learned and judicious Muñoz.

With respect to the birthplace of our illustrious
navigator, were we to enter into the complex discussions of those who, with different arguments of more
or less plausibility, place it in Genoa, Nervi, Savona,
Pradello, Cogoleto, Quinto, Bogliasco, Albisola, Chia-
vara, Oneglia, or the castle of Cuccaro in Monferrato,
—we should but launch upon a sea of difficulties,
with little hope of a successful voyage. We conceive
that the most pertinacious disputant ought to be convinced by an assertion made twice by Columbus in his

will, dated 22nd February 1498, that he was born in the city of Genoa; namely,—" I, being a native of Genoa"; and " I desire my said son Diego, or the person who may succeed to the said inheritance, always to keep and maintain one person of our lineage in the city of Genoa...because from thence I came, and there I was born."*

Having early evinced a strong inclination for the study of geography, geometry, and astronomy, he found at the college of Pavia an excellent opportunity of gaining a more than superficial acquaintance with the principles of those sciences, and at the same time acquired considerable proficiency in the Latin language. The maritime position and commercial engagements of his native city, doubtless suggested and fostered much of that propensity for a nautical life, that he exhibited at so early an age ; and although it appears from several historians that for a short time he worked at his father's trade, yet this must have been simply during his earliest boyhood, for by his own account he commenced the life of a mariner at fourteen years of age. The piratical character of the seafaring life of those days necessarily exposed its followers to unceasing hardships and dangers, and the severity of this early discipline must have most materially tended to render available and permanent those distinguished qualities which have subsequently gained for him the

* " *Siendo yo nacido en Genova*"; and " *mando al dicho Don Diego, mi hijo, a la persona que heredare el dicho mayorazgo que tenga y sostenga siempre en la Ciudad de Genova una persona de nuestro linage...pues que della sali y en ella naci.*"

admiration of the world: indeed no career could have been better calculated to develope his peculiar genius, or add fuel to those enthusiastic aspirations which characterized him to the close of his life.

From the period of his going to sea, which was about the year 1460 until the year 1472, we meet with no distinct mention of his name; though in a letter written by him to their Majesties, in 1495, he says: " *It happened to me that king Réné (whom God has taken to himself) sent me to Tunis to capture the galley Fernandina, and on arriving at the island of San Pedro, in Sardinia, I learned that there were two ships and a caracca with the galley, which so alarmed the crew that they resolved to proceed no further, but to return to Marseilles for another vessel and more people; upon which, being unable to force their inclination, I yielded to their wish, and having first changed the points of the compass, spread all sail, for it was evening, and at daybreak we were within the cape of Carthagena, while all believed for a certainty that they were going to Marseilles.*" The date of this occurrence is unknown, but the expedient of Columbus to alter the point of the needle, reminds us of his subsequent stratagem, of altering his reckoning, to appease his discontented crew during his first great voyage of discovery.

In the year 1472, however, we have evidence of his having been in Savona, from the fact of his signature having been found appended to the will of one Niccolo Monleone, under date of the 20th March of that year.

The document is preserved in Savona, among the notarial archives.

In 1474 we find his name mentioned in a letter addressed by Ferdinand king of Sicily to Louis king of France, the title of which runs thus: *"Literæ à Ferdinando Rege Siciliæ ad Ludovicum XI, Galliæ Regem, per Fæcialem missæ, quibus quæritur, quod Christophorus Columbus triremes suas deprædatus sit, postulatque sibi ablata restitui. Datum in Terra Fogiæ dié 8 Decembr. 1474."* Then follows a letter in five lengthy clauses, in which it is stated that the said vessels were attacked and taken:—*"A Columbo, qui quibusdam navibus præest, Majestatis vestræ subdito."*

The title of Louis's reply runs thus: *"Responsio Ludovici XI quibus promittit restitutionem, excusat tamen Columbum, quod jus sit in Oceano capere naves ab hostilibus terris venientes et saltem bona hostium inde auferre."* These letters are given by Leibnitz, in his *Codex Juris Gentium Diplomaticus, Prodromus*, art. 16 and 17; but on the correction of Nicolas Toinard, he acknowledges, in the preface to his *Mantissa Codicis*, that he had erroneously inserted the Christian name " Christophorus."

Toinard's correction went to shew that Leibnitz had confounded the name of Guillaume de Caseneuve, surnamed Conlomp, Coulon, or Colon, as the Spaniards called him, with that of the illustrious discoverer. This acknowledgment by Leibnitz of his error might seem to render useless any reference to the letters in question; but as Christopher Columbus is stated by

his son, Don Ferdinand, to have been of the same
family as the pirate here mentioned, and also to have
been engaged at sea with him and his nephew, it
becomes interesting to examine what record exists of
these illustrious pirates, and to see how far the assertion of Don Ferdinand bears the semblance of correctness. This Caseneuve, or Colon, is called by
Duclos, in speaking of the very circumstance which
occasioned these letters, in his *Histoire de Louis II,*
"*Vice-Admiral de France, et le plus grand homme de
mer de son temps.*" And Zurita, in his *Libro* 19 *de
los Anales de Aragon,* calls him, "*Colon, capitan de
la Armada del Rey de Francia.*" Garnier, in his
Histoire de France, thus relates the circumstance:
"*Guillaume de Casenove, Vice-Amiral de Normandie,
connu dans notre histoire sous le nom d'Amiral
Coulon, s'était rendu formidable sur toutes les mers
de l'Europe, où il exercait le métier d'armateur :
dans une de ses courses il s'empara de deux riches
frégates chargées pour le compte des plus riches
négocians de Naples, de Florence, et de plusieurs
autres villes d'Italie, qui tout sollicitèrent vivement la
restitution de cette importante prise.*"

Another exploit, in which this Colon was success-
fully engaged, was the taking of eighty Dutch ships
returning from the herring fishery, in the Baltic, in
1479. Again, another sea-fight related by Marc Antonio Sabelico, in the eighth book of his tenth Decade,
is quoted by Don Fernando, where Columbus the
younger (described by Sabelico as the nephew, but by
Zurita as Francis, the son of the famous corsair),

intercepted, between Lisbon and Cape St. Vincent, four richly laden Venetian galleys, on their return from Flanders. Fernando further asserts that his father (Christopher) was present in this engagement, and that after a desperate contest, which lasted from morning till evening, the hand-grenades and other fiery missiles used in the battle, caused a general conflagration among the vessels, which having been lashed together with iron grapplings, could not be separated, and the crews were compelled to leap into the water to escape the fire. He then goes on to say that " his father, who was a good swimmer, finding himself at the distance of two leagues from the land, seized an oar, and by its aid succeeded in reaching the shore. Whereupon, learning that he was not far from Lisbon, where he knew he should find many natives of Genoa, he went thither, and meeting with a gratifying reception, took up his abode in that city." The engagement here described is shown by various French historians to have taken place in 1485, and as it is certain that Columbus was in Lisbon prior to 1474, (for in that year he has a letter addressed to him in the city, by Paolo Toscanelli, in reply to one written by himself from the same place), this relation by Don Ferdinand assumes a very apocryphal aspect.

With respect to his other statement, that his father was of the same name and family as these two renowned corsairs, it is to be remarked, that neither he nor any of the subsequent historians who have claimed this needless honour for the great discoverer, appears to have been acquainted with the real name of the pirates; and as Caseneuve was the strict family name of the latter, and Coulon merely a superadded surname, we may fairly conclude that the claim to consanguinity has no other foundation than the identity in the Spanish language of Columbus's patronymic with the distinguishing surname of the French vice-admiral.

In the *Chronique Scandaleuse* (folio 109) this Caseneuve is said to have had a very handsome mansion, named Gaillart-Bois, in the neighbourhood of Notre Dame d'Escouys, in Normandy, at which Louis XI made a stay of two or three days in the month of June 1475, and returned thither also in the following month and stayed there some time. Spotorno suggests that his name of Coulon may have been derived from a place so called in the province of Berri; so that, in addition to the evidence that he was not of the same name or family with Christopher Columbus, there arises strong reason to believe that he was in reality a Frenchman:* in which case it becomes probable that an event which has been generally attributed to him, or to his still more renowned relative François Caseneuve, would be with greater correctness ascribed to the Genoese navigator, Christopher Columbus. It appears that, in a letter dated Terra d'Otranto, 2nd October 1476 (preserved, according to Bossi, in the royal archives at Milan), addressed to the duke of Milan by two illustrious gentlemen of that city,—the one Guid'Antonio Arcimboldo, and the

---

* Another Caseneuve, probably of this family, is said by De Bry to have been captain of the fourth expedition of the French to Mexico, in the year 1567.

other Giovanni Giacomo Trivulzio—the following story is related. It says that the captain of the Venetian fleet, when stationed off Cyprus to defend the island, had twice encountered a *Genoese* ship, called the "Nave Palavisina," which he had taken to be a Turkish caracca; and in these two engagements one hundred and twenty of the Turks and Genoese had been killed, and in the Venetian squadron thirty had been killed, and two hundred wounded. The captain appears to have had doubts whether he might not have done wrong, and caused offence to the duke of Milan, who might perhaps be an ally of the Genoese: he therefore goes on to say that his only desire had been to meet with his enemies (the Turks) and plunder them; and adds, in confirmation of that assertion, that "a year before he had met with three times as many galleys, who spoke no evil of his good name, and that he found Columbus with ships and galleys, and had cheerfully let him pass by, upon which the cry was raised of 'Viva San Georgio,' and nothing further passed between them." The Columbus here mentioned is shewn, by the cry of "Viva San Georgio," and by the general tenour of the Venetian captain's letter, to have been a Genoese, and with a Genoese crew; and as it appears probable that the Caseneuves were Frenchmen, and would in all probability sail with French crews, it leaves strong reason to presume that the Genoese captain here mentioned was Christopher Columbus, who is allowed by all his early historians to have been engaged in the Mediterranean about the period referred to.

Shortly after his arrival in Portugal he married Doña Felipa Moñiz de Palestrello, whose father, then dead, had been a distinguished navigator under prince Henry, and governor of the island of Porto Santo. This marriage was a fortunate occurrence for Columbus; for, independently of its having been a match of affection, he became by it possessor of his deceased father-in-law's journals, charts, and memoranda. These invaluable documents unfolded to his mind the ideas and experience of the adventurous Portuguese, and supplied food of the most delightful kind to his natural appetite for cosmographical inquiry. He now began to employ his time in making maps and charts, and from the observations and comparisons into which he was naturally led by this occupation, he soon began to perceive how much of the world remained to be explored. To aid the notions suggested by his daily pursuits, the inflamed accounts given by seamen of the recent discoveries of the Portuguese, all lent their force to kindle up the native enthusiasm of his mind. In one instance, he was informed by Antonio Leone, an inhabitant of Madeira, that sailing westward one hundred leagues, he had seen three islands at a distance. Again, one Martin Vicenti, a pilot, related that when at a distance of four hundred and fifty leagues westward of Cape St. Vincent, he had found a piece of wood, carved, but evidently not with an iron instrument.

His wife having inherited some property in Porto Santo, he resided with her a short time there, and as her sister was married to Pedro Correo, a Portuguese

navigator of distinction, the conversations arising out
of their mutual intercourse would naturally turn
upon the subjects which were now become engrossing
to the mind of Columbus. Meanwhile he studied
with deep and careful attention the works of such
geographical authors as supplied suggestions of the
feasibility of a short western passage to India.* These

* Amongst all the authors consulted by Columbus, there was
none for whom he had a greater predilection than the Cardinal
Pierre d'Ailly (Petrus de Aliaco); and it is probable that from the
"Imago Mundi" of that author, he culled all he knew of the opinions
of Aristotle, Strabo, and Seneca, respecting the facility of reaching
India by a western route. His works consist of thirteen small
treatises, four of which,—the first, second, sixth, and seventh—are
on cosmography. There is a magnificent volume in the British
Museum of his works, embodying all these treatises, with the addition of three curious tracts on analogous subjects, by Jean Charlier
de Gerson, chancellor of the university of Paris. The date and
place of printing are wanting, but it is evidently from the types of
John of Westphalia, printed at Louvain about 1480, according to
Serna Santander, and 1483, according to Lambinet. Columbus's
own copy of this work is now in the cathedral of Seville, and forms
one of the most precious items in the valuable library originally
collected by his son Ferdinand, and bequeathed to the cathedral on
condition of its being constantly preserved for public use. The
" Tractatus de Imagine Mundi," which was composed in 1410,
contains a faithful and concise account of the ancient authors who
have given descriptions of the globe; namely, Plotemy, Aristotle,
Pliny, Lucretius, Isidorus de Chara, Averroes, Seneca, etc., whose
opinions the author contrasts with the narrative of Moses and his
commentators. Mr. George Sumner, who has made unwearied personal investigations in Spain for everything that might throw a
light upon the history of Columbus, and who has been privileged
with a sight of this valuable book, has kindly handed the editor
an extract from a letter addressed by him to the Baron von Humboldt,
in which he says that Columbus's copy of *Aliacus* contains many
marginal notes in his own handwriting. Mr. Sumner's letter goes

suggestions were corroborated by the narratives of Marco Polo and Sir John Mandeville, whose reports of the vast extent of Asia eastward led to the reasonable inference, that the westward passage to the eastern confines of that continent, could not demand any considerable length of time.

The natural tendency of his thoughts to nautical enterprise being thus fostered by the works that he studied, and by the animating accounts of recent adventurers, as well as by the glorious prospects which the broad expanse of the unknown world opened up to his view, we find that in the year 1474 his ideas had formed for themselves a determined channel, and his grand project of discovery was established in his mind as a thing to be done, and done by himself. The combined enthusiasm and tenacity of purpose which distinguished his character, caused him to regard his theory, when once formed, as a matter of such undeniable certainty, that no doubts, opposition, or disappointment, could divert him from the pursuit of it.

on to say: "This interesting discovery of the copy of Aliacus which belonged to the admiral is due to Mr. Washington Irving, who lighted upon it accidentally while searching in the library for some other work, not however until he had closed his labours for the *Lives of Columbus and his Companions*. The marginal notes have, I believe, from the examination which I made of them, comparatively little importance; the permission to copy them was however refused me by the librarians. The archives of the Indies were freely opened to me by orders from Madrid, but in the canonical officers of the Columbian Library, I found much the same jealousy that the eastern traveller is sure to encounter among Arab schieks,—a jealousy founded on the belief that the stranger comes among them only to disenter the hidden treasure which lies buried under their ruins."

With these views he commenced a correspondence on the subject with the learned Paolo Toscanelli of Florence, who, to demonstrate his approbation of the design of Columbus, sent him a chart, the most important features of which were laid down from the descriptions of Marco Polo. The coasts of Asia were drawn at a moderate distance from the opposite coasts of Europe and Africa, and the islands of Cipango, Antilla, etc., of whose riches such astonishing accounts had been given by this traveller, were placed at convenient spaces between the two continents.

While all these exciting accounts must have conspired to fan the flame of his ambition, one of the noblest points in the character of Columbus had to be put to the test by the difficulty of carrying his project into effect. The political position of Portugal, engrossed as it was with its wars with Spain, rendered the thoughts of an application for an expensive fleet of discovery worse than useless, and several years elapsed before a convenient opportunity presented itself for making the proposition.

Meanwhile Columbus was not idle. In the year 1477, he tells us, in a letter quoted by his son, Don Ferdinand, that "*he sailed a hundred leagues beyond the island of Thule, the southern part of which is distant from the equinoctial line seventy-three degrees, and not sixty-three, as some assert ; neither does it lie within the line which includes the west of Ptolemy, but is much more westerly. To this island, which is as large as England, the English, especially those from Bristol, go with their merchandize. At the time that I was there the sea was not frozen, but the tides were so great as to rise and fall twenty-six fathoms. It is true that the Thule of which Ptolemy makes mention lies where he says it does, and by the moderns it is called Frislanda."* This island is supposed to have been Iceland, but nothing more is known of the voyage than is contained in this letter. It is moreover supposed by his son, as has been already stated, that he passed a considerable portion of his time at sea, with one or both of the famous pirates of the same name, who were so many years engaged in the Levant; but upon the whole of this portion of his history there rests an impenetrable cloud of obscurity.

About the year 1480, by the joint labours of the celebrated Martin Behaim, and the prince's two physicians, Roderigo and Josef, who were the most able geographers and astronomers in the kingdom, the astrolabe was rendered serviceable for the purposes of navigation, as by its use the seaman was enabled to ascertain his distance from the aquator by the altitude of the sun.

Shortly after this invaluable invention Columbus submitted to the king of Portugal his proposition of a voyage of discovery, and succeeded in obtaining an audience, to advocate his cause. He explained his views with respect to the facility of the undertaking, from the form of the earth, and the comparatively small space that intervened between Europe and the eastern shores of Asia; he proposed, if the king would supply him with ships and men, to take the direct western route to India across the Atlantic; and his application was received at first discouragingly, but the king was at length induced, by the excellent arguments of Columbus, to make a conditional concession, and the result was that the proposition was referred to a council of men supposed to be learned in maritime affairs. This council, consisting of the above mentioned geographers, Roderigo and Joseph, and Cazadilla, bishop of Ceuta, the king's confessor, treated the question as an extravagant absurdity. The king, not satisfied with their judgment, then convoked a second council, consisting of a considerable number of the most learned men in the kingdom; but the result of their deliberations was only confirmative of the verdict of the first junto, and a general sentence of condemnation was passed upon the proposition. As the king still manifested an inclination to make a trial of the scheme of Columbus, and expressed a proportionate dissatisfaction with the decisions of these two juntos, some of his councillors, who were inimical to Columbus and at the same time unwilling to offend the king, suggested a process which coincided with their own views, but which was at once short-sighted, impolitic, and ungenerous. Their plan was to procure from Columbus a detailed account of his design, under the pretence of subjecting it to the examination of the council, and then to dispatch a caravel on the voyage of discovery, under the false pretext of conveying provision to the Cape Verde Islands. King John, contrary to his general character for prudence and generosity, yielded to their insidious advice, and their plan was acted upon. But the caravel which was sent out, after keeping on its westward course for some days, encountered a storm, and the crew, possessing none of the lofty motives of Columbus to support their resolution, returned to Lisbon, ridiculing the scheme in excuse of their own cowardice.   So indignant was Columbus at this unworthy manœuvre, that he resolved to leave Portugal and offer his services to some other country, and towards the end of 1484 he left Lisbon secretly with his son Diego.   The learned and careful Muñoz states his opinion that he went immediately to Genoa, and made a personal proposition to that government, but met with a contemptuous refusal ; great obscurity, however, hangs over his history during the first year after his departure from Portugal.

Columbus, in the letter to the nurse of prince John, which is here translated, asserts that seven years had been spent in treaty, and nine in execution ; so that, deducting seven years from 1492, the year in which he started on his first journey, gives us 1485 as the period of his first application to the court of Spain.   A curious surmise is expressed in a note to Sharon Turner's *History of England in the Middle Ages*, in which the supposition is propounded of the possible identity of Christopher Columbus with a person named Christofre Colyns, who is recorded in some grants in the Harleian MSS. to have been military commandant of Queenborough castle, in the isle of Sheppy, in 1484 and 1485.   This man is distinctly stated in the same grants to have held that post in April 1485, and it may be reasonably conjectured that the cessation of his office would not take place till the accession of Henry

VII, in August of that year, which leaves but little time for his making his way to Genoa, and subsequently reaching Spain, so as to make his application to that court. Moreover, the impoverished condition in which he presented himself at the convent de la Rabida was very incompatible with the probable pecuniary position of a person, who is described by the grants in question not only to have held the prominent position already mentioned, but to have had a ship given him, with an annuity of £100, and an especial grant of money to enable him to supply himself with habiliments of war. We venture, from these considerations, to express an opinion that the supposition proposed by Mr. Turner can be no longer regarded as tenable.

The well known and interesting story of Columbus's visit to the Franciscan convent of Santa Maria de Rabida forms the first incident that we find recorded of him after his arrival in Spain. It is well known that the lively interest which the worthy prior of that convent, Fray Juan Perez de Marchena, took in his guest, was the means, through the anticipated influence of his friend Fernando de Talavera, of first leading Columbus to the Spanish court, under the hope of obtaining the patronage of the king and queen. Talavera, who was prior of the monastery of Prado, and confessor to the queen, possessed great political interest. Juan Perez took advantage of this influential position of his friend, and addressed him a letter, by the hands of Columbus, strongly recommending the project of the latter to his favourable consideration,

h

and requesting his advocacy of it before the sovereigns.   It was in the spring of 1486 that Columbus
first ventured to the Spanish court in the hope of
gaining a favourable audience.   On reaching Cordova,
however, he had the mortification to find that Talavera,
upon whose influence he mainly relied, regarded his
design as unreasonable and preposterous.   The court
also was at that time so engrossed with the war at
Granada, as to place any hope of gaining attention to
his novel and expensive proposition out of the question.   At length, at the close of 1486, the theory
of Columbus, backed as it was by his forcible arguments and earnest manner, gained weight with the
most important personage at court next to the sovereigns themselves.   This was Mendoza, archbishop of
Toledo, and grand cardinal of Spain; who, pleased
with the grandeur of the scheme, and the fervent but
clear-headed reasoning of Columbus, adopted his
cause, and became his staunch protector and friend.
Through his means an audience was procured with
the sovereigns, and the result of the interview was the
expression of a favourable opinion, qualified by the
necessity of an appeal to the judgment of the literati
of the country.   But here again Columbus found
himself in a painful predicament, which it required all
his knowledge and prudence to escape from with
safety.   He was to be examined at Salamanca by a
council of ecclesiastics, and had to propound opinions
which appeared to be at variance with the descriptions
contained in the sacred Scriptures, and that at a period
when the expression of any sentiment approaching to

heresy exposed its owner to the persecution of the
newly established Inquisition. The ignorance of cosmography, and the blind conclusions drawn from
various misinterpreted texts of Scripture, formed
mighty impediments to the pleadings of Columbus,
and he began to find himself in danger of being con-
victed not only of error, but of heresy. One learned
man of the number, however, Diego de Deza, tutor to
prince John, and afterwards archbishop of Seville, appreciated the eloquent and lucid reasonings of the
adventurer, and aiding him with his own powers of
language and erudition, not only gained for him a
hearing, but won upon the judgments of some of the
most learned of the council. Nevertheless, so important a question could not be hastily decided; and the
result of the united pedantry, and sluggish super-
stition of the learned body, was to expose the question
to protracted argumentation or neglect, while Talavera,
who was at its head, and from whom Columbus had
hoped to receive the greatest assistance, was too busied
with political matters to bring it to a conclusion. At
length, in the early part of 1487, the deliberations of
the council were brought to a stand-still, by the departure of the court to Cordova, and were not resumed
till the winter of 1491. During this wearisome period
the bustle and excitement of the memorable campaign
against the Moors, with its alternations of triumphant
festivity, together with the marriage of the princess
Isabella to the prince Alonzo, heir-apparent of Portugal, were far too engrossing to admit of much attention

being given to the schemes of Columbus.* At the close, however, of the year 1491, the learned conclave appears to have recommenced its consultations; but upon being called upon by the sovereigns for a decision, a report was returned to Talavera that the scheme was considered by the general vote of the junto too groundless to be recommended to the interference of the sovereigns. Accordingly Talavera was commanded to inform Columbus that the cares and expenses of the war precluded the possibility of their Highnesses engaging in any new enterprises, but that when it was concluded there would be both the will and the opportunity to consider further upon the subject. Regarding these as nothing better than a courteous evasion of his application, he retired wearied and disappointed from the court, and, but for an attachment which he had formed at Cordova, which made him reluctant to leave Spain, he would in all probability have repaired to France, under the encouragement of a favourable letter which he had received from that quarter.

The ensuing period till 1492 was spent in a succession of vexatious appeals to the Spanish court, during which he had to contend with every obstacle that ignorance, envy, or a pusillanimous economy could suggest.

* It was shortly after this period that Bartholomew Columbus was sent by his brother to king Henry VII, to offer his services in a voyage of navigation; the king is said to have received the offer " con allegro volto "—" with a cheerful countenance"; but his acceptance of the proposition was rendered null by Columbus having in the interim attached himself to the service of queen Isabella.

At length, having overcome all difficulties, he set sail with a fleet of three ships on the 3rd of August 1492, on his unprecedented and perilous voyage. The ordinary difficulties which might be expected to occur in so novel and precarious an adventure were seriously aggravated by the alarming discovery of the variation of the needle, as well as by the mutinous behaviour of his crew; and his life was upon the point of being sacrificed to their impatience, when the fortunate appearance of land, on the morning of the 12th of October, converted their indignation into compunction, and their despondency into unbounded joy.

With reference to the identity of the first landing place of Columbus in America, the learned and industrious Navarrete, whose steady judgment and patience in investigation can be denied by none, uses the following expression: " From a careful examination of the diary of Columbus in his first voyage (inserted in the *Coleccion de Viages*), its courses, descriptions of lands, of islands, coasts and harbours, it appears that this, the first island discovered and occupied by Columbus, and named by him San Salvador, must be the one situated most to the north of those called the Turk Islands, and itself called the Great Turk. Its latitude is 21° 30′ northward of the centre of the island of San Domingo." A communication recently made to the New York Historical Society, by Mr. Gibbs, a resident on Turk's Island, presents several points of evidence strongly confirmative of the correctness of Navarrete's deductions. The most important of Mr. Gibbs's arguments are the following. Colum-

bus states in his journal that there were several
islands in sight from Guanahani.   When Mr. Gibbs
visited the island now called San Salvador, he sent
sailors aloft to look out for land, and himself ascended
the highest part of the island; but though the weather
was clear, no land was visible.   The journal speaks of
soundings to the eastward of Guanahani: there are
none to the eastward of San Salvador.   The Spaniards
sailed round Guanahani in one day: with San Salvador
this would be impossible.   All the marks wanting at
San Salvador are found at Turk's Island.   The journal
describes Guanahani as well wooded, and having much
water; a large lake in the centre, and two several
running streams flowing into the sea.   Turk's Island
has about one-third of its surface covered with lakes
of salt and fresh water; and some of these formerly
communicated with the sea, except at certain seasons
when storms choked up the outlets with sand. A few
years ago vessels sailed into one of the ponds.   The
island, though now without trees, is known to have
been formerly well wooded, and Mr. Gibbs recollects
some remains of the forest existing in his youth.   It
is worthy of notice, too, that the journal makes no
allusion to the Great Bahama Bank, which must have
been passed in approaching San Salvador.*

It is needless to dwell upon the events which followed.   They are for the most part described in the
letter here translated, and are more amply given in
Washington Irving's elaborate and charmingly written
narrative. The main result of this voyage was the dis-

* Vide *Athenæum* for 1846, page 1274.

covery of the islands of St. Salvador, Santa Maria de la Concepcion, Exuma, Isabella, Cuba, Bohio, the Archipelago off the south coast of Cuba (which he names the Jardin del Rey, or King's Garden), the islands of St. Catherine and Hispaniola, on which latter Columbus erected the fortress of La Navidad, and established a colony. He set sail on his return voyage on the 16th January 1493, and, after suffering severely from a storm and a wearisome struggle with the trade winds, reached the island of St. Mary's on the 18th of February. Scarcely had he and his tempest-tossed crew commenced their thanksgivings for their safe return to the abode of civilized men, when the governor of the island, acting under the general orders of the king of Portugal, surrounded them and took them all prisoners. This reception of the admiral on his return to the Old World is well described by Washington Irving, as an earnest of the crosses and troubles with which he was to be requited through life, for one of the greatest benefits that ever man had conferred upon his fellow-beings. Being at length liberated, with an apology, he was invited to the court, and received most graciously by the king and queen, but not without evident manifestations of jealousy and chagrin on the part of some of the courtiers, and propositions to take away his life. The magnanimity of the king prevented this injustice, and leaving Portugal in safety, on the 13th of March, Columbus arrived on the 15th at the little port of Palos, from whence he had sailed on the 3rd of August in the preceding year. His reception in Spain was such as the gran-

deur and dignity of his unrivalled achievement deserved, and his entrance into Barcelona was scarcely
inferior to a Roman triumph.*

* The following remark by Mr. George Sumner has been kindly
supplied by that gentleman, as an interesting item connected with
this period of the history of Columbus:—

From the brilliant description given by Irving and Prescott of the
arrival of Columbus at Barcelona, and of his reception there by the
Catholic sovereigns, it seemed to me as probable that some contemporary account of this arrival and reception, as well as of the
sojourn of Columbus, might be found at Barcelona; and, while
there in the spring of 1844, I searched the admirably arranged archives of Aragon, and also those of the city of Barcelona, for such
notice, but without any success. I could not so much as find a
mention of the name of Columbus.

The *Dietaria*, or day-book, of Barcelona notices the arrival of
ambassadors, the movements of the king and queen, and even
records incidents of as trifling note as those which in our day serve
to fill the columns of a court journal; yet not a word appears in regard to Columbus.

How account for this silence? Is it another evidence of the old
feeling of jealousy between the Aragonese and Castilians, of which
the student of Spanish history meets so many proofs? Such was
the opinion to which I was forced, and such I found also was the
interpretation given to it by the intelligent Archevero, who had
himself gone over this ground a few years since at the request of
Navarrete. The voyage of Columbus was undertaken at the
expense and for the benefit of the crown of Castile. It was not to
Aragon, but to Castilla of Leon, that Columbus gave a new world,
and as the Aragonese did not profit directly by this gift, they saw
fit to treat it and its donor with scornful silence.

In one of the notes to the great work of Capmany,—*Memorias
sobre la ciudad de Barcelona*, 1789—he gives a list of distinguished
men who have enjoyed the hospitality of the city, and among them
places the name of Columbus, making no allusion however to any
contemporary account of his sojourn there.

In the *Dietaria* of Barcelona, under date 15th November 1492,
is the following entry:—" The king, queen, and primogenito,

The seductive adulation of the court and the people did not, however, divert his thoughts from the preparations for a second expedition. A stay of six months sufficed to make all ready for this purpose; during which period a papal bull was obtained, which fixed the famous line of demarcation, determining the right of the Spanish and Portuguese to discovered lands; which line was drawn from the north to the south pole, at a hundred leagues west of the Azores and Cape de Verde islands; the discoveries to the westward were to belong to Spain, and those to the eastward to Portugal. It may be well here to remark that the preparations for Columbus's second armament gave rise to a malignant feeling towards him on the part of Juan Rodriguez Fonseca, bishop of Badajos, which eventually led to such disgraceful ill-usage of the admiral as will remain a stain upon the character of Spain while the name of Columbus exists in the memory of man.

On the 25th September 1493, Columbus took his

entered to-day the city, and lodged in the palace of the bishop of Urgil in the Calle Ancha." This is followed by a description of the festivities which followed. "1493, 4th February.—King and queen went to Alserrat. 14th.—King and queen returned to Barcelona."

As there appears no notice of the king having changed his abode after taking possession of the palace in the Calle Ancha, it was probably there that Columbus recounted to Isabella his adventures and his success. The American pilgrim may still, in the beautiful Alcazar of the Moorish kings, recall the figure of the discoverer of his land, standing in the presence of the Catholic sovereigns of Spain;—in the cotton-spinning town of Barcelona the besom of modern improvement has long since swept away the palace of the bishop of Urgil.

i

departure a second time from Palos, with a fleet of
three large ships of heavy burthen, and fourteen caravels, and after a pleasant voyage reached the island of
Dominica on the 2nd of November. The letter of Dr.
Chanca, which we have here translated, gives an
interesting description of a considerable portion of the
events of this voyage, but it is to be regretted that his
account terminates so abruptly, and the " memorial"
of Columbus to the sovereigns adds but few incidents
of moment to the narrative. We should be strain-
ing the necessary limits of a mere introduction to
these translated documents, were we to undertake to
lead the reader through the various history of this
eventful period of the life of Columbus. Such a task
has been rendered perfectly unnecessary by the much
admired work of Washington Irving. Suffice it that
we state, that the principal geographical information
supplied by this voyage consists in the discovery of the
Caribbee Islands, Jamaica, an Archipelago (named by
Columbus the Queen's Gardens, supposed to be the
Morant Keys), Evangelista, or the Isle of Pines; and
the island of Mona.

He sailed with his fleet finally for Spain on the
28th of April, 1496, and after working their way for
nearly two months against the whole current of the
trade-winds (during which provisions became so reduced, that there was talk of killing, and even eating
the Indian prisoners), they reached the bay of Cadiz on
the 11th of June. The emaciated state of the crew
when they disembarked, presenting so mournful a
contrast with the joyous and triumphant appearance

which they were expected to make, produced a very discouraging impression upon the opinions of the public, and reflected a corresponding depression upon the spirits of Columbus himself. He was reassured, however, by the receipt of a gracious letter from the sovereigns, inviting him to the court; a letter the more gratifying to him that he had feared he was fallen into disgrace. He was received with distinguished favour, and had a verbal concession of his request to be furnished with eight ships for a third voyage. He was doomed, however, to have his patience severely tried by the delay which occurred in the performance of this promise, which was partly attributable to the engrossing character of the public events of the day, and partly to the machinations of his inveterate enemy, the bishop Fonseca.

It was not till the 30th of May 1498, that he set sail from San Lucar, with six of the eight vessels promised, the other two having been despatched to Hispaniola, with provisions, in the beginning of the year. When off Ferro, he despatched three of his six vessels to the same island, with a store of fresh supplies for the colony, while with his remaining three he steered for the Cape Verde Islands, which he reached on the 27th of June. On the 5th of July he left Boavista, and proceeded southward and westward. In the course of this voyage the crews suffered intensely from the heat, having at one time reached the fifth degree of north latitude, but at length land was descried on the 31st of July,—a most providential occurrence, as but one cask of water remained in the ship. The island they came to formed an addition to his discoveries; and as the first land which appeared consisted of three mountains, united at their base, he christened the island, from the name of the Trinity, La Trinidad. It was in this voyage that he discovered terra firma, and the islands of Margarita and Cubagua. His supposition that Paria had formed the original abode of our first parents, is curiously described in our translated letter; and to a careful observer the sagacity of his mode of reasoning is perceptible even in a speculation so fanciful as this. On reaching Hispaniola (to which he was drawn by his anxiety on account of the infant colony), he had the mortification to find that his authority had suffered considerable diminution, and that the colony was in a state of organized rebellion. He had scarcely, by his active, and at the same time politic conduct, brought matters to a state of comparative tranquillity, when a new storm gathered round him from the quarter of the Spanish court. The hatred of his ancient enemies availed itself of the clamour raised against him by some of the rebels who had recently returned to Spain, and charges of tyranny, cruelty, and ambition, were heaped unsparingly upon him. The king and queen, wearied with reiterated complaints, at length resolved to send out a judge, to inquire into his conduct,—injudiciously authorizing him to seize the governorship in the place of Columbus, should the accusations brought against him prove to be valid. The person chosen was Don Francisco de Bobadilla, whose character and qualifications for the office are best demonstrated by the fact, that, on the

day after his arrival in Hispaniola, he seized upon the
government before he had investigated the conduct of
Columbus, who was then absent; he also took up his
residence in his house, and took possession of all his
property, public and private, even to his most secret
papers. A summons to appear before the new
governor was despatched to Columbus, who was at
Fort Concepcion; and in the interval, between the despatch of the summons and his arrival, his brother
(Don Diego) was seized, thrown into irons, and confined on board of a caravel, without any reason being
assigned for his imprisonment. No sooner did the
admiral himself arrive, than he likewise was put in
chains, and thrown into confinement. The habitual
reverence due to his venerable person and exalted
character, made each bystander shrink from the task
of fixing the fetters on him, till one of his own domes-
tics, described by Las Casas as " a graceless and
shameless cook," filled up the measure of ingratitude
that he seemed doomed to experience, by riveting the
irons, not merely with apathy, but with manifest
alacrity. In this shackled condition he was conveyed,
in the early part of October, from prison to the ship
that was to convey him home; and when Andreas
Martin, the master of the caravel, touched with respect
for the years and great merit of Columbus, and deeply
moved at this unworthy treatment, proposed to take
off his irons, he declined the offered benefit, with the
following magnanimous reply: " Since the king has
commanded that I should obey his governor, he shall
find me as obedient to this, as I have been to all his

other orders; nothing but his command shall release me. If twelve years' hardship and fatigue; if continual dangers and frequent famine; if the ocean first opened, and five times passed and repassed, to add a new world, abounding with wealth, to the Spanish monarchy; and if an infirm and premature old age, brought on by these services, deserve these chains as a reward, it is very fit I should wear them to Spain, and keep them by me as memorials to the end of my life." This in truth he did; for he always kept them hung on the walls of his chamber, and desired that when he died, they might be buried with him.

His arrival in Spain in this painful and degraded condition produced so general a sensation of indignation and astonishment, that a warm manifestation in his favour was the immediate consequence. A letter (here translated), written by him to Doña Juana de la Torre, a lady of the court, detailing the wrongs he had suffered, was read to queen Isabella, whose generous mind was filled with sympathy and indignation at the recital. The sovereigns hastened to order him to be set at liberty, and ordered two thousand ducats to be advanced, for the purpose of bringing him to court, with all distinction and an honourable retinue. His reception at the Alhambra was gracious and flattering in the highest degree; the strongest indignation was expressed against Bobadilla, with an assurance that he should be immediately dismissed from his command, while ample restitution and reward were promised to Columbus, and he had every sanction for indulging the fondest hopes of returning in honour and triumph to St. Domingo. But here a grievous disappointment awaited him; his re-appointment was postponed from time to time with various plausible excuses. Though Bobadilla was dismissed, it was deemed desirable to refill his place for two years, by some prudent and talented officer, who should be able to put a stop to all remaining faction in the colony, and thus prepare the way for Columbus to enjoy the rights and dignities of his government, both peacefully and beneficially to the crown. The newly-selected governor was Nicholas de Ovando, who, though described by Las Casas as a man of prudence, justice, and humility, certainly betrayed a want both of generosity and justice, in his subsequent transactions with Columbus. It is possible that the delay manifested by the sovereigns in redeeming their promise, might have continued until the death of Columbus, had not a fresh stimulant to the cupidity of Ferdinand been suggested, by a new project of discovering a strait, of the existence of which Columbus felt persuaded, from his own observations, and which would connect the New World which he had discovered with the wealthy shores of the east. His enthusiasm on the subject was heightened by an emulous consideration of the recent achievements of Vasco de Gama and Cabral, the former of whom had, in 1497, found a maritime passage to India by the Cape, and the latter, in 1500, had discovered for Portugal the vast and opulent empire of Brazil. The prospect of a more direct and safe route to India than that discovered by De Gama, at length gained Columbus the accomplishment of his wish for another armament; and, finally, on the 9th of May 1502, he sailed from Cadiz on his fourth and last voyage of discovery.

It is painful to read the description given of the splendour of the fleet with which Ovando left Spain to assume the government of Hispaniola, and to contrast it with the slender and inexpensive armament granted to Columbus for the purpose of exploring an unknown strait into an unknown ocean, the traversing of whose unmeasured breadth would complete the circumnavigation of the globe. Ovando's fleet consisted of thirty sail, five of them from ninety to one hundred and fifty tons burden, twenty-four caravels of from thirty to ninety tons, and one bark of twenty-five tons; and the number of souls amounted to about two thousand five hundred. The heroic and injured man, to whose unparalleled combination of noble qualities, the very dignity which called for all this state was indebted for its existence, had now in the decline of his years and strength, and stripped both of honour and emolument, to venture forth with four caravels,—the largest of seventy, and the smallest of fifty tons burthen—accompanied by one hundred and fifty men, on one of the most toilsome and perilous enterprises of which the mind can form a conception.

On the 20th of May he reached the Grand Canary, and starting from thence on the 25th, took his departure for the west. Favoured by the trade winds, he made a gentle and easy passage, and reached one of the Caribbee Islands, called by the natives Mantinino (in all probability Martinique), on the 15th of June.

After staying three days at this island, he steered northwards, and touched at Dominica, and from thence directed his course, contrary to his own original intention and the commands of the sovereigns, to St. Domingo. His reason was that his principal vessel sailed so ill as to delay the progress of the fleet, which he feared might be an obstacle to the safety and success of the enterprise, and held this as a sufficient motive for infringing the orders he had received. On his arrival at San Domingo, he found the ships which had brought out Ovando ready to put to sea on their return to Spain. He immediately sent to the governor to explain that his intention in calling at the island was to procure a vessel in exchange for one of his caravels, which was very defective; and further, begged permission for his squadron to take shelter in the harbour, from a hurricane, which, from his acquaintance with the prognostics of the weather, he had foreseen was rapidly approaching. This request was ungraciously refused; upon which Columbus, though denied shelter for himself, endeavoured to avert the danger of the fleet, which was about to sail, and sent back immediately to the governor to entreat that he would not allow it to put to sea for some days. His predictions and requests were treated with equal contempt, and Columbus had not only to suffer these insulting refusals, and the risk of life for himself and squadron, but the loud murmurings of his own crew, that they had sailed with a commander whose position exposed them to such treatment. All he could do was to draw his ships up as close as possible to the

k

shore, and seek the securest anchorage that chance might present him with. Meanwhile the weather appeared fair and tranquil, and the fleet of Bobadilla put boldly out to sea. The predicted storm came on the next night with terrific fury, and all the ships belonging to the governor's fleet, with the exception of one, were either lost, or put back to San Domingo in a shattered condition. The only vessel that escaped was the one which had been freighted with some four thousand gold pieces, rescued from the pillage of Columbus's fortune. Bobadilla, Roldan, and a number of the most inveterate enemies of the admiral, perished in this tremendous hurricane, while his own fleet, though separated and considerably damaged by the storm, all arrived safe at last at Port Hermoso, to the west of San Domingo. He repaired his vessels at Port Hermoso, but had scarcely left the harbour before another storm drove him into Port Brazil. On the 14th of July he left this port, steering for terra firma, and on the 30th discovered the small island of Guanaga or Bonacca, a few leagues east of the bay of Honduras. He continued an eastern course, and discovered the cape now known as Cape Honduras. While moving along this coast, he experienced one of those terrific tempests to which the tropics are liable, and of which he gives so impressive a description in the letter we have translated. At length, after forty days' struggle to make as much as seventy leagues from the cape of Honduras, he reached a cape, by doubling which he found a direct southward course opened to them, offering at the same time an un-obstructed navigation, and a favourable wind. To commemorate this sudden relief from toil and danger, Columbus named this point Cape *Gracias a Dios*, or "thanks to God." A melancholy occurrence took place on the 16th of September, while they were anchored off this coast. The boats had been sent up a large river to procure supplies of wood and water, when, on returning, the encounter of the sea with the rapid current of the river caused so violent and sudden a commotion, that one of the boats was swallowed up, and all on board perished. On the 25th of September he reached Cariay, or Cariari, where he stayed till the 5th of October. The next point was the Bay of Carumbaru, which was the first place on that coast where he met with specimens of pure gold. Leaving this bay on the 17th of October, he sailed along the coast of Veragua, and here he was informed by the Indians of the wealthy country of Ciguare, which he supposed to be some province belonging to the Grand Khan, and also of a river ten days' journey beyond Ciguare, which he conceived to be the Ganges. On the 2nd of November he discovered Puerto Bello, in which harbour he was detained till the 9th by stormy weather; continuing his course eastward till, near the end of the month, he reached a small harbour, to which he gave the name of El Retrete, or the Cabinet. It was here that a continuance of stormy weather, in addition to the murmurs of his crew at being compelled to prosecute an indefinite search, with worm-eaten ships, against opposing currents, determined Columbus on relinquishing his eastward voyage for the present, and to return in search of the gold mines of Veragua. But on altering his course to the westward, he had the mortification to find the wind for which he had long been wishing came now, as if in direct opposition to his adopted course, and for nine days he was exposed to so terrific a storm, that it was a marvel how his crazy vessels could outlive it. At length, after a month's anxiety and suffering, they anchored, on the day of the Epiphany, at the mouth of a river called by the natives Yebra, but which Columbus named Belem, or Bethlehem. Here a settlement was formed, and here occurred the sad disasters and conflicts with the natives, which he describes in his letter from Jamaica, and in which the faithful and zealous Diego Mendez proved an eminently efficient assistant to his much loved master. The history of this unhappy voyage, the toils and perils of which were aggravated to Columbus by extreme bodily suffering, closes by his reaching Jamaica, where he would in all probability have perished, but for the devotedness and activity of Mendez. The highly interesting description of that brave man's exploits on behalf of Columbus, has been quoted by Navarrete from his will, and is here translated. When at length, through the agency of Mendez, two ships arrived from Hispaniola to the assistance of the admiral, he was enabled, on the 28th of June, 1504, to leave his wrecked vessels behind him, and start with revived hopes for San Domingo, which he reached on the 13th of August. His sojourn there was not, as may be judged, calculated to afford him satisfaction or pleasure. The overstrained courtesy of the governor offered but a poor alleviation to the rush of rankling feelings which the past associations and present desolation of the place summoned up to his mind.

On the 12th of September he set sail for Spain; the same tempestuous weather, which had all along tended to make this his last voyage the most disastrous, did not forsake him now. The ship in which he came home sprung her mainmast in four places in one tempest, and in a subsequent storm the foremast was sprung, and, finally on the 7th of November, he arrived, in a vessel as shattered as his own broken and care-worn frame, in the welcome harbour of San Lucar.

The two years which intervened between this period and his death present a picture of black ingratitude on the part of the crown, to this distinguished benefactor of the kingdom, which it is truly painful to contemplate. We behold an extraordinary man, the discoverer of a second hemisphere, reduced by his very success to so low a state of poverty, that in his prematurely infirm old age he is compelled to subsist by borrowing, and to plead in the apologetic language of a culprit for the rights of which the very sovereign whom he has benefited has deprived him. The death of the benignant and high-minded Isabella, in 1505, gave a finishing blow to his hope of obtaining redress, and we find him thus writing subsequent to this period to his old and faithful friend Diego de Deza:—" It appears that his majesty does not think fit to fulfil that which he, with the queen, who is now in glory, promised me by word and seal. For me to contend for the contrary, would be to contend with the wind. I have done all that I could do; I leave the rest to God, whom I have ever found propitious to me in my necessities." The selfish and cold-hearted Ferdinand beheld his illustrious and loyal servant sink, without relief, under bodily infirmity, and the palsying sickness of hope deferred; and at length, on the 20th of May 1506, the generous heart which had done so much without reward and suffered so much without upbraiding, found rest in a world where neither gratitude nor justice is either asked or withheld.

His body was in the first instance buried at Valladolid, in the parish church of Santa Maria de la Antigua, but was transferred, in 1513, to the Cartuja de las Cuevas, near Seville, where a monument was erected over his grave with the memorable inscription,—

A CASTILLA Y A LEON
NUEVO MUNDO DIÓ COLON.

In the year 1536, both his body, and that of his son Diego, who had been likewise buried in the Cartuja, were transported to St. Domingo, and deposited in the cathedral of that city. From hence they were removed to Havanna, in 1795, on the cession of Hispaniola to the French, and the ashes of the immortal discoverer now quietly repose in the cathedral church of that city.*

* I am indebted to Mr. Sumner for the following copy of the inscription on the tomb of Fernando Columbus, in the pavement of the cathedral of Seville, and for the note which accompanies it:—

"Aqui yaze el M. Magnifico S. D. Hernando Colon, el qual

A tardy tribute has been at length paid to his memory by his fellow-citizens of Genoa, and the first stone of a monument in commemoration of his achievements was laid in that city on the 27th of September, 1846.*

The Editor cannot close these remarks without expressing his thanks to Mr. Henry Stevens, than whom

aplicó y gastó toda su vida y hazienda en aumento de las letras, y juntar y perpetuar en esté ciudad todos sus libros de todas las ciencias que en su tiempo halló y en reducirlo a quatro libros, falleció en ésta ciudad a 12 de Julio de 1539 de edad de 50 años 9 meses y 14 dias, fue hijo del valeroso y memorable S. D. Christ. Colon primero que descubrió las Yndias y nuevo mundo en vida de los Cat. R. D. Fernando y D. Ysabel de gloriosa memoria a 11 de Oct. de 1492 con tres galeras y 90 personas, y parti del puerto de Palos a descubrirlas a 3 de Agosto antes, y Bolvio a Castilla con victoria a 7 de illaio del Año Siguiente y torno despues otras dos veces ā poblarlo que descubrio falleció en Valladolid à 20 de Agosto de 1506 años."

ROGA DE DIOS POR ELLOS.

Beneath this is described, in a circle, a globe, presenting the western and part of the eastern hemispheres, surmounted by a pair of compasses. Within the border of the circle is the same inscription as that which was placed over Columbus himself at the Cartuja, with the exception of the word " mundo" being placed before instead of after the word "nuevo."

Throughout all Spain I know of no other inscription to the memory of Columbus. At Valladolid, where he died and where his body lay for some years, there is none that I could discover, neither is there any trace of any at the Cartuja, near Seville, to which his body was afterwards transferred, and in which his brother was buried.

It is a striking confirmation of the reproach of negligence, in regard to the memory of this great man, that in this solitary inscription in old Spain, the date of his death should be inaccurately given.

G. S.

* See *Athenæum*, Oct. 24th, 1846.

few are better acquainted with the literature of America, for minute information on the bibliography of the first letter. He is also indebted to Washington Irving's admirable life of Columbus for very many incidents in the biography, with which no other work could have supplied him.

———

LA LETTERA

DELLISOLE CHE HA TROVATO NUOVAMENTE IL RE DISPAGNA.

(Referred to at p. vi of the Introduction.)

Omnipotente idio, che tucto regge,
donami gratia chio possa cantare
allaude tua & di tua sancta legge,
cosa che piaccia achi stara ascoltare
maxim al popol tuo & alla tua grege,
el qual nō resta mai magnificare,
como al ꝑsēte ha fatto nella Spagna,
delle isole trovate cosa magna.

Io ho gia lecto degli antichi regi
& principi signori stanti in terra,
del re della soria & facti egregi,
& lebactaglie loro & la gran guerra,
& delle giostre gli acquistati pregi
di Bello lessi & selmio dir nō erra,
de persi, medi, & degli ateniensi,
Dāfinione & gli altri egregi immēsi.

Et de lacedemoni le grandi entrate,
di Labores di Oreste & daltri assai,
del Principe Gisippo cose late,
come si legge so che inteso lhai,
di Tholomeo piu cose smisurate,
& del gran Faraone come saprai,
di judici & de regi de giudei,
che afaccia parlavano con lei.

l

Et de latini lessi, & degli albani,
& di quel fiesolano Re Atalante,
de regi & consolati de romani,
& de tribuni lessi cose tante,
dedeci viri electi tanti humani,
& degli īmperadori potrei dir quāte,
cose chi tengo nel mio pecto fisse.
p̄ che sarian nel dir troppo plisse.

che sio volesse tucti efacti dire
disopra nominati & altri assai,
certo farei latua mente stupire
maximi alcuni che nō ludiron mai,
q̃ste cose alte degne magne et mire
che se tu leggi tu letroverrai
invernacula lingua & ī latino,
si come narra un decto dagostino.

Ma chi potessi leggere nel futuro
duno Alexādro magno papa sexto,
della sua creatione il modo puro,
grato a ciascūo anessū mai molesto,
& del primanno suo il magno muro,
che nō glipuo nessuno esser infesto
sesto alexādro pappa borgia ispano,
justo nel giudicare & tucto humano.

Et chi leggesi poi del sua Ferrādo
christianissimo rege xp̃iani
che lisabella tiene al suo comādo,
unica sposa sua, che nelle mani
tanti reami indota allui donando,
gliha dati ītendi ben cō pēsier sani,
che glie re della spagna & di castella
& di leon tolecto villa bella.

Simile re di cordube chiamato,
& poi dimutia re mipar che sia
& digalitia re incoronato,
dalgarbe re & tienla in sua balia,
re digranata sai che conquistato
diragona signor & divalēzia pia
conte mipar che sia dibarzalona,
& disicilia re isola buona.

Di quāta altura principe mipare
& disardigna tien la signoria,
& di corsica sifa simil chiamare,
di q̃lla parte che glha in sua balia
& conte di serdeina appellare,
& dirosello conte par che sia
simile re mi pare che dimaiorica,
l'altro reame e poi della minorica.

Et poi signor dibiscaia & molina,
delalsesiras signor chiamato,
dellasturias terra peregrina,
p. tucto il mondo q̃sto e nominato,
tucto fedele della legge divina,
chi altro crede e mal dallui trattato
come sivede che nō e mai satio,
dimarrani giudei far ogni stratio.

Pero il signore lha semp̃ ivicto facto,
che si puo uno agusto nominare,
ogni sua lega triegua legge o pacto,
mai nō sividde dallui maculare
lui nō derise mai savio ne macto
limosine per dio sempre fa fare
della chiesa zeloso a tucte lhore
come fedel, p̃iano, & pio signore.

Come mōstra lamagna ābascieria,
che glha mandato adar lubidiēza
al suo sesto Alexādro anima pia
che mai sivide tal magnificenza
in tucte cose la sua signoria
dimōstrā aver fra gli altri grā potēza
ī q̃sti magni ābascidor sispecchi
chi nol credessi nōci p̃sti orecchi.

Se io volessi e sua titoli dire,
o auditore io ti potrei tediare,
de sua reame io ti farei stupire,
sol que che lisabelela volse dare
indota a q̃sto Re o questo sire,
quando luso p marito pigliare
q̃sta isabella e dispagna Regina,
honesta doña savia & peregrina.

Hor vo tornar almio primo tractato
dellisole trovate incognite a te
in q̃sto anno presente q̃sto e stato
nel millequatrocento novātatre,
uno che xp̃ofan colōbo chiamato,
che e stato in corte der prefecto Re
ha molte volte questa stimolato,
el Re ch'cerchi acrescere il suo stato.

Dicendo, signor mio, io vo cercare
p che comprēdo che ce molta terra
che nostri antichi nō seppō trovare
& spero dacquistarle senza guerra,
se vostra signoria si vuol degnare
ajuto darmi che so que non erra
lamente mia spera nel signore
chimbrieve cidara rengo & honore.

Voi mectetē la roba io la persona
non sara vostra signoria disfacta,
ispesse volte la fortuna dona
ꝑ piccol prezo assai & non e macta
che sua sperāza tucto il mōdo sprona
savio e colùi che dicercar sadacta
ꝑ che dice elvāgelio ĩ legge nuova
che chicercādo va spesso truova.

Hō poi cħ lebbe ilre piu volte udito
& facto carisposta sorridendo
xꝓfani ripigliando come ardito
q̃sto āno il re secōdo ch' io cōprēdo
prese di dargli aiuto per partito
& disse il tuo sperare oggi cōmēdo
piglia una nave cō due carovelle
di q̃ste mie armate le piu belle.

Et comādo de poi che gli sia dato
danari & roba q̃l che fa mestiero,
& poi dimolta gēte accompagnato
divotamente & cō buō pensiero,
al sommo dio che fu racomandato,
& alla madre sua & sancto piero,
& prese q̃ste cose, & poi licentia
dalre & laregina & sua clementia.

Et navico piu giorni per perduto,
cō pena, con affanni & grāde stento,
pensa che ua in mare no e mai tuto,
ma semꝓ cōbactēdo ĩ acqua & uēto
ꝑdesi spesso elguadagno eltrebuto,
& nōgli gioua dire io menepento
ma come piacꝗ, adio cħ mai nōerra
in trentatre giornate pose in terra.

Et messe dua desua huomini armati
a cercar ple terre che han trouate,
seforse siscoprissin qualche aguati,
ma caminaron ben per tre giornate
che nōsi furon mai indrieto uolti,
& nō trouaron mai uille o brigate,
si che simarauiglia che camina
& piu chi e restato alla marina.

Ma niēte di manco quella terra
era di uari fructi molto ornata,
se chi ha scripto i qua neldir nōerra,
mōtagne e ue daltura ismisurata,
& molti fiumi lacircūda & serra,
doue trouorun poi molta brigata,
sēza pāni, uestite, o arme, o scudi,
ma tucti emēbri loro si erano nudi.

Saluo chalcuna donna che coperte
tiene leparte genitale immonde,
cō bambagia tessuta, & di po certe
lhauen coperte con diuerse frōde,
& come uidon questi lediserte
forte fuggendo ciascun fina scōde,
& questi dua in drieto si tornauano,
& axꝓofano lo facto racontauano.

Et xꝓofano & glialtri dismontati
armati tucti il paese cercando
isole molte & huomini trouati
come tu intenderai qui ascoltando
& glistendardi del Re ha rizati,
& a ciascuno il suo nome mutando,
come dira questa pistola magna,
da xꝓosano scripta al Re di spagna.

Perchio so, signor mio, c̃ gr̄a piacer̃
hara la uostra magna signoria
quando potra intendere o sapere,
delle cose che io presi in mia balia,
p uirtu del signore & suo potere,
& simil dellà madre sua maria,
dal partir mio a tr̄etatre giornate,
molte isole & gr̄a ḡete iho trouate.

Lisola prima chio trouai, signore,
io lho p nome facta nominare
isola magna di san Saluadore,
& la seconda poi feci chiamare
conceptio Marie a suo honore,
di poi laterza feci baptezare
per uostra signoria c̃ t̄ato ornata
isola ferrandina lho nominata,

Et la quarta Isabella fo chiamare,
p la Regina che t̄anto honorata,
& alla quinta il nome uolsi dare
che lisola Giouanna fia chiamata,
& la festa dun nome uolsi ornare
che c̄ogruo miparse a q̃lla fiata,
che Laspagnuola qlla sichiamasse,
per che mipar che cosi meritasse.

Enomi son dellisole trouate
nel india, signor mio, como uiscriuo,
& questa & laltre sopra nominate
notitia auoi nedo signor mio diuo
trec̄eto uc̃tun miglio ho caminate,
& peruenuto alfin colsancto uliuo
dalla gioūana alla spagnuola elmar̃
ciqū̄ataquattro miglia largo apare.

Et per septentrione lanauicai
cinquantaquattro miglia dimarina,
doue che alla spagna io arriuai,
inuerso loriente sauicina,
& per lalinea recta io caminai
da onde la spagnuola li confina
son c̄iquec̄esessantaquattro miglia,
e lalargheza che q̄sta isola piglia.

Et q̄sta & tucte laltre e molto forte,
ma q̄sta sopra laltre par fortissima,
potresi inanzi dare a tucti morte
ch̄ una parte sacquisti piccolissima,
certo questo eildestino qsto e lesorte,
ch̄ uostra signoria fan felicissima,
e dotata di fructe molte & uarie,
& liti, & porti, & cose necessarie,

Et molti fiumi, & maxime mōtagne,
che son dalteza molto smisurate,
arbori, fonte, uccegli, & cose magne,
chauostri tempi nō san mai trouate,
certo lamente mia signor ne piagne,
per lalegreza delle cose ornate,
di tucte cose cie se io non erro,
saluo ch̄ nōsi truoua acciaio o ferro.

Sonci di septe o uer docto ragioni
di palme che mifan marauigliare,
& se alzando gliocchi poni
pini uison che laria par toccare,
passere lu signuoli & altri doni,
che nonsi potre mai tucto narrare,
della bambagia un pondo ce infinito
& daltre cose assai ce inquesto lito.

Arbori cison duna ragion fioriti
del mese di novembre chenoi siano
come ī ispagna, & ne suo degno liti,
liarberi sō elmagio, elmōte, elpiano,
si che no altri stiano tucti stupiti
p labōdantia che trouata habbiano,
sonci gli arberi uerdi & lelor foglie,
chi credo che nō pdā mai lespoglie.

Di reubararo ce tanta abōdantia,
& dicenamo daltra spetieria,
loro & largento, el metallo ciauāza,
maxime un fiume che per q̃sta uia,
che nō puo questa terra farne senza,
doue ho trouato cō mia fantasia,
che dimoltoro e piena quella rena,
sicome lacqua di quel fiume mena.

Simil, signore, io uiuoglio auisare,
che inq̃stisola ce molta pianura,
doue difizi molti sipuon fare,
& castelle cipta cō magne mura,
che nō bisogna poi di dubitare,
ne dhauer chi cista nulla paura,
molte terre cison da feminare,
& depascer lebestie & nutricare.

Ho po trouati certi fiumicelli,
cħ tucti menano oro & nō gia poco,
& molti porti grādi & da far belli,
che abōdanza ce dacqua diloco,
lherbe & leselue facte co pennelli
nō son si belle & nō cisusa foco,
glhuomini sono affabile formati,
timidi semp̃ & alfuggir parati.

Sonci assai uille ma son piccolecte,
dhuomini & dōne son tucte calcate,
glihabitacoli qui son capānecte
semplici sono & credule brigate,
& ben che sieno nudi stāno necte,
si che signor dibuona uoglia state,
& credon che no siā di cielo ī terra,
mādati per cāpargli dogni guerra.

Portano alcun certe cāne appuntate,
socto lebraccia come noi lespade,
archi cō frecce dicanne tagliate,
& uāno īsieme assai come lesquadr̃
di capegli & di barbe molto ornate,
nō son micidial persone o ladre,
ma tucto q̃l cħ glhiāno ī lor potere
celodarebbon p farci piacere.

Et parmi che cifia grā diferenza
da questa isola a q̃lla di Giouāna
darbori, fructi, & dherbe & dip̃sēza,
nōci manca senon la sancta māna,
doro ce tanto cha uostra potenza
chi guerra far sipensa ī uan safāna
oltre alla roba acquistate lhonore,
tucti son prōti acreder al signore.

Questi popoli grādi & infiniti,
come p segni ciāno dimōstrato,
ledōne & lor figluoli & lor mariti
ciascuno spera desser baptezato,
priego il signor iesu che puo glīuiti
apossedere el suo regno beato
di quāto ben cagion signor sarete
coluostro auxilio che dato mhauete.

Iho menati qui certi indiani
c̄h cōprēdā di q̃sta alcun līguaggio
tal che parlando con cēni dimani
q̃lcū diq̃sti c̄he piu sperto & saggio
dicon di farsi a noi tucti xp̃iani
tal chiho p̃so signor mio uātaggio
& di legname una bastia fo fare
& lagente uimecto per guardare.

Et forniti glilascio per uno anno
darme diuectouaglia ben chi spero
che nō haranno molestia ne dāno
p che gli lascio cō un buon pensiero,
humili mansueti tucti stanno,
sic̄h auxilio iluostro signor chiero,
mandimi uostra signoria piacente
allaude del signore omnipotente.

Chi nō uede signor lisole degne,
& lericheze o nobil creatura,
& lauarieta darbori & legne,
& deglhuomini & dōne lor figura,
nō sa c̄h sia delmōdo lesue ī segne,
chi nō esce delcerchio di sua mura,
nō puo perfectamente idio laudare
chi nō gusta lecose che sa fare.

Signor mio dolce, lapiaceuoleza
di q̃sta gente io non saprei narrare,
per una stringa che poco sipreza
uolson tanto oro aun diquesti dare
c̄h tre ducati & mezo o che richeza
hare potuto inqueste parte fare,
ma io ho comādato alla mia gente
che ciascun doni & nō pigli niēte.

Per far lor grata uostra signoria
dimolta roba io ho facto donare
di quella dimie gente & della mia,
come scodelle & piacti damāgiare,
& uetri & panni chera in mia balia,
senza riserbo alcuno per me fare
p chio glho conosciuti tanto grati,
iglho come fedeli & buō tractati.

Vero e cħ sono assai prōti alfugire
per che non sono usati di uedere
gente che usin panni da uestire,
ma per che uegan noi tucto sapere,
ciascun diloro ciadora come sire,
& lalor roba da mangiare o bere,
nō ho ueduto fare ne tuo ne mio,
ma lauita comune alparer mio.

Volsano ancora p una bocte trista,
& per un pezo darco che nō uale,
tre once doro darmi & similmista,
tanta bambagia che mezo quintale,
ma poi chi hebbi questa cosa uista
parsemi dipigliar niente male,
& ho cōmesso aciaschedun de mia
chedipigliare niente ardito sia.

Nō e fra loro alcuna briga o secta,
ma pacifici tucti insieme stanno,
di parole & di facti mai saspecta,
di far uēdecta alcūa īgiuria o dāno,
beato a q̃llo che seguir sidilecta,
acompagnati abraccio semp̃ uāno,
io glho uisti si buoni recti & grati,
chc abuō fine idio glhara chiamati.

Nō e fra loro idolatria nessuna,
tucti lemani al ciel tengono alzate,
nō adoran pianeti, o sole, o luna,
ma lelor mente al ciel tucte leuate,
dicon la gloria ī ciel esser sol una,
dellaqual pàtria credon cħ mādate
lenostre barche siano & noi ī terra,
a far pace colciel dogni lor guerra.

Io nho cō meco semp̃ alcū menato
equali feci per forza pigliare,
q̃ndo alpricipio ī terra fui smōtato,
non potendo inaltra forma fare
pelueloce fuggir mai ascoltato
nō era lemie uoci olmio parlare,
& q̃sti che per forza allhor pigliai,
son per amor uenuti sempre mai.

Semp̃ mangiare, o bere, & adormire,
acanto a me io glho si ben tractati,
cħ gliaferman p certo & usan dire
cħ dalregno del ciel no siā mādati,
uanocci inanzi gridando uenire,
debba ciascuno auedere ebeati,
si chalpresente ognū corre auedere
& portan tucti damāgiare & bere.

Da luna isola allaltra q̃sti uāno
cō certe barche che inquesta isola e,
lequal dun legno solo facte stanno,
& son chiamate queste canoe,
sō lūghe strecte & par quasi uolādo
andare achiunche messo dētro ce,
bencħ sien grossamente lauorate
cō sassi & legni & ossi son cauate.

Et hōne uista alcuna tāto grāde
che octanta persone cista dentro,
& ciascūo hal suo remo & leumāde
nauica q̃sti & con buon sētimeto
la roba luno allaltro li sispande
q̃l chio uscriuo signor nulla mēto
& uanno baractando tucti quāti
come sefussin quasi mercatanti.

Inqueste isole tucte nominate
nō ho ueduta nulla differenza
dincarnati diuisi o dibrigate,
ma tucti quasi son duna presenza
& dun cōstume tucti cōstumate
huomini & dōne sō pie dicremēza,
tucti hāno una loquela & un parlã̄
che uifarē, signor, marauigliare.

Che par che util cosa questa sia
acōuerrirgli a nostra sancta fede,
che come scriuo auostra signoria
ciascun disposto ce, & gia lacrede
dique che han uista lapresenza mia
no glho tucti ueduti ne siuede
cñglie margior giouāna senza sotia
che nōe linghilterra con lascotia.

Son duo p̃uincíe chio nō ho cercate,
secondo che q̄sti altri decto hāno,
una cene la qual queste brigate
dican che quelle gente che uistāno
son con le code tucte quante nate
& Anaan elnome posto lehanno,
poi caminai p̃ la spagnuola ciglia
p̃ cinquecēsessantoquattro miglia.

Doue e lauilla laqual io pigliai,
doue io feci larocca o uer bastia
che la piu bella che io uedessi mai,
come iho scripto a uostra signoria
non miricorda se adir uimandai
inquesta brieue epistolecta mia
elnōe ch̄ io lho posto & forse auisto
natiuita del nostro Iesu Xp̄o.

In queste isole tucti questi stāno
contenti duna dōna ciascheduno,
ma q̄sti principali tucti mhanno
uēti lequal son date lor per uno,
& luno allaltro mai torto nō fanno,
che a cio far nō ce pronto nessuno,
& nelle cose tucte da mangiare
nulla diuision uiueggo fare.

Et ben che i q̄ste parti caldo sia,
lastate eluerno ce digran freddura,
ma p che mangiā molta spetieria
lacarne loro alfreddo molto dura
inquesta parte nulla cosa ria,
sitruoua diche questi habbin paura,
saluo che ce unisola allentrare
dellindia per uoler qui arriuare.

In nella quale sta gente uillana
da q̄sti nō mipar che siano amati,
p ch̄ dice māgiā carne humana,
pero nō son da questi qui prezati,
hanno assai legni q̄sta gente strana,
da nauicare & hanno gio rubati,
aquesti di scorrendo dogni banna
cō archi ī mano & cō frecce dicāna.

Non e da q̄sti a quegli differenza,
senō innecapegli che q̄gli hanno
lunghi come ledōne & dipresenza
son come q̄sti & fāno molto dāno,
aq̄ste ch̄ son pprio essa clemenza,
si che ingelosia sempre nestanno,
ma spero che lauostra signoria
sapra purgare una tal maltaia.

Una isola cie decta mactanino,
nella qual le donne sole stanno,
& questo iniquo popol glie uicino,
& ausar con q̄ste spesso uanno,
ma q̄sto popol tucto feminino
exercitio di dōne mai nō fanno,
ma cō gliarchi trahēdo tuctauia,
che par per certo una grā fantasia.

Et uanno queste ben tucte coperte,
nō gia di pāni lini, o lani, o ueli,
ma derbe & giūchi, & q̄ste cose certe
son che di qua nōe lēzuoli o teli
unaltra isola poi legente offerte,
femine & maschi nascō senza peli,
manzi uoglio cōfuso esser nel dire
chi uoglia alcuna cosa preterire.

Et dove q̄sti senza peli sono,
piu oro cie chihabbia ācor trouata
di q̄l chi scriuo o parlando ragiono,
signore, io ne son ben giustificato
auostra signoria un magno dono
iho per portar meco preparato
di tucti q̄sti luoghi iuo menare
gente che possin cio testificare.

Pero, giusto signor, di Spagna degno,
stia uostra signoria dibuona uoglia
chīho cresciuto tāto iluostro regno,
cħ chi ua īuidia po crepar didoglia
doro & dargento passarete el segno
tal cħ trarra elnimico di sua soglia,
ma q̃l chi so cħ molto piu prezate
son queste gēte a xp̃o preparate.

Reubarbero assai & aloe,
mastice, cinamono, & spetierie,
tanta richeza, signor mio, qui e
che discaccia da me leuoglie rie,
piu allegreza, signor mio, fare,
si fussi certo che per tucte uie
q̃sta scripta uenissi asaluamento
nel mōdo nō sare huom piu cōtēto.

Nō miacascaltro degno mio signore
scriuere auostra magna signoria,
raccomandomi a q̃lla a tucte lhore,
laqual cōserui ilfigluol di Maria
parato semp̃mai per uostro amore
amecter q̃sta breue uita mia
aquindici de febraio q̃sta sife
nel mille quattrocento nouāta tre.

Magnifici & discreti circūstanti
q̃sta e gran cosa certo da pensare,
cħl nostro redēptor̃ cō tucti esancti
nō resta mai legratie sue mandare
douerebbon di q̃sto tucti quanti
ebaptizati a x̃po festa fare,
chi ue chi uimādo & chi ue andato
prepari dio alsuo regno beato.

Questa ha cōposto de dati Giuliano
apreghiera del magno caualiere
messer Giouanphilippo ciciliano,
che fu di Sixto quarto suo scudiere
& commessario suo & capitano,
a q̃lle cose che fur di mestiere
allaude del signor sicanta & dice
che ciconduca al suo regno felice.

⸿ FINIS LAUS DEO.

⸿ Finita lastoria della īuētione delle nuoue isole dicānaria
īdiane tracto duna pistola dixp̄ofano colōbo, & p̃messer
Giuliano dati tradocta dilatino i uersi uulgari allaude
della christiana religione & ap̃ghiera delmagnifico
caualiere messer Giouāfilippo del ignamine
domestico familiare dello illustrissimo
Redispagna xp̃ianissimo a
di. xxvi. doctobre.
14.93.

Florentie.

SELECT LETTERS

OF

CHRISTOPHER COLUMBUS.

ETC.

FIRST VOYAGE OF COLUMBUS.

A Letter addressed to the noble Lord Raphael Sanchez, Treasurer to their most invincible Majesties, Ferdinand and Isabella, King and Queen of Spain, by Christopher Columbus, to whom our age is greatly indebted, treating of the islands of India recently discovered beyond the Ganges, to explore which he had been sent eight months before under the auspices and at the expense of their said Majesties.

KNOWING that it will afford you pleasure to learn that I have brought my undertaking to a successful termination, I have decided upon writing you this letter to acquaint you with all the events which have occurred in my voyage, and the discoveries which have resulted from it.   Thirty-three days after

---

EPISTOLA CHRISTOFORI COLOM.

Cui ætas nostra multum debet, de Insulis Indiæ supra Gangem nuper inventis, ad quas perquirendas, octavo antea mense, auspiciis et ære invictissimorum Ferdinandi ac Elizabeth Hispaniarum Regum, missus fuerat: ad magnificum Dominum Raphaelem Sanxis, eorumdem Serenissimorum Regum Thesaurarium, missa: quam generosus ac litteratus vir Leander de Cosco ab hispano idiomate in latinum convertit: tertio Kalendas Maii, MCCCCXCIII, Pontificatus Alex. VI, anno I.

QUONIAM susceptæ provinciæ rem perfectam me consecutum fuisse gratum tibi fore scio, has constitui exarare, quæ te uniuscujusque rei in hoc nostro itinere gestæ inventæque admoneant.   Tricesimo tertio die postquam Gadibus discessi, in mare indicum perveni, ubi

B   .

my departure from Cadiz[1] I reached the Indian sea, where I discovered many islands, thickly peopled, of which I took possession without resistance in the name of our most illustrious Monarch, by public proclamation and with unfurled banners. To the first of these islands, which is called by the Indians Guanahani, I gave the name of the blessed Saviour (San Salvador), relying upon whose protection I had reached this as well as the other islands; to each of these I also gave a name, ordering that one should be called Santa Maria de la Concepcion,[2] another Fernandina,[3] the third Isabella,[4] the fourth Juana,[5] and so with all the rest respectively. As soon as we arrived at that, which as I have said was named Juana, I

---

plurimas insulas innumeris habitatas hominibus reperi, quarum omnium pro felicissimo Rege nostro, præconio celebrato, et vexillis extensis, contradicente nemine, possessionem accepi : primæque earum Divi Salvatoris nomen imposui, cujus fretus auxilio tam ad hanc quam ad ceteras alias pervenimus ; eam vero Indi Guanahanyn vocant. Aliarum etiam unamquamque novo nomine nuncupavi : quippe aliam insulam Sanctæ Mariæ Conceptionis, aliam Fernandinam, aliam Isabelam, aliam Joannam, et sic de reliquis appellari jussi. Quamprimum in eam insulam (quam dudum Joannam vocari

[1] A strange mistake has crept into the Latin versions of this letter; in all the editions of which it is stated that Cadiz was the point from which Columbus sailed on his first voyage. In the journal of that voyage, published by Mr. Navarrete, as well as in the accounts given by Don Fernando Columbus, and all other historians, it is distinctly said that he sailed from *Palos*, on the third of August. The question is important, not simply as affecting the correctness of the letter, but also the length of time in which the voyage was accomplished; for as Columbus reached the island of St. Salvador, or Guanahani, on the morning of the twelfth of October, it is apparent, that more than twice the number of days here mentioned, transpired between his leaving Spain and arriving at the West Indies. The mistake evidently consists in the word "Gadibus" having been by some circumstance, at which we can only guess, carelessly exchanged for Gomera, whence Columbus started, according to the journal, on the eighth of September, which leaves an interval exactly coinciding with the thirty-three days here mentioned.

[2] North Caico.   [3] Little Inagua.   [4] Great Inagua.   [5] Cuba.

proceeded along its coast a short distance westward, and found it to be so large and apparently without termination, that I could not suppose it to be an island, but the continental province of Cathay. Seeing, however, no towns or populous places on the sea coast, but only a few detached houses and cottages, with whose inhabitants I was unable to communicate, because they fled as soon as they saw us, I went further on, thinking that in my progress I should certainly find some city or village. At length, after proceeding a great way and finding that nothing new presented itself, and that the line of coast was leading us northwards (which I wished to avoid, because it was winter, and it was my intention to move southwards; and because moreover the winds were contrary), I resolved not to attempt any further progress, but rather to turn back and retrace my course to a certain bay that I had observed, and from which I afterwards dispatched two of our men to ascertain whether there were a king or any cities in that province. These men reconnoitred the country for three days, and found a most numerous population, and great numbers of houses, though small, and built without any regard to order : with

---

dixi) appulimus ; juxta ejus litus occidentem versus aliquantulum processi, tamque eam magnam nullo reperto fine inveni, ut non insulam sed continentem Cathai provinciam esse crediderim ; nulla tamen videns oppida, municipiave in maritimis sita confinibus, præter aliquos vicos et prædia rustica, cum quorum incolis loqui nequibam ; quare simul ac nos videbant, surripiebant fugam. Progrediebar ultra, existimans aliquam me urbem villasve inventurum: denique videns quod longe admodum progressis nihil novi emergebat, et hujusmodi via nos ad septentrionem deferebat (quod ipse fugere exoptabam, terris etenim regnabat bruma), ad austrumque erat in voto contendere, nec minus venti flagitantibus succedebant; constitui alios non operiri successus : et sic retrocedens, ad portum quemdam, quem signaveram, sum reversus ; unde duos homines ex nostros in terram missi, qui investigarent, esset ne Rex in ea provincia, urbesve aliquæ. Hi per tres dies ambularunt, invenerunt-que innumeros populos et habitationes, parvas tamen et absque ullo which information they returned to us. In the mean time I had learned from some Indians whom I had seized, that that country was certainly an island: and therefore I sailed towards the east, coasting to the distance of three hundred and twenty-two miles, which brought us to the extremity of it; from this point I saw lying eastwards another island, fifty-four miles distant from Juana, to which I gave the name of Española:[6] I went thither, and steered my course eastward as I had done at Juana, even to the distance of five hundred and sixty-four miles along the north coast.[7] This said island of Juana is exceedingly fertile, as indeed are all the others; it is surrounded with many bays, spacious, very secure, and surpassing any that I have ever seen; numerous large and healthful

---

regimine; quapropter redierunt. Interea ego jam intellexeram à quibusdam Indis, quos ibidem susceperam, quod hujusmodi provincia insula quidem erat : et sic perrexi orientem versus, ejus semper stringens litora, usque ad milliaria CCCXXII, ubi ipsius insulæ sunt extrema. Hinc aliam insulam ad orientem prospexi, distantem ab hac Joanna milliar. LIV, quam protinus Hispanam dixi, in eamque concessi, et direxi iter quasi per septentrionem, quemadmodum in Joanna ad orientem, milliaria DLXIV. Quæ dicta Joanna et aliæ ibidem insulæ quam fertilissimæ exsistunt. Hæc multis atque tutissimis et latis, nec aliis quos unquam viderim comparandis portibus est circumdata : multi maximi et salubres hanc interfluunt

[6] Hispaniola, or San Domingo.

[7] Naverrete, the learned and industrious compiler of these original letters, in his translation of this first letter from the Latin into the Spanish language, has mistakenly attributed to the preposition "per" the sense of the Spanish word "hacia" (towards), a meaning which can under no circumstances be given to the word, but in this case renders the passage unintelligible. The editor has translated "per septentrionem" "along the north coast" of the island, such a rendering of the preposition being perfectly grammatical, while it gives to the whole sentence a meaning consistent with the course which Columbus in reality took. There are, moreover, two sentences in the immediate context of the original, where, when the sense of "towards" is intended to be expressed, it is unmistakeably given by the words "versus" and "ad".

rivers intersect it, and it also contains many very lofty mountains. All these islands are very beautiful, and distinguished by a diversity of scenery; they are filled with a great variety of trees of immense height, and which I believe to retain their foliage in all seasons; for when I saw them they were as verdant and luxuriant as they usually are in Spain in the month of May,—some of them were blossoming, some bearing fruit, and all flourishing in the greatest perfection, according to their respective stages of growth, and the nature and quality of each: yet the islands are not so thickly wooded as to be impassable. The nightingale and various birds were singing in countless numbers, and that in November, the month in which I arrived there. There are besides in the same island of Juana seven or eight kinds of palm trees, which, like all the other trees, herbs, and fruits, considerably surpass ours in height and beauty. The pines also are very handsome, and there are very extensive fields and meadows, a variety of birds, different kinds of honey, and many sorts of metals, but no iron. In that island also which I have before said we named Española, there are mountains of very great size and beauty, vast plains, groves, and very fruitful fields, admirably adapted

---

fluvii: multi quoque et eminentissimi in ea sunt montes. Omnes hæ insulæ sunt pulcherrimæ, et variis distinctæ figuris, perviæ, et maximâ arborum varietate sidera lambentium plenæ, quas nunquam foliis privari credo: quippe vidi eas ita virentes atque decoras, ceu mense Maio in Hispania solent esse; quarum aliæ florentes, aliæ fructuosæ, aliæ in alio statu, secundum uniuscujusque qualitatem vigebant. Garriebat philomela, et alii passeres varii ac innumeri, mense Novembri, quo ipse per eas deambulabam. Sunt præterea in dicta insula Joanna septem vel octo palmarum genera, quæ proceritate et pulchritudine, quemadmodum ceteræ omnes arbores, herbæ fructusque, nostras facile exsuperant. Sunt et mirabiles pinus, agri, et prata vastissima, variæ aves, varia mella, variaque metalla, ferro excepto. In ea autem, quam Hispanam supra diximus nuncupari, maximi sunt montes ac pulchri, vasta rura, nemora, campi feracissimi, seri pascique et condendis ædificiis aptissimi:

for tillage, pasture, and habitation. The convenience and excellence of the harbours in this island, and the abundance of the rivers, so indispensable to the health of man, surpass anything that would be believed by one who had not seen it. The trees, herbage, and fruits of Española are very different from those of Juana, and moreover it abounds in various kinds of spices, gold, and other metals. The inhabitants of both sexes in this island, and in all the others which I have seen, or of which I have received information, go always naked as they were born, with the exception of some of the women, who use the covering of a leaf, or small bough, or an apron of cotton which they prepare for that purpose. None of them, as I have already said, are possessed of any iron, neither have they weapons, being unacquainted with, and indeed incompetent to use them, not from any deformity of body (for they are well-formed), but because they are timid and full of fear. They carry however in lieu of arms, canes dried in the sun, on the ends of which they fix heads of dried wood sharpened to a point, and even these they dare not use habitually; for it has often occurred when I have sent two or three

---

portuum in hac insula commoditas et præstantia, fluminum copia, salubritate admixta hominum, quod, nisi quis viderit, credulitatem superat. Hujus arbores, pascua et fructus multum ab illis Joannæ differunt. Hæc præterea Hispana diverso aromatis genere, auro metallisque abundat. Hujus quidem et omnium aliarum, quas ego vidi et quarum cognitionem habeo, incolæ utriusque sexûs nudi semper incedunt, quemadmodum eduntur in lucem; præter aliquas feminas, quæ folio frondeve aliqua aut bombycino velo pudenda operiunt quod ipsæ sibi ad id negotii parant. Carent hi omnes (ut supra dixi) quocumque genere ferri: carent et armis, utpote sibi ignotis, nec ad eas sunt apti, non propter corporis deformitatem (quum sint bene formati), sed quia sunt timidi ac pleni formidine; gestant tamen pro armis arundines sole perustas, in quarum radicibus hastile quoddam ligneum siccum et in mucronem attenuatum figunt, neque his audent jugiter uti: nam sæpe evenit, quum miserim duos vel tres homines ex meis ad aliquas villas, ut cum eorum of my men to any of the villages to speak with the natives, that they have come out in a disorderly troop, and have fled in such haste at the approach of our men, that the fathers forsook their children and the children their fathers. This timidity did not arise from any loss or injury that they had received from us; for, on the contrary, I gave to all I approached whatever articles I had about me, such as cloth and many other things, taking nothing of theirs in return: but they are naturally timid and fearful. As soon however as they see that they are safe, and have laid aside all fear, they are very simple and honest, and exceedingly liberal with all they have; none of them refusing any thing he may possess when he is asked for it, but on the contrary inviting us to ask them. They exhibit great love towards all others in preference to themselves: they also give objects of great value for trifles, and content themselves with very little or nothing in return. I however forbad that these trifles and articles of no value (such as pieces of dishes, plates, and glass, keys, and leather straps) should be given to them, although if they could obtain them, they imagined themselves to be possessed of the most beautiful trinkets in the world. It even happened that a sailor

---

loquerentur incolis, exisse agmen glomeratum ex Indis, et ubi nostros appropinquare videbant, fugam celeriter arripuisse, despretis à patre liberis, et è contra ; et hoc non quod cuipiam eorum damnum aliquod vel injuria illata fuerit, immo ad quoscumque appuli, et quibuscum verbum facere potui, quidquid habebam sum elargitus pannum aliaque permulta, nulla mihi facta versura ; sed sunt naturâ pavidi ac timidi. Ceterum ubi se cernunt tutos omni metu repulso, sunt admodum simplices ac bonæ fidei, et in omnibus quæ habent liberalissimi : roganti quod possidet inficiatur nemo, quin ipsi nos ad id poscendum invitant. Maximum erga omnes amorem præ se ferunt: dant quæque magna pro parvis, minima licet re nihilove contenti. Ego attamen prohibui, ne tam minima et nullius pretii hisce darentur, ut sunt lancis, paropsidum vitrique fragmenta: item clavi, lingulæ ; quamquam si hoc poterant adipisci, videbatur eis pulcherrima mundi possidere jocalia. Accidit enim quemdam

received for a leather strap as much gold as was worth three
golden nobles, and for things of more trifling value offered
by our men, especially-newly coined blancas, or any gold
coins, the Indians would give whatever the seller required;
as, for instance, an ounce and a half or two ounces of gold, or
thirty or forty pounds of cotton, with which commodity they
were already acquainted. Thus they bartered, like idiots, cotton
and gold for fragments of bows, glasses, bottles, and jars;
which I forbad as being unjust, and myself gave them many
beautiful and acceptable articles which I had brought with me,
taking nothing from them in return; I did this in order that
I might the more easily conciliate them, that they might be
led to become Christians, and be inclined to entertain a regard
for the King and Queen, our Princes and all Spaniards, and
that I might induce them to take an interest in seeking out,
and collecting, and delivering to us such things as they possessed in abundance, but which we greatly needed. They
practise no kind of idolatry, but have a firm belief that all
strength and power, and indeed all good things, are in heaven,
and that I had descended from thence with these ships and
sailors, and under this impression was I received after they

---

navitam tantum auri pondus habuisse pro una ligula, quanti sunt
tres aurei solidi, et sic alios pro aliis minoris pretii, præsertim pro
blanquis novis, et quibusdam nummis aureis, pro quibus habendis
dabant quicquid petebat venditor, puta unciam cum dimidia et duas
auri: vel triginta et quadraginta bombycis pondo, quod ipsi jam
noverant. Item arcuum, amphoræ, hydriæ, doliique fragmenta
bombyci et auro tamquam bestiæ comparabant; quod quia iniquum
sane erat, vetui, dedique eis multa pulchra et grata, quæ mecum
tuleram, nullo interveniente præmio, ut eos mihi facilius concilia-
rem, fierentque Christicolæ, et ut sint proni in amorem erga Regem,
Reginam Principesque nostros, et universas gentes Hispaniæ, ac
studeant perquirere et coacervare, eaque nobis tradere quibus ipsi
affluunt et nos magnopere indigemus. Nullam hi norunt idolola-
triam, immo firmissimè credunt omnem vim, omnem potentiam,
omnia denique bona esse in cœlo, mæque inde cum his navibus et

had thrown aside their fears. Nor are they slow or stupid, but of very clear understanding; and those men who have crossed to the neighbouring islands give an admirable description of everything they observed; but they never saw any people clothed, nor any ships like ours. On my arrival at that sea, I had taken some Indians by force from the first island that I came to, in order that they might learn our language, and communicate to us what they knew respecting the country; which plan succeeded excellently, and was a great advantage to us, for in a short time, either by gestures and signs, or by words, we were enabled to understand each other. These men are still travelling with me, and although they have been with us now a long time, they continue to entertain the idea that I have descended from heaven; and on our arrival at any new place they published this, crying out immediately with a loud voice to the other Indians, "Come, come and look upon beings of a celestial race" : upon which both women and men, children and adults, young men and old, when they got rid of the fear they at first entertained, would come out in throngs, crowding the roads to see us,

---

nautis descendisse ; atque hoc animo ibi fui susceptus postquam metum repulerant. Nec sunt segnes aut rudes, quin summi ac perspicacis ingenii ; et homines, qui transfretant mare illud, non sine admiratione uniuscujusque rei rationem reddunt ; sed nunquam viderunt gentes vestitas, neque naves hujusmodi. Ego statim ac ad mare illud perveni, é prima insula quosdam Indos violenter arripui, qui ediscerent à nobis, et nos pariter docerent ea quorum ipsi in hisce partibus cognitionem habebant, et ex voto successit : nam brevi nos ipsos, et hi nos, tum gestu ac signis, tum verbis intellexerunt, magnoque nobis fuere emolumento. Veniunt modo mecum, tamen qui semper putant me desiluisse é cœlo, quamvis diu nobiscum versati fuerint, hodieque versentur, et hi erant primi, qui id quocumque appellebamus nunciabant, alii deinceps aliis elata voce dicentes, Venite, venite, et videbitis gentes æthereas. Quamobrem tam feminæ quam viri tam impuberes quam adulti, tam juvenes quam senes, deposita formidine paulo ante concepta, nos certatim visebant magna iter some bringing food, others drink, with astonishing affection and kindness.   Each of these islands has a great number of canoes, built of solid wood, narrow and not unlike our double-banked boats in length and shape, but swifter in their motion: they steer them only by the oar. These canoes are of various sizes, but the greater number are constructed with eighteen banks of oars, and with these they cross to the other islands, which are of countless number, to carry on traffic with the people.   I saw some of these canoes that held as many as seventy-eight rowers.   In all these islands there is no difference of physiognomy, of manners, or of language, but they all clearly understand each other, a circumstance very propitious for the realization of what I conceive to be the principal wish of our most serene King, namely, the conversion of these people to the holy faith of Christ, to which indeed, as far as I can judge, they are very favourable and well-disposed. I said before, that I went three hundred and twenty-two miles in a direct line from west to east, along the coast of the island of

---

stipante caterva, aliis cibum, aliis potum afferentibus, maximo cum amore ac benevolentia incredibili.   Habet unaquæque insula multas scaphas solidi ligni, etsi angustas, longitudine tamen ac forma nostris biremibus similes, cursu autem velociores : reguntur remis tantum modo. Harum quædam sunt magnæ, quædam parvæ, quædam in medio consistunt: plures tamen biremi qua remigent duodeviginti transtris majores, cum quibus in omnes illas insulas quæ innumeræ sunt trajicitur, cumque his suam mercaturam exercent, et inter eos commercia fiunt.   Aliquas ego harum biremium seu scapharum vidi, quæ vehebant septuaginta et octoginta remiges. In omnibus his insulis nulla est diversitas inter gentis effigies, nulla in moribus atque loquela, quin omnes se intelligunt adinvicem, quæ res perutilis est ad id quod Serenissimum Regem nostrum exoptare præcipué reor, scilicet eorum ad sanctam Christi fidem conversionem, cui quidem, quantum intelligere potui, facillimi sunt et proni. Dixi quemadmodum sum progressus antea insulam Joannam per rectum tramitem occassus in orientem milliar. cccxxii. Secundum quam viam et intervallum itineris possum dicere hanc Joannam esse ma-

Juana;[8] judging by which voyage, and the length of the passage, I can assert that it is larger than England and Scotland united; for independent of the said three hundred and twenty-two miles, there are in the western part of the island two provinces which I did not visit; one of these is called by the Indians Anam, and its inhabitants are born with tails. These provinces extend to a hundred and fifty-three miles in length, as I have learnt from the Indians whom I have brought with me, and who are well acquainted with the country. But the extent of Española is greater than all Spain from Catalonia to Fontarabia, which is easily proved, because one of its four sides which I myself coasted in a direct line, from west to east, measures five hundred and forty miles. This island is to

---

jorem Anglia et Scotia simul: namque ultra dicta cccxxii milliaria in ea parte quæ ad occidentem prospectat duæ, quas non petii, supersunt provinciæ, quarum alteram Indi Anam vocant, cujus accolæ caudati nascuntur. Tenduntur in longitudinem ad milliaria cliii, ut ab his quos veho mecum Indis percepi, qui omnes has callent insulas. Hispanæ vero ambitus major est tota Hispania a Cologna usque ad Fontem Rabidum; hincque facile arguitur, quod quartum ejus latus, quod ipse per rectam lineam occidentis in orientem trajeci, milliaria continet dxl. Hæc insula est affectanda, et affectata,

[8] Here a somewhat similar mistake to that which occurred in page four has been made by Navarrete, in his translation from the Latin; the accusative "insulam Joannam" comes after the neuter verb "progressus sum" without the intervention of a preposition; but it is evident from the sense that the missing word was intended to express that Columbus proceeded *along* the island; whereas Navarrete has translated it thus: "He dicho que anduve en recta direccion de poniente a oriente trescientas veinte y dos millas para llegar a la isla Juanna." *Anglice.* "I have said that I proceeded three hundred and twenty-two miles in a straight line from west to east *to arrive at* the island of Juana," a mode of proceeding which was in the first place geographically impossible, and in the next place would destroy the basis upon which Columbus founds his estimate of the size of the island, when compared with England and Scotland. There is no doubt that "per" is the preposition understood, while Mr. Navarrete has incautiously adopted "versus" instead of it.

be regarded with especial interest, and not to be slighted; for
although as I have said I took possession of all these islands
in the name of our invincible King, and the government of
them is unreservedly committed to his said Majesty, yet there
was one large town in Española of which especially I took
possession, situated in a remarkably favourable spot, and in
every way convenient for the purposes of gain and commerce.
To this town I gave the name of Navidad del Señor, and
ordered a fortress to be built there, which must by this time
be completed, in which I left as many men as I thought
necessary,[9] with all sorts of arms, and enough provisions for
more than a year.   I also left them one caravel, and skilful
workmen both in ship-building and other arts, and engaged

non spernenda, in qua, etsi aliarum omnium ut dixi pro invictissimo
Rege nostro solemniter possessionem accepi, earumque imperium
dicto Regi penitus committitur, in opportuniori tamen loco, atque
omni lucro et commercio condecenti, cujusdam magnæ villæ, cui
Nativitatis Domini nomen dedimus, possessionem peculiariter accepi:
ibique arcem quamdam erigere extemplo jussi, quæ modo jam debet
esse peracta, in qua homines, qui necessarii sunt visi, cum omni ar-
morum genere, et ultra annum victu opportuno reliqui; item quamdam caravelam, et pro aliis construendis tam in hac arte quam in
ceteris peritos, ac ejusdem insulæ Regis erga nos benevolentiam et

[9] There appears to be a doubt as to the exact number of men left by
Columbus at Española, different accounts variously giving it as thirty-
seven, thirty-eight, thirty-nine, and forty.   There is, however, a list of
their names included in one of the diplomatic documents printed in
Navarrete's work, which makes the number amount to forty, independent
of the governor Diego de Arana, and his two lieutenants Pedro Gutierrez
and Rodrigo de Escobedo.   All these men were Spaniards, with the exception of two ; one an Irishman named William Ires, a native of Galway,
and one an Englishman, whose name was given as Tallarte de Lajes, but
whose native designation it is difficult to guess at.   The document in
question, was a proclamation to the effect that the heirs of those men
should, on presenting at the office of public business at Seville, sufficient
proof of their being the next of kin, receive payment in conformity with
the royal order to that purpose, issued at Burgos, on the twentieth of
December, 1507.

the favor and friendship of the King of the island in their behalf, to a degree that would not be believed, for these people are so amiable and friendly that even the King took a pride in calling me his brother. But supposing their feelings should become changed, and they should wish to injure those who have remained in the fortress, they could not do so, for they have no arms, they go naked, and are moreover too cowardly; so that those who hold the said fortress, can easily keep the whole island in check, without any pressing danger to themselves, provided they do not transgress the directions and regulations which I have given them. As far as I have learned, every man throughout these islands is united to but one wife, with the exception of the kings and princes, who are allowed to have twenty: the women seem to work more than the men. I could not clearly understand whether the people possess any private property, for I observed that one man had the charge of distributing various things to the rest, but especially meat and provisions and the like. I did not find, as some of us had expected, any cannibals amongst them, but on the contrary men of great deference and kindness. Neither are they black, like the Ethiopians: their hair is smooth and straight:

---

familiaritatem incredibilem. Sunt enim gentes illæ amabiles admodum et benignæ, eo quod rex prædictus me fratrem suum dici gloriabatur. Et si animum revocarent et iis qui in arce manserunt nocere velint, nequeunt, quia armis carent, nudi incedunt, et nimium timidi: ideo dictam arcem tenentes dumtaxat possunt totam eam insulam nullo sibi imminente discrimine, dummodo leges quas dedimus ac regimen non excedant, facile detinere. In omnibus his insulis, ut intellexi, quisque uni tantum conjugi acquiescit, præter Principes aut Reges quibus viginti habere licet. Feminæ magis quam viri laborare videntur, nec bene potui intelligere an habeant bona propria; vidi enim, quod unus habebat aliis impartiri, præsertim dapes, obsonia et hujusmodi. Nullum apud eos monstrum reperi, ut plerique existimabant, sed homines magnæ reverentiæ atque benignos. Nec sunt nigri velut æthiopes: habent crines planos ac demissos; non degunt ubi radiorum solaris emicat calor:

for they do not dwell where the rays of the sun strike most vividly,—and the sun has intense power there, the distance from the equinoctial line being, it appears, but six-and-twenty degrees. On the tops of the mountains the cold is very great, but the effect of this upon the Indians is lessened by their being accustomed to the climate, and by their frequently indulging in the use of very hot meats and drinks. Thus, as I have already said, I saw no cannibals, nor did I hear of any, except in a certain island called Charis,[10] which is the second from Española on the side towards India, where dwell a people who are considered by the neighbouring islanders as most ferocious : and these feed upon human flesh. The same people have many kinds of canoes, in which they cross to all the surrounding islands and rob and plunder wherever they can ; they are not different from the other islanders, except that they wear their hair long, like women, and make use of the bows and javelins of cane, with sharpened spear-points fixed on the thickest end, which I have before described, and therefore they are looked upon as ferocious, and regarded by the other Indians with unbounded fear; but I think no more

---

permagna namque hic est solis vehementia, propterea quod ab æqui-noctiali linea distat (ut videtur) gradus sex et viginti. Ex montium cacuminibus maximum quoque viget frigus, sed id quidem mode-rant Indi tum loci consuetudine, tum rerum calidissimarum quibus frequenter et luxuriosè vescuntur præsidio. Itaque monstra aliqua non vidi, neque eorum alicubi habui cognitionem, excepta quadam insula Charis nuncupata, quæ secunda ex Hispana in Indiam trans-fretantibus existit, quam gens quædam, à finitimis habita ferocior, incolit : hi carne humana vescuntur. Habent prædicti biremium genera plurima, quibus in omnes indicas insulas trajiciunt, depræ-dant, surripiuntque quæcumque possunt. Nihil ab aliis differunt, nisi quod gerunt more femineo longos crines, utuntur arcubus et spiculis arundineis, fixis, ut diximus, in grossiori parte attenuatis hastilibus : ideoque habentur feroces ; quare ceteri Indi inexhausto

[10] Query Carib, the Indian name of Porto Rico.

of them than of the rest. These are the men who form unions with certain women, who dwell alone in the island Matenin,[11] which lies next to Española on the side towards India; these latter employ themselves in no labour suitable to their own sex, for they use bows and javelins as I have already described their paramours as doing, and for defensive armour have plates of brass, of which metal they possess great abundance. They assure me that there is another island larger than Española, whose inhabitants have no hair, and which abounds in gold more than any of the rest. I bring with me individuals of this island and of the others that I have seen, who are proofs of the facts which I state. Finally, to compress into few words the entire summary of my voyage and speedy return, and of the advantages derivable therefrom, I promise, that with a little assistance afforded me by our most invincible sovereigns, I will procure them as much gold as they need, as great a quantity of spices, of cotton, and of mastic (which is only found in Chios), and as many men for the service of the navy as their Majesties may require. I promise also rhubarb and other sorts of drugs,

———————

metu plectuntur: sed hos ego nihil facio plus quam alios. Hi sunt qui coeunt cum quibusdam feminis, quæ solæ insulam Mathenim primam ex Hispana in Indiam trajicientibus inhabitant. Hæ autem feminæ nullum sui sexûs opus exercent: utuntur enim arcubus et spiculis, sicuti de earum conjugibus dixi, muniunt sese laminis æneis, quarum maxima apud eas copia exsistit. Aliam mihi insulam affirmant supradicta Hispana majorem; ejus incolæ carent pilis auroque inter alias potissimum exuberat. Hujus insulæ et aliarum, quas vidi, homines mecum porto, qui horum quæ dixi testimonium perhibent. Denique ut nostri discessûs et ceteris reversionis compendium ac emolumentum brevibus astringam, hoc polliceor, me nostris Regibus invictissimis, parvo eorum fultum auxilio, tantum auri daturum, quantum eis fuerit opus, tantum vero aromatum, bombycis, masticis, quæ apud Chium dumtaxat invenitur, tamque ligni aloes, tantum servorum hydrophilatorum, quantum eorum

[11] One of the Virgin Islands—which, is uncertain.

which I am persuaded the men whom I have left in the aforesaid fortress have found already and will continue to find;
for I myself have tarried no where longer than I was compelled
to do by the winds, except in the city of Navidad, while I provided for the building of the fortress, and took the necessary
precautions for the perfect security of the men I left there. Although all I have related may appear to be wonderful and
unheard of, yet the results of my voyage would have been more
astonishing if I had had at my disposal such ships as I required.
But these great and marvellous results are not to be attributed
to any merit of mine, but to the holy Christian faith, and to the
piety and religion of our Sovereigns; for that which the unaided
intellect of man could not compass, the spirit of God has
granted to human exertions, for God is wont to hear the
prayers of his servants who love his precepts even to the performance of apparent impossibilities. Thus it has happened to
me in the present instance, who have accomplished a task to
which the powers of mortal men had never hitherto attained;
for if there have been those who have anywhere written or
spoken of these islands, they have done so with doubts and
conjectures, and no one has ever asserted that he has seen
them, on which account their writings have been looked upon

---

majestas voluerit exigere: item reubarbarum et aliorum aromatum
genera, quæ ii quos in dicta arce reliqui, jam invenisse atque inven-
turos existimo: quandoquidem ego nullibi magis sum moratus (nisi
quantum me coegerunt venti) præterquam in villa Nativitatis, dum
arcem condere, et tuta omnia esse providi. Quæ etsi maxima et
inaudita sunt multo tamen majora forent, si naves mihi, ut ratio
exigit, subvenissent. Verum multum ac mirabile hoc nec nostris
meritis correspondens, sed sanctæ christianæ fidei, nostrorumque
regum pietati ac religioni, quia, quod humanus consequi non pote-
rat intellectus, id humanis concessit divinus. Solet enim Deus
servos, quique sua præcepta diligunt, etiam in impossibilibus exau-
dire, ut nobis in præsentia contigit, qui consecuti sumus, quæ hac-
tenus mortalium vires minimè attigerant; nam si harum insularum
quidpiam aliqui scripserunt aut locuti sunt, omnes per ambages et

as little else than fables.   Therefore let the king and queen, our princes and their most happy kingdoms, and all the other provinces of Christendom, render thanks to our Lord and Saviour Jesus Christ, who has granted us so great a victory and such prosperity.   Let processions be made, and sacred feasts be held, and the temples be adorned with festive boughs. Let Christ rejoice on earth, as he rejoices in heaven in the prospect of the salvation of the souls of so many nations hitherto lost.   Let us also rejoice, as well on account of the exaltation of our faith, as on account of the increase of our temporal prosperity, of which not only Spain, but all Christendom will be partakers.

Such are the events which I have briefly described. Farewell.

Lisbon, the 14th of March.

CHRISTOPHER COLUMBUS,

Admiral of the Fleet of the Ocean.

---

conjecturas, nemo se eas vidisse asserit: unde prope videbatur fabula.   Igitur Rex et Regina, Principes, ac eorum regna felicissima, cunctæque aliæ Christianorum provinciæ, Salvatori Domino nostro Jesu Christo agamus gratias, qui tanta nos victoria munereque donavit. Celebrentur processiones, peragantur solemnia sacra, festâque fronde velentur delubra.   Exsultet Christus in terris, quemadmodum in cœlis exsultat, quum tot populorum perditas antehac animas salvatum iri prævidet.   Lætemur et nos, tum propter exaltationem nostræ fidei, tum propter rerum temporalium incrementa, quorum non solum Hispania, sed universa Christianitas est futura particeps.   Hæc gesta sic breviter enarrata. Vale.   Ulisbonæ pridie idus Martii.

CHRISTOFORUS COLOM,

Oceanæ classis præfectus.

D

SECOND VOYAGE OF COLUMBUS.[1]

A Letter addressed to the Chapter of Seville by Dr. Chanca,[2] native of that city, and physician to the fleet of Columbus, in his second voyage to the West Indies, describing the principal events which occurred during that voyage.

MOST noble sir,—Since the occurrences which I relate in private letters to other persons, are not of such general interest as those which are contained in this epistle, I have resolved to give you a distinct narrative of the events of our

---

SEGUNDA VIAGE DE COLON.

La Carta del Doctor Chanca, que escribió a la Cindad de Sevilla.

Muy magnífico Señor : Porque las cosas que yo particularmente escribo á otros en otras cartas no son igualmente comunicables como las que en esta escritura van, acordé de escribir distintamente las

[1] The description of the second voyage of Columbus, has been given in Latin by Peter Martyr, of Anghiera, in lib. ii, of his " Decades"; but as Doctor Chanca, a native of Seville, who was physician to the fleet in that voyage, and was an eye-witness of the events he related, has written an account of it in a letter to the Chapter of Seville, it has been deemed advisable to take his account in preference to that of Peter Martyr, which is made up only from information gathered from hearsay. Moreover, Dr. Chanca's description, while it in no way contradicts that of Peter Martyr, is more agreeably written, and mentions some few incidents that are omitted in the narrative of the latter.

[2] Doctor Chanca was appointed physician to Columbus's fleet by a dispatch of the 23rd of May, 1493 ; and on the 24th, the chief accountants were instructed to pay him salary and rations as scrivener in the Indies.

voyage, as well as to treat of the other matters which form the subject of my petition to you. The news I have to communicate are as follows : The expedition which their Catholic Majesties sent, by Divine permission, from Spain to the Indies, under the command of Christopher Columbus, admiral of the ocean, left Cadiz on the twenty-fifth of September, of the year ,[3] with wind and weather favorable for the voyage. This wind lasted two days, during which time we managed to make fifty leagues; the weather then changing, we made little or no progress for the next two days; it pleased God, however, after this, to restore us fine weather, so that in two days more we reached the Great Canary. Here we put into harbour, which we were obliged to do, to repair one of the ships which made a great deal of water; we remained all that day, and on the following set sail again, but were several times becalmed, so that we were four or five days before we reached Gomera. We

---

nuevas de acá y las otras que á mi conviene suplicar á vuestra Señoría, é las nuevas son las siguientes: Que la flota que los Reyes Católicos, nuestros Señores, enviaron de España para las Indias é gobernacion del su Almirante del mar Océano Cristóbal Colon por la divina permision, parte de Caliz á veinte y cinco de Setiembre del año de   años con tiempo é viento convenible á nuestro camino, é duró este tiempo dos dias, en los cuales pudimos andar al pie de cincuenta leguas: y luego nos cambió el tiempo otros dos, en los cuales anduvimos muy poco ó no nada; plogó á Dios que pasados los dias nos tornó buen tiempo, en manera que en otros dos llegamos á la Gran Canaria donde tomamos puerto, lo cual nos fue necesario por reparar un navío que hacia mucha agua, y estovimos ende todo aquel dia, é luego otra dia partimos é fizonos algunas calmerías, de manera que estovimos en llegar al Gomero cuatro ó cinco dias, y en la Gomera fue necesario estar

The curate of Los Palacios makes mention of Dr. Chanca, and had this same narration before him, as may be seen in the one hundred and twentieth chapter of his manuscript "History of their Catholic Majesties". (M. F. de Navarrete).

[3] A similar gap in the original : it should say *of the year* 1493.

had to remain at Gomera one day to lay in our stores of meat, wood, and as much water as we could stow, preparatory to the long voyage which we expected to make without seeing land: thus through the delay at these two ports, and being fixed in a calm one day after leaving Gomera, we were nineteen or twenty days before we arrived at the Island of Ferro. After this we had, by the goodness of God, a return of fine weather, more continuous than any fleet ever enjoyed during so long a voyage; so that leaving Ferro on the thirteenth of October, within twenty days we came in sight of land: and we should have seen it in fourteen or fifteen days, if the ship *Capitana* had been as good a sailer as the other vessels; for many times the others had to shorten sail, because they were leaving us much behind. During all this time we had great good fortune, for throughout the voyage we encountered no storm, with the exception of one on St. Simon's eve, which for four hours put us in considerable jeopardy.

On the first Sunday after All Saints, namely the third of November, about dawn, a pilot of the ship *Capitana* cried out: "The reward, I see the land!"

---

algun dia por facer provisiones de carne, leña é agua la que mas pudiesen, por la larga jornada que se esperaba hacer sin ver mas tierra: ansi que en la estada destos puertos y en un dia despues de partidos de la Gomera, que nos fizo calma, que tardamos en llegar fasta la isla del Fierro, estovimos diez y nueve ó veinte dias : desde aqui por la bondad de Dios nos tornó buen tiempo, el mejor que nunca flota llevó tan largo camino, tal que partidos del Fierro á trece de Octubre dentro de veinte dias hobimos vista de tierra : y vieramosla á catorce ó quince si la nao Capitana fuera tan buena velera como los otros navíos, porque muchas veces los otros navíos sacaban velas porque nos dejaban mucho atras. En todo este tiempo hobimos mucha bonanza, que en él ni en todo el camino no hobimos fortuna, salvo la víspera de S. Simon que nos vino una que por cuatro horas nos puso en harto estrecho. El primero domingo despues de Todos Santos, que fue á tres dias de Noviembre, cerca del alba, dijo un piloto de la nao Capitana : albricias, que tenemos tierra. Fue el alegría tan grande en la gente que era maravilla oir

The joy of the people was so great, that it was wonderful to hear their cries and exclamations of pleasure; and they had good reason to be delighted; for they had become so wearied of bad living, and of working the water out of the ships, that all sighed most anxiously for land. The pilots of the fleet, reckoned on that day, that between leaving Ferro and first reaching land, we had made eight hundred leagues; others said seven hundred and eighty (so that the difference was not great), and three hundred more between Ferro and Cadiz, making in all eleven hundred leagues; I do not therefore feel as one who had not seen enough of the water. On the morning of the aforesaid Sunday, we saw lying before us an island, and soon on the right hand another appeared : the first[4] was high and mountainous, on the side nearest to us ; the other[5] flat, and very thickly wooded : as soon as it became lighter, other islands began to appear on both sides ; so that on that day, there were six islands to be seen lying in different direc-

---

las gritas y placeres que todos hacian, y con mucha razon, que la gente venian ya tan fatigados de mala vida y de pasar agua, que con muchos deseos sospiraban todos por tierra. Contaron aquel dia los pilotos del armada desde la isla de Fierro hasta la primera tierra que vimos unas ochocientas leguas, otros setecientas é ochenta, de manera que la diferencia no era mucha, é mas trescientas que ponen de la isla de Fierro fasta Caliz, que eran por todos mil é ciento ; ansí que no siento quien no fuese satisfecho de ver agua. Vimos el Domingo de mañana sobredicho, por proa de los navíos, una isla y luego á la man derecha parecio otra : la primera era la tierra alta de sierras por aquella parte que vimos, la otra era tierra llana, tambien muy llena de árboles muy espesos, y luego que fue mas de dia comenzó á parecer á una parte é á otra islas ; de manera que aquel dia eran seis islas á diversas partes, y las mas harto grandes. Fuimos enderezados para ver aquella que primero habiamos visto, é

[4] The island of Dominica, which is so called from having been discovered on a Sunday. (M. F. de Navarrete.)

[5] The island Marigalante, which was so called from the name of the ship in which Columbus sailed. (M. F. de Navarrete.)

tions, and most of them of considerable size.   We directed
our course towards that which we had first seen, and reaching
the coast, we proceeded more than a league in search of a
port where we might anchor, but without finding one : all that
part of the island which we could observe, appeared mountainous, very beautiful, and green even up to the water, which
was delightful to see, for at that season, there is scarcely any
thing green in our own country.   When we found that there
was no harbour there, the admiral decided that we should
go to the other island, which appeared on the right, and which
was at four or five leagues distance : one vessel however still
remained on the first island all that day seeking for a harbour,
in case it should be necessary to return thither.   At length,
having found a good one, where they saw both people and dwellings, they returned that night to the fleet, which had put into
harbour at the other island,[6] and there the admiral, accompanied
by a great number of men, landed with the royal banner in his
hands, and took formal possession on behalf of their Majesties.
This island was filled with an astonishingly thick growth of
wood ; the variety of unknown trees, some bearing fruit and

---

llegamos por la costa andando mas de una legua buscando puerto
para sorgir, el cual todo aquel espacio nunca se pudo hallar.   Era
en todo aquello que parecia desta isla todo montaña muy hermosa y
muy verde, fasta el agua que era alegria en mirarla, porque en aquel
tiempo no hay en nuestra tierra apenas cosa verde.   Despues que
allí no hallamos puerto acordó el Almirante que nos volviesemos á
la otra isla que parescia á la mano derecha, que estaba desta otra
cuatro ó cinco leguas.   Quedó por entonces un navío en esta isla
buscando puerto todo aquel dia para cuando fuese necesario venir á
ella, en la cual halló buen puerto é vido casas é gentes, é luego se
tornó aquella noche para donde estaba la flota que habia tomado
puerto en la otra isla, donde decendió el Almirante é mucha gente
con él con la bandera Real en les manos, adonde tomó posesion por
sus Altezas en forma de derecho. En esta isla habia tanta espesura
de arboledas que era maravilla, é tanta diferencia de árboles no co-

[6] Marigalante.

some flowers, was surprising, and indeed every spot was covered
with verdure. We found there a tree whose leaf had the
finest smell of cloves that I have ever met with ; it was like a
laurel leaf, but not so large : but I think it was a species of
laurel. There were wild fruits of various kinds, some of which
our men, not very prudently, tasted ; and upon only touching
them with their tongues, their countenances became inflamed,[7]
and such great heat and pain followed, that they seemed to
be mad, and were obliged to resort to refrigerants to cure
themselves. We found no signs of any people in this island,
and concluded it was uninhabited ; we remained only two
hours, for it was very late when we landed, and on the following morning we left for another very large island,[8] situated
below this at the distance of seven or eight leagues. We
approached it under the side of a great mountain, that seemed
almost to reach the skies, in the middle of which rose a peak,
higher than all the rest of the mountain, whence many streams
diverged into different channels, especially towards the part

---

nocidos á nadie que era para espantar, dellos con fruto, dellos con
flor, ansí que todo era verde. Allí hallamos un arbol, cuya hojo
tenia el mas fino olor de clavos que nunca ví, y era como laurel,
salvo que no era ansi grande ; yo ansí pienso que era laurel su
especia. Allí habia frutas salvaginas de diferentes maneras, de las
quales algunos no muy sabios probaban, y del gusto solamente to-
cándoles con las lenguas se les hinchaban las caras, y les venia tan
grande ardor y dolor que parecian que rabiaban, los cuales se reme-
diaban con cosas frias. En esta isla no hallamos gente nin señal
della, creimos que era desboblada, en la cual estovimos bien
dos horas, porque cuando allí llegamos era sobre tarde, é luego
otro dia de mañana partimos para otra isla que parescia en bajo
desta que era muy grande, fasta la cual desta que habria siete ú
ocho leguas, llegamos á ella hácia la parte de una gran montaña que
parecia que queria llegar al cielo, en medio de la cual montaña estaba un pico mas alto que toda la otra montaña, del cual se ver-

[7] One would infer from this that it was the fruit of the manzanillo, which
produces similar effects. (M. F. de Navarrete.)   [8] Guadaloupe.

at which we arrived. At three leagues distance, we could see an immense fall of water, which discharged itself from such a height that it appeared to fall from the sky; it was seen from so great a distance that it occasioned many wagers to be laid on board the ships, some maintaining that it was but a series of white rocks, and others that it was water. When we came nearer to it, it showed itself distinctly, and it was the most beautiful thing in the world to see from how great a height and from what a small space so large a fall of water was discharged. As soon as we neared the island the admiral ordered a light caravel to run along the coast to search for a harbour; the captain put into land in a boat, and seeing some houses, leapt on shore and went up to them, the inhabitants fleeing at sight of our men; he then went into the houses and there found various household articles that had been left unremoved, from which he took two parrots, very large and quite different from any we had before seen; he found a great quantity of cotton, both spun and prepared for spinning, and articles of food, of all of which he brought away a portion; besides these, he also brought away four or five bones

---

tian á diversas partes muchas aguas, en especial hácia la parte donde ibamos: de tres leguas paresció un golpe de agua tan gordo como un buey, que se despeñaba de tan alto como si cayera del cielo: parescia de tan lejos, que hobo en los navíos muchas apuestas, que unos decian que eran peñas blancas y otros que era agua. Desque llegamos mas á cerca vídose lo cierto, y era la mas hermosa cosa del mundo de ver de cuan alto se despeñaba é de tan poco logar nacia tan gran golpe de agua. Luego que llegamos cerca mandó el Almirante á una carbela ligera que fuese costeando á buscar puerto, la cual se adelantó y llegando á la tierra vido unas casas, é con la barca saltó el Capitan en tierra é llegó á las casas, en las cuales halló su gente, y luego que los vieron fueron huyendo, é entró en ellas, donde halló las cosas que ellos tienen, que no habian llevado nada, donde tomó dos papagayos muy grandes y muy diferenciados de cuantos se habian visto. Halló mucho algodon hilado é por hilar, é cosas de sus mantenimientos, é de todo trajo un poco, en es-of human arms and legs. On seeing these we suspected that we were amongst the Caribbee islands, which are inhabited by cannibals; for the admiral, guided by the information respecting their situation which he had received from the Indians of the islands discovered in his former voyage, had directed his course with a view to their discovery, both because they were the nearest to Spain, and because this was the direct track for the island of Española, where he had left some of his people. Thither, by the goodness of God and the wise management of the admiral, we came in as straight a track as if we had sailed by a well known and frequented route. This island is very large, and on the side where we arrived it seemed to us to be twenty-five leagues in length. We sailed more than two leagues along the shore in search of a harbour; on the part towards which we moved appeared very high mountains, and on that which we left extensive plains; on the sea coast there were a few small villages, whose inhabitants fled as soon as they saw the sails : at length after proceeding two leagues we found a port late in the evening. That night the admiral resolved that some of the men should

---

pecial trajo cuatro ó cinco huesos de brazos é piernas de hombres. Luego que aquello vimos sospechamos que aquellas islas eran las de Caribe, que son habitadas de gente que comen carne humana, porque el Almirante por las señas que le habian dado del sitio destas islas, el otro camino, los indios de las islas que antes habian descubierto, habia enderezado el camino por descubrirlas, porque estaban mas cerca de España, y tambien porque por allí se hacia el camino derecho para venir á la isla Española, donde antes habia dejado la gente, á los cuales, por la bondad de Dios y por el buen saber del Almirante, venimos tan derechos como si por camino sabido é seguido vinieramos. Esta isla es muy grande, y por el lado nos pareció que habia de luengo de costa veinte é cinco leguas : fuimos costeando por ella buscando puerto mas de dos leguas ; por la parte donde ibamos eran montañas muy altas, á la parte que dejamos parecian grandes llanos, á la orilla de la mar habia algunos poblados pequeños, é luego que veian las velas huian todos. Andadas dos land at break of day in order to confer with the natives, and learn what sort of people they were; although it was suspected, from the appearance of those who had fled at our approach, that they were naked, like those whom the admiral had seen in his former voyage. In the morning several detachments under their respective captains sailed forth; one of them arrived at the dinner hour, and brought away a boy of about fourteen years of age, as it afterwards appeared, who said that he was one of the prisoners taken by these people. The others divided themselves, and one party took a little boy whom a man was leading by the hand, but who left him and fled; this boy they sent on board immediately with some of our men; others remained, and took certain women, natives of the island, together with other women from among the captives who came of their own accord. One captain of this last company, not knowing that any intelligence of the people had been obtained, advanced farther into the island and lost himself, with the six men who accompanied him: they could not find their way back until after four days, when they lighted upon the sea shore, and following the

---

leguas hallamos puerto y bien tarde. Esa noche acordó el Almirante que á la madrugada saliesen algunos para tomar lengua é saber que gente era, no embargante la sospecha é los que ya habian visto ir huyendo, que era gente desnuda como la otra que ya el Almirante habia visto el otro viage. Salieron esa madrugada ciertos Capitanes; los unos vinieron á hora de comer é trageron un mozo de fasta catorce años, á lo que despues se sopo, é él dijo que era de los que esta gente tenian cativos. Los otros se dividieron, los unos tomaron un mochacho pequeño, al cual llevaba un hombre por la mano, é por huir lo desamparó. Este enviaron luego con algunos dellos, otros quedaron, é destos unos tomaron ciertas mugeres naturales de la isla, é otras que se vinieron de grado, que eran de las cativas. Desta compañía se apartó un Capitan no sabiendo que se habia habido lengua con seis hombres, el cual se perdió con los que con él iban, que jamas sopieron tornar, fasta que á cabo de cuatro dias toparon con la costa de la mar, é siguiendo por ella tornaron á

line of coast returned to the fleet.[8] We had already looked
upon them as killed and eaten by the people that are called
Caribbees; for we could not account for their long absence in
any other way, since they had among them some pilots who by
their knowledge of the stars could navigate either to or from
Spain, so that we imagined that they could not lose themselves
in so small a space.   On this first day of our landing several
men and women came on the beach up to the water's edge,
and gazed at the ships in astonishment at so novel a sight;
and when a boat pushed on shore in order to speak with them,
they cried out, "tayno, tayno," which is as much as to say,
"good, good," and waited for the landing of the sailors,
standing by the boat in such a manner that they might
escape when they pleased.   The result was, that none of the
men could be persuaded to join us, and only two were taken

----

topar con la flota.   Ya los teniamos por perdidos é comidos de
aquellas gentes que se dicen los Caribes, porque no bastaba razon
para creer que eran perdidos de otra manera, porque iban entre
ellos pilotos, marineros que por la estrella saben ir é venir hasta
España, creiamos que en tan pequeño espacio no se podian perder.
Este dia primero que allí decendimos andaban por la playa junto
con el agua muchos hombres é mugeres mirando la flota, é maravillándose de cosa tan nueva, é llegándose alguna barca á tierra á
hablar con ellos, diciéndolos *tayno tayno*, que quiere decir *bueno*,
esperaban en tanto que no salian del agua, junto con él moran, de
manera que cuando ellos querian se podian salvar : en conclusion,
que de los hombres ninguno se pudo tomar por fuerza ni por grado, salvo dos que se seguraron é despues los trajeron por fuerza

[9] It was Diego Marquez, the caterer, who with eight other men went
on shore into the interior of the island, without permission from the admiral, who caused him to be sought for by parties of men with trumpets,
but without success.   One of those who were sent out with this object,
was Alonzo Ojeda, who took with him forty men, and on their return they
reported that they had found many aromatic plants, a variety of birds, and
some considerable rivers.   The wanderers were not able to find their way
to the ships until the eighth of November. (M. F. Navarrete's note, from
Bartholomeo de las Casas' Manuscript History, chap. 84.)

by force, who were secured and led away. More than twenty
of the female captives were taken with their own consent,
and other women natives of the island were surprised and
carried off: several of the boys, who were captives, came to us
fleeing from the natives of the island who had taken them
prisoners. We remained eight days in this port in consequence of the loss of the aforesaid captain, and went many
times on shore, passing amongst the dwellings and villages
which were on the coast; we found a vast number of human
bones and skulls hung up about the houses, like vessels
intended for holding various things. There were very few
men to be seen here, and the women informed us that this was
in consequence of ten canoes having gone to make an attack
upon other islands. These islanders appeared to us to be
more civilized than those that we had hitherto seen; for
although all the Indians have houses of straw, yet the houses
of these people are constructed in a much superior fashion,
are better stocked with provisions, and exhibit more evidences
of industry, both on the part of the men and the women.
They had a considerable quantity of cotton, both spun and

---

alli. Se tomaron mas de veinte mugeres de las cativas, y de su
grado se venian otras naturales de la isla, que fueron salteadas é
tomadas por fuerza. Ciertos mochachos cabtivos se vinieron á
nosotros huyendo de los naturales de la isla que los tenian cabtivos.
En este puerto estovimos ocho dias á causa de la pérdida del sobredicho Capitan, donde muchas veces salimos á tierra andando por sus
moradas é pueblos, que estaban á la costa, donde hallamos infinitos
huesos de hombres, é los cascos de las cabezas colgados por las
casas á manera de vasijas para tener cosas. Aquí no parescieron
muchos hombres ; la causa era, segun nos dijeron las mugeres, que
eran idas diez canoas con gentes á saltear á otras islas. Esta gente
nos pareció mas pulítica que la que habita en estas otras islas que
habemos visto, aunque todos tienen las moradas de paja ; pero estos las tienen de mucho mejor hechura, é mas proveidas de mantenimientos, é parece en ellas mas industria ansi veril como femenil.
Tenian mucho algodon hilado y por hilar, y muchas mantas de al-

prepared for spinning, and many cotton sheets, so well woven as to be no way inferior to those of our country. We enquired of the women, who were prisoners in the island, what people these islanders were : they replied that they were Caribbees. As soon as they learned that we abhorred such people, on account of their evil practice of eating human flesh, they were much delighted; and, after that, if they brought forward any woman or man of the Caribbees, they informed us (but secretly), that they were such, still evincing by their dread of their conquerors, that they belonged to a vanquished nation, though they knew them all to be in our power.

We were enabled to distinguish which of the women were natives, and which were captives, by the Caribbees wearing on each leg two bands of woven cotton, the one fastened round the knee, and the other round the ankle; by this means they make the calves of their legs large, and the above-mentioned parts very small, which I imagine that they regard as a matter of refinement: by this peculiarity we distinguished them. The habits of these Caribbees are brutal. There are three islands : the one called Turuqueira; the other, which was the

---

godon tan bien tejidas que no deben nada á las de nuestra patria. Preguntamos á las mugeres, que eran cativas en esta isla, que qué gente era esta ; respondieron que eran Caribes. Despues que entendieron que nosotros aborreciamos tal gente por su mal uso de comer carne de hombres, holgaban mucho, y sí de nuevo traian alguna muger ó hombre de los Caribes, secretamente decian que eran Caribes, que allí donde estaban todos en nuestro poder mostraban temor dellos como gente sojuzgada, y de allí conocimos cuáles eran Caribes de las mugeres é cuáles nó, porque las Caribes traian en las piernas en cada una dos argollas tejidas de algodon, la una junto con la rodilla, la otra junto con los tobillos ; de manera que les hacen las pantorrillas grandes, é de los sobredichos logares muy ceñidas, que esto me parece que tienen ellos por cosa gentil, ansi que por esta diferencia conocemos los unos de los otros. La costumbre desta gente de Caribes es bestial : son tres islas, esta se llama Turuqueira, la otra que primero vimos se llama Ceyre, la tercera first that we saw, is called Ceyre; the third is called Ayay: there is a resemblance amongst all these, as if they were of one race, and they do no injury to each other; but each and all of them wage war against the other neighbouring islands, and for the purpose of attacking them, make voyages of a hundred and fifty leagues at sea, with their numerous canoes, which are a small kind of craft with one mast. Their arms are arrows, in the place of iron weapons, and as they have no iron, some of them point their arrows with tortoise-shell, and others make their arrow heads of fish spines, which are naturally barbed like coarse saws: these prove dangerous weapons to a naked people like the Indians, and may inflict severe injury, but to men of our nation, are not very formidable. In their attacks upon the neighbouring islands, these people take as many of the women as they can, especially those who are young and beautiful, and keep them as concubines; and so great a number do they carry off, that in fifty houses no men were to be seen; and out of the number of the captives, more than twenty were young girls. These women also say that the Caribbees use them with such cruelty as would scarcely

se llama Ayay; estos todos son conformidad como si fuesen de un linage, los cuales no se hacen mal: unos é otros hacen guerra á todas las otras islas comarcanas, los cuales van por mar ciento é cincuenta leguas á saltear con muchas canoas que tienen, que son unas fustas pequeñas de un solo madero. Sus armas son frechas en lugar de hierros; porque no poseen ningun hierro, ponen unas puntas fechas de huesos de torgugas los unos, otros de otra isla ponen unas espinas de un pez fechas dentadas, que ansi lo son naturalmente, á manera de sierras bien recias, que para gente desarmada, como son todos, es cosa que les puede matar é hacer harto daño; pero para gente de nuestra nacion no son armas para mucho temer. Esta gente saltea en las otras islas, que traen las mugeres que pueden haber, en especial mozas y hermosas, las cuales tienen para su servicio, é para tener por mancebas, é traen tantas que en cincuenta casas ellos no parecieron, y de las cativas se vinieron mas de veinte mozas. Dicen tambien estas mugeres que estos usan de una cruel-be believed ; and that they eat the children which they bear to them, and only bring up those which they have by their natural wives. Such of their male enemies as they can take alive, they bring to their houses to make a feast of them, and those who are dead they devour at once. They say that man's flesh is so good, that there is nothing like it in the world ; and this is pretty evident, for of the bones which we found in their houses, they had gnawed everything that could be gnawed, so that nothing remained of them, but what from its great hardness, could not be eaten : in one of the houses we found the neck of a man, undergoing the process of cooking. When they take any boys prisoners, they dismember them, and make use of them until they grow up to manhood, and then when they wish to make a feast they kill and eat them ; for they say that the flesh of boys and women is not good to eat. Three of these boys came fleeing to us thus mutilated.

At the end of four days arrived the captain who had lost himself with his companions, of whose return we had by this time given up all hope; for other parties had been twice sent out to seek him, one of which came back on the same day

---

dad que parece cosa increible ; que los hijos que en ellas han se los comen, que solamente crian los que han en sus mugeres naturales. Los hombres que pueden haber, los que son vivos llevánselos á sus casas para hacer carnicería dellos, y los que han muertos luego se los comen. Dicen que la carne del hombre es tan buena que no hay tal coso en el mundo ; y bien parece porque los huesos que en estas casas hallamos todo lo que se puede roer todo lo tenian roido, que no habia en ellos sino lo que por su mucha dureza no se podia comer. Allí se halló en una casa cociendo en una olla un pezcuezo de un hombre. Los mochachos que cativan cortanlos el miembro, é sirvense de ellos fasta que son hombres, y despues cuando quieren facer fiesta mátanlos é cómenselos, porque dicen que la carne de los mochachos é de las mogeres no es buena para comer. Destos mochachos se vinieron para nosotros huyendo tres, todos tres cortados sus miembros. E á cabo de cuatro dias vino el Capitan que se habia perdido, de cuya venida estabamos ya bien desesperados, that he rejoined us, without having gained any information respecting the wanderers : we rejoiced at their arrival, regarding it as a new accession to our numbers.   The captain and the men who accompanied him brought back some women and boys, ten in number : neither this party, nor those who went out to seek them, had seen any of the men of the island, which must have arisen either from their having fled, or possibly from there being but very few men in that locality; for, as the women informed us, ten canoes had gone away to make an attack upon the neighbouring islands.   The wanderers had returned from the mountains in such an emaciated condition, that it was distressing to see them; when we asked them how it was that they lost themselves, they said that the trees were so thick and close that they could not see the sky; some of them who were mariners had climbed the trees to get a sight of the stars, but could never see them, and if they had not found their way to the sea coast, it would have been impossible to have returned to the fleet.   We left this island eight days after our arrival.[9]   The next day at noon we saw another

---

porque ya los habian ido á buscar otras cuadrillas por dos veces, é aquel dia vino la una cuadrilla sin saber dellos ciertamente.   Holgamos con su venida como si nuevamente se hobieran hallado : trajo este Capitan con los que fueron con él diez cabezas entre mochachos y mugeres.   Estos ni los otros que los fueron á buscar, nunca hallaron hombres porque se habien huido, ó por ventura que en aquella comarca habia pocos hombres, porque segun se supo de las mugeres eran idas diez canoas con gentes á saltear á otras islas. Vino él é los que fueron con él tan destrozados del monte, que era lástima de los ver : decian, preguntándoles como se habien perdido, dijeron que era la espesura de los árboles tanta que el cielo no podian ver, é que algunos de ellos, que eran marineros, habian subido por los árboles para mirar el estrella, é que nunca la podieron ver, é que si no toparan con el mar fuera imposible tornar á la flota. Partimos desta isla ocho dias despues que allí llegamos.   Luego

[10] They left on Sunday the 10th of November.   (M. F. de Navarrete.)

island,[11] not very large, at about twelve leagues distance from the one we were leaving; the greater part of the first day of our departure we were kept close in to the coast of this island by a calm, but as the Indian women whom we brought with us said that it was not inhabited, but had been dispeopled by the Carribees, we made no stay in it. On that evening we saw another island:[12] and in the night finding there were some sandbanks near, we dropped anchor, not venturing to proceed until the morning. On the morrow another island[13] appeared, of considerable size, but we touched at none of these because we were anxious to convey consolation to our people who had been left in Española; but it did not please God to grant us our desire, as will hereafter appear. Another day at the dinner hour we arrived at an island[14] which seemed to be worth finding, for judging by the extent of cultivation in it, it appeared very populous. We went thither and put into harbour, when the admiral immediately sent on shore a well manned barge to hold speech with the Indians, in order to ascertain what race

---

otro dia á medio dia vimos otra isla, no muy grande, que estaria desta otra doce leguas; porque el primero dia que partimos lo mas del dia nos fizo calma, fuimos junto con la costa desta isla, é dijeron las Indias que llevabamos que no era habitada, que los Caribes la habian despoblado, é por esto no paramos en ella. Luego esa tarde vimos otra : á esa noche, cerca desta isla, fallamos unos bajos, por cuyo temor sorgimos, que no osamos andar fasta que fuese de dia. Luego á la mañana paresció otra isla harto grande : á ninguna destas no llegamos por consolar los que habian dejado en la Española, é no plogó á Dios segun que abajo parecerá. Otro dia á hora de comer llegamos á una isla é pareciónos mucho bien, porque parecia muy poblada, segun las muchas labranzas que en ella habia. Fuimos allá é tomamos puerto en la costa : luego mandó el Almirante ir á tierra una barca guarnecida de gente para si pudiese tomar lengua para saber que gente era, é tambien porque habiamos me-

---

11 The island Montserrat. (M. F. de Navarrete.)
12 The admiral called it Santa Maria la Redonda. (M. F. de Navarrete.)
13 Santa Maria la Antigua.   14 The island of St. Martin.

they were, and also because we considered it necessary to
gain some information respecting our course; although it
afterwards plainly appeared that the admiral, who had never
made that passage before, had taken a very correct route.
But since doubtful questions ought always by investigation
to be reduced as nearly to a certainty as possible, he wished
that communication should be held with the natives at once,
and some of the men who went in the barge leapt on shore
and went up to a village, whence the inhabitants had already
withdrawn and hidden themselves. They took in this island
five or six women and some boys, most of whom were captives,
like those in the other island; we learned from the women
whom we had brought with us, that the natives of this place also
were Caribbees. As this barge was about to return to the ships
with the capture which they had taken, a canoe came along
the coast containing four men, two women, and a boy; and
when they saw the fleet they were so stupified with amazement, that for a good hour they remained motionless at the
distance of nearly two gunshots from the ships. In this position they were seen by those who were in the barge and also

---

nester informarnos del camino, caso quel Almirante, aunque nunca
habia fecho aquel camino, iba muy bien encaminado segun en cabo
pareció. Pero porque las cosas dubdosas se deben siempre buscar
con la mayor certinidad que haberse pueda, quiso haber allí lengua,
de la cual gente que iba en la barca ciertas personas saltaron en
tierra, é llegaron en tierra á un poblado de donde la gente ya se
habia escondido. Tomaron allí cinco ó seis mugeres y ciertos mochachos, de las cuales las mas eran tambien de las cativas como en
la otra isla, porque tambien estos eran de los Caribes, segun ya sabiamos por la relacion de las mugeres que traiamos. Ya que esta
barca se queria tornar á los navíos con su presa que habia fecho por
parte debajo; por la costa venia una canoa en que venian cuatro
hombres é dos mugeres é un mochaco, é desque vieron la flota ma-
ravillados se embebecieron tanto que por una grande hora estovieron
que no se movieron de un lugar casi dos tiros de lombarda de los
navíos. En esto fueron vistos de los que estaban en la barca é aun

by all the fleet. Meanwhile those in the barge moved towards the canoe, but so close in shore, that the Indians, in their perplexity and astonishment as to what all this could mean, never saw them, until they were so near that escape was impossible; for our men pressed on them so rapidly that they could not get away, although they made considerable effort to do so.

When the Caribbees saw that all attempt at flight was useless, they most courageously took to their bows, both women and men; I say most courageously, because they were only four men and two women, and our people were twenty-five in number. Two of our men were wounded by the Indians, one with two arrow-shots in his breast, and another with one in his side, and if it had not happened that they carried shields and wooden bucklers, and that they got near them with the barge and upset their canoe, most of them would have been killed with their arrows. After their canoe was upset, they remained in the water swimming and occasionally wading (for there were shallows in that part), still using their bows as much as they could, so that our men had enough to do to take them: and after all there was one of

---

de toda la flota. Luego los de la barca fueron para ellos tan junto con la tierra, que con el embebecimiento que tenian, maravillándose é pensando que cosa seria, nunca los vieron hasta que estovieron muy cerca dellos, que no les pudieron mucho huir aunque harto trabajaron por ello; pero los nuestros aguijaron con tanta priesa que no se les pudieron ir. Los Caribes desque vieron que el hoir no les aprovechaba, con mucha osadia pusieron mano á los arcos, tambien las mugeres como los hombres; é digo con mucha osadia porque ellos no eran mas de cuatro hombres y dos mugeres, é los nuestros mas de veinte é cinco, de los cuales firieron dos, al uno dieron dos frechadas en los pechos é al otro una por el costado, é sino fuera porque llevaban adargas é tablachutas, é porque los invistieron presto con la barca é les trastornaron su canoa, asaetearan con sus frechas los mas dellos. E despues de trastornada su canoa quedaron en el agua nadando, é á las veces haciendo pie, que allí habia unos bajos, é tovieron harto que hacer en tomarlos, que to-them whom they were unable to secure till he had received a mortal wound with a lance, and whom thus wounded they took to the ships. The difference between these Caribbees and the other Indians, with respect to dress, consists in their wearing their hair very long, while the others have it clipt irregularly and paint their heads with crosses and a hundred thousand different devices, each according to his fancy; which they do with sharpened reeds. All of them, both the Caribbees and the others, are beardless, so that it is a rare thing to find a man with a beard: the Caribbees whom we took had their eyes and eyebrows stained, which I imagine they do from ostentation and to give them a more formidable appearance. One of these captives said, that in an island belonging to them called Cayre (which is the first we saw, though we did not go to it), there is a great quantity of gold; and that if we were to take them nails and tools with which to make their canoes, we might bring away as much gold as we liked. On the same day we left that island, having been there no more than six or seven hours; and steering for

---

davía cuanto podian tiraban, é con todo eso el uno no lo pudieron tomar sino mal herido de una lanzada que murió, el cual trajeron ansi herido fasta los navíos. La diferencia destos á los otros indios en el hábito, es que los de Caribe tienen el cabello muy largo, los otros son tresquilados é fechas cien mil diferencias en las cabezas de cruces, é de otras pinturas en diversas maneras, cada uno como se le antoja, lo cual se hacen con cañas agudas. Todos ansi los de Caribe como los otros es gente sin barbas, que por maravilla hallarás hombre que las tenga. Estos Caribes que allí tomaron venian tiznados los ojos é las cejas, lo cual me parece que hacen por gala, é con aquello parescian mas espantables; el uno destos dice que en una isla dellos, llamada Cayre, que es la primera que vimos, á la cual no llegamos, hay mucho oro; que vayan allá con clavos é contezuelas para hacer sus canoas, é que traerán cuanto oro quisieren. Luego aquel dia partimos de esta isla, que no estariamos allí mas de seis ó siete horas, fuemos para otra tierra que pareció á ojo que another point of land[15] which appeared to lie in our intended course, we reached it by night. On the morning of the following day we coasted along it, and found it to be a large extent of country, but not continuous, for it was divided into more than forty islets.[16] The land was very high and most of it barren, an appearance which we have never observed in any of the islands visited by us before or since: the surface of the ground seemed to suggest the probability of its containing metals. None of us went on shore here, but a small latteen caravel went up to one of the islets and found in it some fishermen's huts; the Indian women whom we brought with us said they were not inhabited. We proceeded along the coast the greater part of that day, and on the evening of the next we discovered another island called Burenquen,[17] which we judged to be thirty leagues in length, for we were coasting along it the whole of one day. This island is very beautiful and apparently fertile: hither the Caribbees come

---

estaba en el camino que habiamos de facer : llegamos noche cerca della. Otro dia de mañana fuimos por la costa della : era muy gran tierra, aunque no era muy continua, que eran mas de cuarenta y tantos islones, tierra muy alta, é la mas della pelada, la cual no era ninguna ni es de las que antes ni despues habemos visto. Parescia tierra dispuesta para haber en ella metales: á esta no llegamos para saltar en tierra, salvo una carabela latina llegó á un islon de estos, en el cual hallaron ciertas casas de pescadores. Las Indias que traiamos dijeron que no eran pobladas. Andovimos por esta costa lo mas deste dia, hasta otro dia en la tarde que llegamos á vista de otra isla llama Burenquen, cuya costo corrimos todo un dia : juzgábase que ternia por aquella banda treinta leguas. Esta isla es muy hermosa y muy fértil á parecer : á esta vienen los de Caribe á con-

15 The island of *Santa Cruz*, where they anchored on Thursday the fourteenth of November. (M. F. de Navarrete.

16 The admiral named the largest of these islands *St. Ursula*, and all the others *The eleven thousand Virgins*. (M. F. de Navarrete.)

17 The island of *Porto Rico*, to which the admiral gave the name of *St. John the Baptist*. (M. F. de Navarrete.)

with the view of subduing the inhabitants, and often carry away many of the people. These islanders have no boats nor any knowledge of navigation; but, as our captives inform us, they use bows as well as the Caribbees, and if by chance when they are attacked they succeed in taking any of their invaders, they will eat them in like manner as the Caribbees themselves in the contrary event would devour them. We remained two days in this island, and a great number of our men went on shore, but could never get speech of the natives, who had all fled, from fear of the Caribbees. All the above-mentioned islands were discovered in this voyage, the admiral having seen nothing of them in his former voyage; they are all very beautiful and possess a most luxuriant soil, but this last island appeared to exceed all the others in beauty. Here terminated the islands, which on the side towards Spain had not been seen before by the admiral, although we regard it as a matter of certainty that there is land more than forty leagues beyond the foremost of these newly discovered islands, on the side nearest to Spain. We believe this to be the case, because two days before we saw land we observed some birds called rabihorcados (or pelicans, marine birds of prey which

---

quistar, de la cual llevaban mucha gente; estos no tienen fustas ningunas nin saben andar por mar; pero, segun dicen estos Caribes que tomamos, usan arcos como ellos, é si por caso cuando los vienen á saltear los pueden prender tambien se los comen como los de Caribe á ellos. En un puerto desta isla estovimos dos dias, donde saltó mucha gente en tierra; pero jamas podimos haber lengua, que todos se fuyeron como gente temorizadas de los Caribes. Todas estas islas dichas fueron descubiertas deste camino, que fasta aquí ninguna dellas habia visto el Almirante el otro viage, todos son muy hermosas é de muy buena tierra; pero esta paresció mejor á todos: aquí casi se acabaron las islas que fácia la parte de España habia dejado de ver el Almirante, aunque tenemos por cosa cierta que hay tierra mas de cuarenta leguas antes de estas primeras hasta España, porque dos dias antes que viesemos tierra vimos unas aves que llaman rabihorcados, que son aves de rapiña marinas é ni sido not sit or sleep upon the water), making circumvolutions in the air at the close of evening previous to taking their flight towards land for the night. These birds could not be going to settle at more than twelve or fifteen leagues distance, because it was late in the evening, and this was on our right hand on the side towards Spain; from which we all judged that there was land there still undiscovered; but we did not go in search of it, because it would have taken us round out of our intended route. I hope that in a few voyages it will be discovered. It was at dawn that we left the before-mentioned island of Burenquen,[18] and on that day before nightfall we caught sight of land, which though not recognized by any of those who had come hither in the former voyage, we believed to be Española, from the information given us by the Indian women whom we had with us: and in this island we remain at present.[19] Between Española and Burenquen[20] another island appeared at a distance, but of no great size. When we reached Española the land, at the part where we approached it, was low and very

---

entan ni duermen sobre el agua, sobre tarde rodeando sobir en alto, é despues tiran su via á buscar tierra para dormir, las cuales no podrian ir á caer segun era tarde de doce ó quince leguas arriba, y esto era á la man derecha donde veniamos hasta la parte de España; de donde todos juzgaron allí quedar tierra, lo cual no se buscó porque se nos hacia rodeo para la via que traimos. Espero que á pocos viages se hallará. Desta isla sobredicha partimos una madrugada, é aquel dia, antes que fuese noche, hobimos vista de tierra, la cual tampoco era conocida de ninguno de los que habian venido el otro viage; pero por las nuevas de las indias que traimos sospechamos que era la Española, en la cual agora estamos. Entre esta isla é la otra de Buriquen parecia de lejos otra, aunque no era grande. Desque llegamos á esta Española, por el comienzo de alla era tierra baja y muy llana, del conocimiento de la cual aun estaban todos

[18] Porto Rico.
[19] On Friday, the twenty-second of November, the admiral first caught sight of the island of Española. (M. F. de Navarrete.)
[20] La Mona and Monito. (M. F. de Navarrete.)

flat, [21] on seeing which, a general doubt arose as to its identity; for, neither the admiral nor his companions, on the previous voyage, had seen it on this side.

The island being large, is divided into provinces; the part which we first touched at, is called Hayti; another province adjoining it, they call Xamana; and the next province is named Bohio, where we now are. These provinces are again subdivided, for they are of great extent. Those who have seen the length of its coast, state that it is two hundred leagues long, and I, myself, should judge it not to be less than a hundred and fifty leagues: as to its breadth, nothing is hitherto known; it is now forty days since a caravel left us with the view of circumnavigating it, and is not yet returned. The country is very remarkable, and contains a vast number of large rivers, and extensive chains of mountains, with broad open valleys, and the mountains are very high: it does not appear that the grass is ever cut throughout the year. I do not think they have any winter in this part, for near Navidad (at Christmas) were found many birds-nests, some containing the

---

dubdosos si fuese la que es, porque aquella parte nin el Almirante ni los otros que con él vinieron habian visto, é aquesta isla como es grande es nombrada por provincias, e á esta parte que primero llegamos llaman Hayti, y luego á la otra provincia junta con esta llaman Xamaná, é á la otra Bohio, en la cual agora estamos; ansi hay en ellas muchas provincias porque es gran cosa, porque segun afirman los que la han visto por la costa de largo, dicen que habrá doscientas leguas: á mi me parece que á lo menos habrá ciento é cincuenta; del ancho della hasta agora no se sabe. Alla es ido cuarenta dias ha á rodearla una carabela, la cual no es venida hasta hoy. Es tierra muy singular, donde hay infinitos rios grandes é sierras grandes é valles grandes rasos, grandes montañas: sospecho que nunca se secan las yerbas en todo el año. Non creo que hay invierno ninguno en esta nin en las otras, porque por Navidad se fallan muchos nidos de aves, dellas con pájaros, é dellas con hue-

[21] Cape Engaño, in the island of Española.

young birds, and others containing eggs. No four-footed animal has ever been seen in this or any of the other islands, except some dogs of various colours, as in our own country, but in shape like large house-dogs; and also some little animals, in colour, size, and fur, like a rabbit, with long tails, and feet like those of a rat; thèse animals climb up the trees, and many who have tasted them, say they are very good to eat :[22] there are not any wild beasts. There are great numbers of small snakes, and some lizards, but not many; for the Indians consider them as great a luxury as we do pheasants : they are of the same size as ours, but different in shape. In a small adjacent island[23] (close by a harbour called Monte Christo, where we stayed several days), our men saw an enormous kind of lizard, which they said was as large round as a calf, with a tail as long as a lance, which they often went out to kill: but bulky as it was, it got into the sea, so that they could not catch it. There are, both in this and the other islands, an infinite number of birds like those in our own country, and

---

vos. En ella ni en las otras nunca se ha visto animal de cuatro pies, salvo algunos perros de todas colores como en nuestra patria, la hechura como unos gosques grandes ; de animales salvages no hay. Otrosí, hay un hanimal de color de conejo é de su pelo, el grandor de un conejo nuevo, el rabo largo, los pies é manos como de raton, suben por los árboles, muchos los han comido, dicen que es muy bueno de comer : hay culebras muchas no grandes ; lagartos aunque no muchos, porque los indios hacen tanta fiesta dellos como hariamos allá con faisanes, son del tamaño de los de allá, salvo que en la hechura son diferentes, aunque en una isleta pequeña, que está junto con un puerto que llaman Monte Christo, donde estovimos muchos dias, vieron muchos dias un lagarto muy grande que decian que seria de gordura de un becerro, é atan complido como una lanza, é muchas veces salieron por lo matar, é con la mucha espesura se les metia en la mar, de manera que no se pudo haber dél derecho. Hay en esta isla y en las otras infinitas aves de las de nuestra patria, é otras muchas que allá nunca se vieron :

[22] In all probability a species of *capromys*.
[23] Cabra, or Goat island, between Puerto de Plata and Cas Rouge Point.

many others such as we had never seen. No kind of domestic fowl has been seen here, with the exception of some ducks in the houses in Zuruquia; these ducks were larger than those of Spain, though smaller than geese,—very pretty, with tufts on their heads, most of them as white as snow, but some black.

We ran along the coast of this island nearly a hundred leagues, concluding, that within this range we should find the spot where the admiral had left some of his men, and which we supposed to be about the middle of the coast. As we passed by the province called Xamaná, we sent on shore one of the Indians, who had been taken in the previous voyage, clothed, and carrying some trifles, which the admiral had ordered to be given him. On that day died one of our sailors, a Biscayan, who had been wounded in the affray with the Caribbees, when they were captured, as I have already described, through their want of caution. As we were proceeding along the coast, an opportunity was afforded for a boat to go on shore to bury him, the boat being accompanied by two caravels to protect it. When they reached the shore, a great number of Indians came out to the boat, some of them wearing necklaces and ear-rings of gold, and expressed

---

de las aves domésticas nunca se ha visto acá ninguna, salvo en la Zuruquia habia en las casas unas ánades, las mas dellas blancas como la nieve é algunas dellas negras, muy lindas, con crestas rasas, mayores que las de allá, menores que ánsares. Por la costa desta isla corrimos al pie de cien leguas porque hasta donde el Almirante habia dejado la gente, habria en este compás, que será en comedio ó en medio de la isla. Andando por la provincia della llamada Xamaná, en derecho echamos en tierra uno de los indios quel otro viage habian llevado vestido, é con algunas cosillas quel Almirante le habia mandado dar. Aquel dia se nos murió un marinero vizcaino que habia seido herido de los Caribes, que ya dije que se tomaron, por su mala guarda, é porque ibamos por costa de tierra, dióse lugar que saliese una barca á enterrarlo, é fueron en reguarda de la barca dos carabelas cerca con tierra. Salieron á la barca en llegando en tierra muchos indios, de los cuales algunos traian oro a wish to accompany the Spaniards to the ships; but our men refused to take them, because they had not received permission from the admiral. When the Indians found that they would not take them, two of them got into a small canoe, and went up to one of the caravels that had put in to shore; they were received on board with great kindness, and taken to the admiral's ship, where, through the medium of an interpreter, they related that a certain king had sent them to ascertain who we were, and to invite us to land, adding that they had plenty of gold, and also of provisions, to which we should be welcome. The admiral desired that shirts, and caps, and other trifles, should be given to each of them, and said that as he was going to the place where Guacamari dwelt, he would not stop then, but that on a future day he should have the opportunity of seeing him, and with that they departed. We continued our route till we came to an harbour called Monte Cristi, where we remained two days, in order to observe the position of the land; for the admiral had an objection to the spot where his men had been left with the view of forming a station. We went on shore therefore to survey the forma-

---

al cuello, é á las orejas; querian venir con los cristianos á los navíos, é no los quisieron traer, porque no llevaban licencia del Almirante; los cuales desque vieron que no los querian traer se metieron dos dellos en una canoa pequeña, é se vinieron á una carabela de las que se habian acercado á tierra, en la cual los recibieron con su amor, é trajéronlos á la nao del Almirante, é dijeron, mediante un interprete, que un Rey fulano los enviaba á saber que gente eramos, é á rogar que quisiesemos llegar á tierra, porque tenian mucho oro é le darian dello, é de lo que tenian de comer: el Almirante les mandó dar sendas camisas é bonetes é otras cosillas, é les dijo que porque iba á donde estaba Guacamarí non se podria detener, que otro tiempo habria que le pudiese ver, é con esto se fueron. No cesamos de andar nuestro camino fasta llegar á un puerto llamado Monte Cristi, donde estuvimos dos dias para ver la disposicion de la tierra, porque no habia parecido bien al Almirante el logar donde habia dejado la gente para hacer asiento. Decendimos en tierra

tion of the land : there was a large river of excellent water
close by ;[24] but the ground was inundated, and very ill-calcu-
lated for habitation. As we went on making our observations
on the river and the land, some of our men found two dead
bodies by the river's side, one with a rope round his neck,
and the other with one round his foot : this was on the first
day of our landing. On the following day they found two
other corpses farther on, and one of these was observed to
have a great quantity of beard ; this was regarded as a very
suspicious circumstance by many of our people, because, as I
have already said, all the Indians are beardless. This harbour
is twelve leagues[25] from the place where the Spaniards had been
left under the protection of Guacamari, the king of that province, whom I suppose to be one of the chief men of the
island. After two days we set sail for that spot, but as it was
late when we arrived there,[26] and there were some shoals, where
the admiral's ship had been lost, we did not venture to put in

para ver la dispusicion : habia cerca de allí un gran rio de muy
buena agua ; pero es toda tierra anegada é muy indispuesta para
habitar. Andando veyendo el rio é tierra hallaron algunos de los
nuestros en una parte dos hombres muertos junto con el rio, el uno
con un lazo al pescuezo y el otro con otro al pie, esto fue el primero dia. Otro dia siguiente hallaron otros dos muertos mas adelante de aquellos, el uno destos estaba en disposicion que se le pudo
conocer tener muchas barbas. Algunos de los nuestros sospecharon
mas mal que bien, é con razon, porque los indios son todos desbar-
bados, como dicho he. Este puerto está del lugar donde estaba la
gente cristiana doce leguas : pasados dos dias alzamos velas para el
lugar donde el Almirante habia dejado la sobredicha gente, en compañía de un Rey destos indios, que se llamaba Guacamarí, que
pienso ser de los principales desta isla. Este dia llegamos en derecho de aquel lugar ; pero era ya tarde, é porque allí habia unos
bajos donde el otro dia se habia perdido la nao en que habia ido el

[24] The river of Santiago.   [25] It is only seven leagues.
[26] The admiral anchored at the entrance of the harbour of Navidad, on
Wednesday, the twenty-seventh of November, towards midnight, and on
the following day, in the afternoon, put into the harbour. (Navarrete.)

close to the shore, but remained that night at a little less than a league from the coast, waiting until the morning, when we might enter securely. On that evening, a canoe, containing five or six Indians, came out at a considerable distance from where we were, and approached us with great celerity. The admiral believing that he insured our safety by keeping the sails set, would not wait for them; they, however, perseveringly rowed up to us within gunshot, and then stopped to look at us; but when they saw that we did not wait for them, they put back and went away. After we had anchored that night at the spot in question,[27] the admiral ordered two guns to be fired, to see if the Spaniards, who had remained with Guacamari, would fire in return, for they also had guns with them; but when we received no reply, and could not perceive any fires, nor the slightest symptom of habitations on the spot, the spirits of our people became much depressed, and they began to entertain the suspicion which the circumstances were naturally calculated to excite. While all were in this desponding mood, and when four or five hours of the night had passed

---

Almirante, no osamos tomar el puerto cerca de tierra fasta que otro dia de mañana se desfondase é pudiesen entrar seguramente : quedamos aquella noche no una legua de tierra. Esa tarde, viniendo para allí de lejos, salió una canoa en que parescian cinco ó seis indios, los cuales venian á prisa para nosotros. El Almirante creyendo que nos seguraba hasta alzarnos, no quiso que los esperasemos, é porfiando llegaron hasta un tiro de lombarda de nosotros, é parabanse á mirar, é desde allí desque vieron que no los esperabamos dieron vuelta é tornaron su via. Despues que surgimos en aquel lugar sobredicho tarde, el Almirante mandó tirar dos lombardas á ver si respondian los cristianos que habian quedado con el dicho Guacamarí, porque tambien tenian lombardas, los cuales nunca respondieron ni menos parescian huegos ni señal de casas en aquel lugar, de lo qual se deconsoló mucho la gente é tomaron la sospecha que de tal caso se debia tomar. Estando ansi todos muy tristes, pasadas cuatro ó cinco horas de la noche, vino la misma

[27] The Bay of Caracol, four leagues west of Fort Dauphin.

away, the same canoe which we had seen in the evening, came up, and the Indians with a loud voice addressed the captain of the caravel, which they first approached, inquiring for the admiral; they were conducted to the admiral's vessel, but would not go on board till he had spoken to them, and they had asked for a light, in order to assure themselves that it was he who conversed with them. One of them was a cousin of Guacamari, who had been sent by him once before: it appeared, that after they had turned back the previous evening, they had been charged by Guacamari with two masks of gold as a present; one for the admiral, the other for a captain who had accompanied him on the former voyage. They remained on board for three hours, talking with the admiral in the presence of all of us, he showing much pleasure in their conversation, and inquiring respecting the welfare of the Spaniards whom he had left behind. Guacamari's cousin replied, that those who remained were all well, but that some of them had died of disease, and others had been killed in quarrels that had arisen amongst them: he said also that the province had been invaded, by two kings named Caonabó and

---

canoa que esa tarde habiamos visto, é venia dando voces, preguntando por el Almirante un Capitan de una carabela donde primero llegaron: trajéronlos á la nao del Almirante, los cuales nunca quisieron entrar hasta que el Almirante los hablase; demandaron lumbre para lo conocer, é despues que lo conocieron entraron. Era uno dellos primo del Guacamarí, el cual los habia enviado otra vez. Despues que se habian tornado aquella tarde traian caratulas de oro que Guacamarí enviaba en presente; la una para el Almirante é la otra para un Capitan quel otro viage habia ido con él. Estovieron en la nao hablando con el Almirante en presencia de todos por tres horas mostrando mucho placer, preguntándoles por los Cristianos que tales estaban: aquel pariente dijo que estaban todos buenos, aunque entre ellos habia algunos muertos de dolencia é otros de diferencia que habia contecido entre ellos, é que Guacamarí estaba en otro lugar ferido en una pierna é por eso no habia venido, pero que otro dia vernia; porque otros dos Reyes, llamado el uno

Mayreni, who had burned the habitations of the people; and that Guacamari was at some distance, lying ill of a wound in his leg, which was the occasion of his not appearing, but that he would come on the next day. The Indians then departed, saying they would return on the following day with the said Guacamari, and left us consoled for that night. On the morning of the next day, we were expecting that Guacamari would come; and, in the meantime, some of our men landed by command of the admiral, and went to the spot where the Spaniards had formerly been: they found the building which they had inhabited, and which they had in some degree fortified with a palisade, burnt and levelled with the ground; they found also some rags and stuffs which the Indians had brought to throw upon the house. They observed too that the Indians who were seen near the spot, looked very shy, and dared not approach, but, on the contrary, fled from them. This appeared strange to us, for the admiral had told us that in the former voyage, when he arrived at this place, so many came in canoes to see us, that there was no keeping them off; and as we now saw that they were suspicious of us, it gave us

---

Caonabó y el otro Mayrení, habian venido á pelear con él é que le habian quemado el logar; é luego esa noche se tornaron diciendo que otra dia vernian con el dicho Guacamarí, é con esto nos dejaron por esa noche consolados. Otro dia en la mañana estovimos esperando que viniese el dicho Guacamarí, é entretanto saltaron en tierra algunos por mandado del Almirante, é fueron al lugar donde solian estar, é halláronle quemado un cortijo algo fuerte con una palizada, donde los Cristianos habitaban, é tenian lo suyo quemado é derribado, é ciertas bernias é ropas que los indios habian traido á echar en la casa. Los dichos indios que por allí parecian andaban muy cahareños, que no se osaban allegar á nosotros, antes huian; lo cual no nos pareció bien porque el Almirante nos habia dicho que en llegando á quel lugar salian tantas canoas dellos á bordo de los navíos á vernos que no nos podriamos defender dellos, é que en el otro viage ansi lo facian; é como agora veiamos que estaban sospechosos de nosotros no nos parecia bien, con todo halagándoles a very unfavourable impression. We threw trifles, such as buttons and beads, towards them, in order to conciliate them, but only four, a relation of Guacamari's and three others, took courage to enter the boat, and were rowed on board. When they were asked concerning the Spaniards, they replied that all of them were dead: we had been told this already by one of the Indians whom we had brought from Spain, and who had conversed with the two Indians that on the former occasion came on board with their canoe, but we had not believed it. Guacamari's kinsman was asked who had killed them: he replied that king Caonabó and king Mayreni had made an attack upon them, and burnt the buildings on the spot, that many were wounded in the affray, and among them Guacamari, who had received a wound in his thigh, and had retired to some distance: he also stated that he wished to go and fetch him; upon which some trifles were given to him, and he took his departure for the place of Guacamari's abode. All that day we remained in expectation of them, and when we saw that they did not come, many suspected that the Indians who had been on board the night before, had been drowned; for

---

aquel dia é arrojándolos algunas cosas, ansi como cascabeles é cuentas, hobo de asegurarse un su pariente del dicho Guacamarí é otros tres, los cuales entraron en la barca é trajéronlos la nao. Despues que le preguntaron por los Cristianos dijeron que todos eran muertos, aunque ya nos lo habia dicho un indio de los que llevabamos de Castilla que lo habian hablado los dos indios que antes habian venido á la nao, que se habian quedado á bordo de la nao con su canao, pero no le habiamos creido. Fue preguntado á este pariente de Guacamarí quien los habia muerto: dijo que el Rey de Canoabó y el Rey Mayrení, é que le quemaron las cosas del lugar, é que estaban dellos muchos heridos, é tambien el dicho Guacamarí estaba pasado un muslo, y él que estaba en otro lugar y que él queria ir luego allá á lo llamar, al cual dieron algunas cosas, é luego se partió para donde estaba Guacamarí. Todo aquel dia los estobimos esperando, é desque vimos que no venian, muchos tenian sospecha que se habian ahogado los indios que antenoche habian venido, they had had wine given them two or three times, and they had come in a small canoe that might be easily upset. The next morning the admiral went on shore, taking some of us with him; we went to the spot where the settlement had been, and found it utterly destroyed by fire, and the clothes of the Spaniards lying about upon the grass, but on that occasion we saw no dead body. There were many different opinions amongst us; some suspecting that Guacamari himself was concerned in the betrayal and death of the Christians; others thought not, because his own residence was burnt: so that it remained a very doubtful question. The admiral ordered all the ground which had been occupied by the fortifications of the Spaniards to be searched, for he had left orders with them to bury all the gold that they might get. While this was being done, the admiral wished to examine a spot at about a league's distance, which seemed to be suitable for building a town, for there was yet time to do so;—and some of us went thither with him, making our observations of the land as we went along the coast, until we reached a village of seven or eight houses, which the Indians for-

---

porque los habian dado á beber dos ó tres veces de vino, é venian en una canoa pequeña que se les podria trastornar. Otro dia de mañana salió á tierra el Almirante é algunos de nosotros, é fuemos donde solia estar la villa, la cual nos vimos toda quemada é los vestidos de los cristianos se hallaban por aquella yerba. Por aquella hora no vimos ningun muerto. Habia entre nosotros muchas razones diferentes, unos sospechando que el mismo Guacamarí fuese en la traicion ó muerte de los Cristianos, otros les parecia que no, pues estaba quemada su villa, ansí que la cosa era mucho para dudar. El Almirante mandó catar todo el sitio donde los Cristianos estaban fortalecidos porquel los habia mandado que desque toviesen alguna cantidad de oro que lo enterrasen. Entretanto que esto se hacia quiso llegar á ver á cerca de una legua do nos parecia que podria haber asiento para poder edificar una villa porque ya era tiempo, adonde fuimos ciertos con él mirando la tierra por la costa, fasta que llegamos á un poblado donde habia siete ú ocho casas; las

H

sook when they saw us approach, carrying away what they could, and leaving the things which they could not remove, hidden amongst the grass, around the houses. These people are so degraded that they have not even the sense to select a fitting place to live in; those who dwell on the shore, build for themselves the most miserable hovels that can be imagined, and all the houses are so covered with grass and dampness, that I wonder how they can contrive to exist. In these houses we found many things belonging to the Spaniards, which it could not be supposed they would have bartered; such as a very handsome Moorish mantle, which had not been unfolded since it was brought from Spain, stockings and pieces of cloth, also an anchor belonging to the ship which the admiral had lost here on the previous voyage; with other articles, which the more confirmed our suspicions. On examining some things which had been very cautiously sewn up in a small basket, we found a man's head wrapped up with great care; this we judged might be the head of a father, or mother, or of some person whom they much regarded: I have since heard that many were found in the same state, which makes me

---

quales habian desamparado los indios luego que nos vieron ir, é llevaron lo que pudieron é lo otro dejaron escondido entre yerbas junto con las casas, que es gente tan bestial que no tienen discrecion para buscar lugar para habitar, que los que viven á la marina es maravilla cuan bestialmente edifican, que las casas enderedor tienen tan cubiertas de yerba ó de humidad, que estoy espantado como viven. En aquellas casas hallamos muchas cosas de los Cristianos, las cuales no se creian que ellos hobiesen rescatado, ansí como una almalafa muy gentil, la cual no se habia descogido de como la llevaron de Castilla, é calzas é pedazos de paños, é una ancla de la nao quel Almirante habia allí perdido el otro viage, é otras cosas, de las cuales mas se esforzó nuestra opinion; y de acá hallamos, buscando las cosas que tenian guardadas en una esportilla mucho cosida é mucho á recabdo, una cabeza de hombre mucho guardada. Allí juzgamos por entonces que seria la cabeza de padre ó madre, ó de persona que mucho querian. Despues he oido que hayan hallado

believe that our first impression was the true one. After this
we returned. We went on the same day to the site of the
settlement; and when we arrived, we found many Indians,
who had regained their courage, bartering gold with our men:
they had bartered to the extent of a mark : we also learned
that they had shown where the bodies of eleven of the dead
Spaniards were laid, which were already covered with the
grass that had grown over them; and they all with one voice
asserted that Caonabó and Mayreni had killed them; but notwithstanding all this, we began to hear complaints that one
of the Spaniards had taken three women to himself, and
another four; from whence we drew the inference that jealousy
was the cause of the misfortune that had occurred. On the
next morning, as no spot in that vicinity appeared suitable for
our making a settlement, the admiral ordered a caravel to go
in one direction to look for a convenient locality, while some
of us went with him another way. In the course of our ex-
plorations, we discovered a harbour, of great security; the
neighbourhood of which, so far as regarded the formation of
the land, was excellent for habitation ; but as it was far from
any mine of gold, the neighbourhood of which was very de-

---

muchas desta manera, por donde creo ser verdad lo que allí juzgamos ; desde allí nos tornamos. Aquel dia venimos por donde estaba
la villa, y cuando llegamos hallamos muchos indios que se habian
asegurado y estaban rescatando oro : tenian rescatado fasta un marco:
hallamos que habian mostrado donde estaban muertos once cristianos, cubiertos ya de la yerba que habia crecido sobre ellos, é todos
hablaban por una boca que Caonabó é Mayreni los habian muerto ;
pero con todo eso asomaban queja que los Cristianos uno tenia tres
mugeres, otro cuatro, donde creemos quel mal que les vino fue de
zelos. Otro dia de mañana, porque en todo aquello no habia logar
dispuesto para nosotros poder hacer asiento, acordó el Almirante
fuese una carabela á una parte para mirar lugar conveniente, é algunos que fuimos con él fuimos á otra parte, á do hallamos un
puerto muy seguro é muy gentil disposicion de tierra para habitar,
pero porque estaba lejos de donde nos deseabamos que estaba la

sirable, the admiral decided that we should settle in some spot
which would give us greater certainty of attaining that object,
provided the position of the land should prove equally convenient.   On our return, we found the other caravel arrived,
in which Melchior and four or five other trustworthy men had
been exploring with a similar object.   They reported that as
they went along the coast, a canoe came out to them in which
were two Indians, one of whom was the brother of Guacamari,
and was recognized by a pilot who was in the caravel. When
he questioned them as to their purpose, they replied that
Guacamari sent to beg the Spaniards to come on shore, as he
was residing near, with as many as fifty families around him.
The chief men of the party then went on shore in the boat,
proceeded to the place where Guacamari was, and found him
stretched on his bed, complaining of a severe wound.   They
conferred with him, and inquired respecting the Spaniards;
his reply was, in accordance with the account already given
by the others, viz.—that they had been killed by Caonabó
and Mayreni, who also had wounded him in the thigh; and in
confirmation of his assertion, he showed them the limb bound

mina de oro, no acordó el Almirante de poblar sino en otra parte
que fuese mas cierta si se hallase conveniente disposicion. Cuando
venimos deste lugar hallamos venida la otra carabela que habia ido
á la otra parte á buscar el dicho lugar, en la cual habia ido Melchior e otros cuatro ó cinco hombres de pro.   E yendo costeando
por tierra salió á ellos una canoa en que venian dos indios, el uno
era hermano de Guacamarí, el cual fue conocido por un piloto
que iba en la dicha carabela, é preguntó quien iba allí, al cual,
dijeron los hombres prencipales, dijeron que Guacamarí les ro-
gaba que se llegasen á tierra, donde él tenia su asiento con fasta
cincuenta casas.   Los dichos prencipales saltaron en tierra con
la barca é fueron donde él estaba, el cual fallaron en su cama
echado faciendo del doliente ferido.   Fablaron con él preguntán-
dole por los Cristianos : respondió concertando con la mesma
razon de los otros, que era que Caonabó é Mayreni los habian muerto, é que á él habian ferido en un muslo, el cual mostró ligado :

up : on seeing which, they concluded that his statement was correct. At their departure he gave to each of them a jewel of gold, according to his estimation of their respective merits. The Indians beat the gold into very thin plates, in order to make masks of it, and set it in a cement which they make for that purpose : other ornaments they make of it, to wear on the head and to hang in the ears and nostrils, for these also they require it to be thin ; it is not the massiveness of the gold that they admire in their ornaments, but its showy appearance. Guacamari desired them by signs and as well as he was able, to tell the admiral that as he was thus wounded, he prayed him to have the goodness to come to see him. This adventure the aforesaid sailors related to the admiral when he arrived. The next morning he resolved to go thither, for the spot could be reached in three hours, being scarcely three leagues distance from the place where we were ; but as it would be the dinner-hour when we arrived, we dined before we went on shore. After dinner, the admiral gave orders that all the captains should come with their barges to proceed to the shore, for already on that morning, previous to our de-

---

los que entonces lo vieron ansí les pareció que era verdad como él lo dijo : al tiempo del despedirse dió á cada uno dellos una joya de oro, á cada uno como le pareció que lo merescia. Este oro facian en fojas muy delgadas, porque lo quieren para facer carátulas é para poderse asentar en betun que ellos facen, si así no fuese no se asentaria. Otro facen para traer en la cabeza é para colgar en las orejas é narices, ansí que todavía es menester que sea delgado, pues que ellos nada desto hacen por riqueza salvo por buen parecer. Dijo el dicho Guacamarí por señas e como mejor pudo, que porque él estaba ansí herido que dijesen al Almirante que quisiese venir á verlo. Luego quel Almirante llegó los sobredichos le contaron este caso. Otro dia de mañana acordó partir para allá, al cual lugar llegariamos dentro de tres horas, porque apenas habria dende donde estábamos allá tres leguas ; ansí que cuando allí llegamos era hora de comer : comimos ante de salir en tierra. Luego que hobimos comido mandó el Almirante que todos los Capitanes viniesen con

parture, the aforesaid brother of Guacamari had come to speak
with the admiral to urge his visit.   Then the admiral went on
shore accompanied by all the principal officers, so richly
dressed that they would have made a distinguished appearance
even in any of our chief cities : he took with him some articles
as presents, having already received from Guacamari a certain
quantity of gold, and it was reasonable that he should make
a commensurate response to his acts and expressions of good-
will : Guacamari had also provided himself with a present.
When we arrived, we found him stretched upon his bed, which
was made of cotton net-work, and, according to their custom,
suspended. He did not arise, but made from his bed the best
gesture of courtesy of which he was capable.   He showed
much feeling ; with tears in his eyes lamented the death of
the Spaniards, and began speaking on the subject, with explaining to the best of his power, how some died of disease,
others had gone to Caonabó in search of the mine of gold,
and had there been killed, and that the rest had been attacked
and slain in their own town.   According to the appearance
of the dead bodies, it was not two months since this had hap-

---

sus barcas para ir en tierra, porque ya esa mañana antes que parti-
esemos de donde estábamos habia venido el sobredicho su hermano
á hablar con el Almirante, é á darle priesa que fuese al lugar donde
estaba el dicho Guacamarí.   Allí fue el Almirante á tierra é toda
la gente de pro con él, tan ataviados que en una cibdad prencipal
parecieran bien : llevó algunas cosas para le presentar porque ya
habia recibido dél alguna cantidad de oro, é era razon le respondiese
con la obra é voluntad quel habia mostrado. El dicho Guacamarí
ansí mismo tenia aparejado para hacerle presente. Cuando llegamos hallámosle echado en su cama, como ellos lo usan, colgado en
el aire, fecha una cama de algodon como de red ; no se levantó,
salvo dende la cama hizo el semblante de cortesia como él mejor
sopo, mostró mucho sentimiento con lágrimas en los ojos por la
muerte de los Cristianos, é comenzó á hablar en ello mostrando,
como mejor podia, como unos murieron de dolencia, é como otros
se habian ido á Caonabó á buscar la mina del oro é que allí los

pened. Then the admiral presented him with eight marks
and a half of gold, six hundred and five pieces of jewellery, of
various colours, and a cap of similar jewel-work, which I think
they ought to value very highly, because in it was a jewel, for
which the admiral, when presenting it, expressed great vene-
ration. It appears to me that these people put more value
upon copper than gold. The surgeon of the fleet and myself
being present, the admiral told Guacamari that we were
skilled in the treatment of human disorders, and wished that
he would shew us his wound; he replied that he was willing;
upon which I said it would be necessary that he should, if
possible, go out of the house, because we could not see well
on account of the place being darkened by the throng of
people; to this he consented, I think more from timidity than
inclination, and left the house leaning on the arm of the
admiral. After he was seated, the surgeon approached him
and began to untie the bandage; then he told the admiral
that the wound was made with a *ciba*, by which he meant
with a stone. When the wound was uncovered, we went up

---

habian muerto, é los otros que se los habian venido á matar allí en
su villa. A lo que parecian los cuerpos de los muertos no habia
dos meses que habia acaecido. Esa hora el presentó al Almirante
ocho marcos y medio de oro, é cinco ó seiscientos labrados de pe-
dreria de diversos colores, é un bonete de la misma pedrería, lo
cual me parece deben tener ellos en mucho. En el bonete estaba un
joyel, lo cual le dió en mucha veneracion. Pareceme que tienen
en mas el cobre quel oro. Estábamos presentes yo y un zurugiano
de armada ; entonces dijo el Almirante al dicho Guacamarí que
nosotros eramos sabios de las enfermedades de los hombres que nos
quisiese mostrar la herida : él respondió que le placia, para lo cual
yo dije que seria necesario, si pudiese, que saliese fuera de casa,
porque con la mucha gente estaba escura é no se podria ver bien ;
lo cual él fizo luego, creo mas de empacho que de gana ; arrimán-
dose á el salió fuera. Despues de asentado, llegó el zurugiano á
él é comenzó de desligarle : entonces dijo al Almirante que era
ferida fecha con ciba, que quiere decir con piedra. Despues que

to examine it: it is certain that there was no more wound on that leg than on the other, although he cunningly pretended that it pained him much.   Ignorant as we were of the facts, it was impossible to come to a definite conclusion There were certainly many proofs of an invasion by a hostile people, so that the admiral was at a loss what to do; he with many others thought, however, that for the present, and until they could ascertain the truth, they ought to conceal their distrust; for after ascertaining it, they would be able to claim whatever indemnity they thought proper.   That evening Guacamari accompanied the admiral to the ships, and when they showed him the horses and other objects of interest, their novelty struck him with the greatest amazement: he took supper on board, and returned that evening to his house. The admiral told him that he wished to settle there and to build houses; to which he assented, but said that the place was not wholesome, because it was very damp: and so it most certainly was.

All this passed through the interpretation of two of the Indians who had gone to Spain in the last voyage,

---

fue desatada llegamos á tentarle.   Es cierto que no tenia mas mal en aquella que en la otra, aunque él hacia del raposo que le dolia mucho.   Ciertamente no se podia bien determinar porque las razones eran ignotas, que ciertamente muchas cosas habia que mostraban haber venido á él gente contraria.   Ansimesmo el Almirante no sabia que se hacer : paresció le, é á otros muchos, que por entonces fasta bien saber la verdad que se debia disimular, porque despues de sabida, cada que quisiesen, se podia dél recibir enmienda.   E aquella tarde se vino con el Almirante á las naos, é mostráronle caballos é cuanto ahí habia, de lo cual quedó muy maravillado como de cosa estraña á él ; tomó colacion en la nao, é esa tarde luego se tornó á su casa : el Almirante dijo que queria ir á habitar allí con él é queria facer casas, y él respondió que le placia, pero que el lugar era mal sano porque era muy humido, é tal era él por cierto.   Esto todo pasaba estando por intérpretes dos indios de los que el otro viage habian ido á Castilla, los cuales habian que-who were the sole survivors of seven who had embarked with us; five died on the voyage, and these but narrowly escaped. The next day we anchored in that port: Guacamari sent to know when the admiral intended leaving, and was told that he should do so on the morrow. The same day Guacamari's brother, and others with him, came on board, bringing gold to barter: on the day of our departure also they bartered a great quantity of gold. There were ten women on board, of those which had been taken in the Caribbee islands, principally from Boriquen, and it was observed that the brother of Guacamari spoke with them; we think that he told them to make an effort to escape that night; for certainly during our first sleep they dropped themselves quietly into the water, and went on shore, so that by the time they were missed they had reached such a distance that only four could be taken by the boats which went in pursuit, and these were secured when just leaving the water: they had to swim considerably more than half a league. The next morning the admiral sent to desire that Guacamari would cause search to be made for the women who had escaped in the night, and

---

dado vivos de siete que metimos en el puerto, que los cinco se murieron en el camino, los cuales escaparon á uña de caballo. Otro dia estuvimos surtos en aquel puerto; é quiso saber cuando se partiria el Almirante: le mandó decir que otro dia. En aquel dia vinieron á la nao el sobredicho hermano suyo é otros con él, é trajeron algun oro para rescatar. Ansí mesmo el dia que allá salimos se rescató buena cantidad de oro. En la nao habia diez mugeres de las que se habian tomado en las islas de Cariby; eran las mas dellas de Boriquen. Aquel hermano de Guacamarí habló con ellas: creemos que les dijo lo que luego esa noche pusieron por obra, y es que al primer sueño muy mansamente se echaron al agua é se fueron á tierra, de manera que cuando fueron falladas menos iban tanto trecho que con las barcas no pudieron tomar mas de las cuatro, las cuales tomaron al salir del agua; fueron nadando mas de una gran media legua. Otro dia de mañana envió el Almirante á decir á Guacamarí que le enviase aquellas mugeres que la noche antes se

I

that he would send them back to the ships. When the messengers arrived they found the place forsaken and not a soul there; this strongly confirmed the suspicions of many, but others said they might have removed to another village, as was their custom. That day we remained quiet, because the weather was contrary for our departure. On the next morning the admiral resolved that as the wind was adverse, it would be well to go with the boats to inspect a port on the coast at two leagues distance further up,[28] to see if the formation of the land was favourable for a settlement; and we went thither with all the ship's boats, leaving the ships in the harbour. As we moved along the coast the people manifested a sense of insecurity, and when we reached the spot to which we were bound all the natives had fled. While we were walking about this place we found an Indian stretched on the hill-side, close by the houses, with a gaping wound in his shoulder caused by a dart, so that he had been disabled from fleeing any further. The natives of this island fight with sharp darts, which they discharge from cross-bows in the same manner as boys in

---

habian huido, é que luego las mandase buscar. Cuando fueron hallaron el lugar despoblado, que no estaba persona en el ; ahí tornaron muchos fuerte á afirmar su sospecha, otros decian que se habria mudado á otra poblacion quellos ansí lo suelen hacer. Aquel dia estovimos allí quedos por que el tiempo era contrario para salir: otro dia de mañana acordó el Almirante, pues que el tiempo era contrario, que seria bien ir con las barcas á ver un puerto la costa arriba, fasta el cual habria dos leguas, para ver si habria dispusicion de tierra para hacer habitacion ; donde fuemos con todas las barcas de los navíos dejando los navíos en el puerto. Fuimos corriendo toda la costa, é tambien estos no se seguraban bien de nosotros ; llegamos á un lugar de donde todos eran huidos. Andando por él fallamos junto con las casas, metido en el monte, un indio ferido de una vara, de una ferida que resollaba por las espaldas, que no habia podido huir mas lejos. Los desta isla pelean con unas varas agudas, las cuales tiran con unas tiranderas como las que tiran los mochachos las varillas en

[28] Port Dauphin.

Spain shoot their small arrows, and which they send with considerable skill to a great distance; and certainly upon an unarmed people these weapons are calculated to do serious injury. The wounded man told us that Caonabó and his people had wounded him and burnt the houses of Guacamari. Thus we are still kept in uncertainty respecting the death of our people, on account of the paucity of information on which to form an opinion, and the conflicting and equivocal character of the evidence we have obtained. We did not find the position of the land in this port favourable for healthy habitation, and the admiral resolved upon returning along the upper coast by which we had come from Spain, because we had had tidings of gold in that direction. But the weather was so adverse that it cost more labour to sail thirty leagues in a backward direction than the whole voyage from Spain; so that, what with the contrary wind and the length of the passage, three months had elapsed since we first set foot on land. It pleased God, however, that through the check upon our progress caused by contrary winds, we succeeded in finding the best and most suitable spot that we could have selected for a

---

Castilla, con las cuales tiran muy lejos asaz certero. Es cierto que para gente desarmada que pueden hacer harto daño. Este nos dijo que Caonabó é los suyos lo habian ferido, é habian quemado las casas á Guacamarí. Ansí quel poco entender que los entendemos é las razones equívocas nos han traido á todos tan afuscados que fasta agora no se ha podido saber la verdad de la muerte de nuestra gente, é no hallamos en aquel puerto dispusicion saludable parer hacer habitacion. Acordó el Almirante nos tornásemos por la costa arriba por do habiamos venido de Castilla, porque la nueva del oro era fasta allá. Fuenos el tiempo contrario, que mayor pena nos fue tornar treinta leguas atrás que venir desde Castilla, que con el tiempo contrario é la largueza del camino ya eran tres meses pasados cuando decendimos en tierra. Plugó á nuestro Señor que por la contrariedad del tiempo que no nos dejó ir mas adelante, hobimos de tomar tierra en el mejor sitio y dispusicion que pudieramos escoger, donde hay mucho buen puerto é gran pesquería, settlement, where there was an excellent harbour[29] and abundance of fish, an article of which we stood in great need from the scarcity of meat. The fish caught here are very singular and more wholesome than those of Spain. The climate does not allow the fish to be kept from one day to another, for all animal food speedily becomes unwholesome, on account of the alternate heat and damp.

The land is very rich for all purposes; near the harbour there are two rivers; one large,[30] and another of moderate breadth somewhat near to it: the water is of a very remarkable quality. On the bank of it is being built a city called Marta,[31] one side of which is bounded by the water with a ravine of cleft rock, so that at that part there is no need of fortification; the other half is girt with a plantation of trees so thick that a rabbit could scarcely pass through it; and so green that fire will never be able to burn it. A channel has been commenced for a branch of the river, which the managers say they will lead through the middle of the settlement, and will place on it mills of all kinds requiring to be worked by water. Great quantities of

---

de la cual tenemos mucha necesidad por el carecimiento de las carnes. Hay en esta tierra muy singular pescado mas sano quel de España. Verdad sea que la tierra no consiente que se guarde de un dia para otro porque es caliente é humida, é por ende luego las cosas introfatibles ligeramente se corrompen. La tierra es muy gruesa para todas cosas; tiene junto un rio prencipal é otro razonable, asaz cerca de muy singular agua: edificase sobre la ribera dél una cibdad Marta, junto quel lugar se deslinda con el agua, de manera que la metad de la cibdad queda cercada de agua con una barranca de peña tajada, tal que por allí no ha menester defensa ninguna; la otra metad está cercada de una arboleda espesa que apenas podrá un conejo andar por ella; es tan verde que en ningun tiempo del mundo fuego la podrá quemar: hase comenzado á traer un brazo del rio, el cual dicen los maestros que trairán por medio del lugar, é asentarán en él moliendas é sierras de agua, é

[29] Port Isabelique, or Isabella, ten leagues to the east of Monte Cristi.
[30] The river Isabella.   [31] The infant city of Isabella.

vegetables have been planted, which certainly attain a more luxuriant growth here in eight days than they would in Spain in twenty. We were frequently visited by numbers of Indians, among whom were some of their caciques or chiefs, and many women. They all come loaded with *ages*,[32] a sort of turnip, very excellent for food, which we dressed in various ways. This food was so nutritious as to prove a great support to all of us after the privations we endured when at sea, which were more severe then ever were suffered by man; for as we could not tell what weather it would please God to send us on our voyage, we were obliged to limit ourselves most rigorously with regard to food, in order that, at all events, we might at least have the means of supporting life: this *age* the Caribbees call *nabi*, and the Indians *hage*. The Indians barter gold, provisions, and every thing they bring with them, for tags of laces, beads, and pins, and pieces of porringers and dishes. They all, as I have said, go naked as they were born, except the women of this island, who some of them wear a covering of cotton, which they bind round their hips, while others use

---

cuanto se pudiere hacer con agua. Han sembrado mucha hortaliza, la cual es cierto que crece mas en ocho dias que en España en veinte. Vienen aquí continuamente muchos indios é caciques con ellos, que son como capitanes dellos, é muchas indias : todos vienen cargados de *ages*, que son como nabos, muy excelente manjar, de los cuales facemos acá muchas maneras de manjares en cualquier manera ; es tanto cordial manjar que nos tiene á todos muy consolados, porque de verdad la vida que se trajo por la mar ha seido la mas estrecha que nunca hombres pasaron, é fue ansí necesario porque no sabiamos que tiempo nos haria, ó cuanto permitiría Dios que estoviesemos en el camino ; ansí que fue cordura estrecharnos, porque cualquier tiempo que viniera pudieramos conservar la vida. Rescatan el oro é mantenimientos é todo lo que traen por cabos de agujetas, por cuentas, por alfileres, por pedasos de escudillas é de plateles. A este *age* llaman los de Caribi *nabi*, é los indios *hage*. Toda esta gente, como dicho tengo, andan como nacieron, salvo las

[32] Yams.

grass and leaves of trees. When they wish to appear full-dressed, both men and women paint themselves, some black, others white, and various colours, in so many devices that the effect is very laughable: they shave some parts of their heads, and in others wear long tufts of matted hair, which have an indescribably ridiculous appearance: in short, whatever would be looked upon in our country as characteristic of a madman, is here regarded by the highest of the Indians as a mark of distinction.

In our present position, we are in the neighbourhood of many mines of gold, not one of which, we are told, is more than twenty or twenty-five leagues off: the Indians say that some of them are in Niti, in the possession of Caonabó, who killed the Christians; the others are in another place called Cibao, which, if it please God, we shall see with our eyes before many days are over; indeed we should go there at once, but that we have so many things to provide that we are not equal to it at present. One third of our people have fallen sick within the last four or five days, which I think has principally arisen from the toil and privations of the journey;

---

mugeres de esta isla traen cubiertas sus verguenzas, dellos con ropa de algodon que les ciñen las caderas, otras con yerbas é fojas de árböles. Sus galas dellos é dellas es pintarse, unos de negro, otros de blanco é colorado, de tantos visajes que en verlos es bien cosa de reir; las cabezas rapadas en logares, é en logares con vedijas de tantas maneras que no se podria escrebir. En conclusion, que todo lo que allá en nuestra España quieren hacer en la cabeza de un loco; acá el mejor dellos vos lo terná en mucha merced. Aquí estamos en comarca de muchas minas de oro, que segun lo que ellos dicen no hay cada una dellas de veinte ó veinte é cinco leguas: las unas dicen que son en Niti, en poder de Caonabó, aquel que mató los cristianos; otras hay en otra parte que se llama Cibao, las cuales, si place á nuestro Señor, sabremos é veremos con los ojos antes que pasen muchos dias, porque agora se ficiera sino porque hay tantas cosas de proveer que no bastamos para todo, porque la gente ha adolecido en cuatro ó cinco dias el tercio della, creo la another cause has been the variableness of the climate; but I hope in our Lord that all will be restored to health. My idea of this people is, that if we could converse with them, they would all become converted, for they do whatever they see us do, making genuflections before the altars at the Ave Maria and the other parts of the devotional service, and making the sign of the cross. They all say that they wish to be Christians, although in truth they are idolaters, for in their houses they have many kinds of figures: when asked what such a figure was, they would reply it is a thing of *Turey*, by which they meant " of Heaven." I made a pretence of throwing them on the fire, which grieved them so that they began to weep : they believe that everything we bring comes from heaven, and therefore call it *Turey*, which, as I have already said, means heaven in their language. The first day that I went on shore to sleep, was the Lord's day: the little time that we have spent on land, has been so much occupied in seeking for a fitting spot for the settlement, and in providing necessaries, that we have had little opportunity of becoming acquainted with the productions of the soil, yet although the

---

mayor causa dello ha seido el trabajo é mala pasada del camino ; allende de la diversidad de la tierra ; pero espero en nuestro Señor que todos se levantarán con salud. Lo que parece desta gente es que si lengua toviesemos que todos se convertirian, porque cuanto nos veen facer tanto facen, en hincar las rodillas á los altares, é al Ave Maria, é á las otras devociones é santiguarse : todos dicen que quieren ser cristianos, puesto que verdaderamente son idólatras, porque en sus casas hay figuras de muchas maneras ; yo les he preguntado que es aquello, dicenme que es cosa de *Turey*, que quiere decir del cielo. Yo acometi á querer echarselos en el fuego é haciaseles de mal que querian llorar : pero ansi piensan que cuanto nosotros traemos que es cosa del cielo, que á todo llaman *Turey*, que quiere decir cielo. El dia que yo salí á dormir en tierra fue el primero dia del Señor : el poco tiempo que habemos gastado en tierra ha seido mas en hacer donde nos metamos, é buscar las cosas necesarias, que en saber las cosas que hay en la tierra, pero aunque ha

time has been so short, many marvellous things have been
seen. We have met with trees bearing wool, of a sufficiently
fine quality (according to the opinion of those who are acquainted with the art) to be woven into good cloth; there are
so many of these trees that we might load the caravels with
wool, although it is troublesome to collect, for the trees are
very thorny,[33] but some means may be easily found of over-
coming this difficulty. There are also cotton trees as large as
peach trees, which produce cotton in the greatest abundance.
We found trees producing wax as good both in colour and smell
as bees-wax and equally useful for burning, indeed there is
no great difference between them. There are vast numbers
of trees which yield surprisingly fine turpentine, and a great
abundance of tragacanth, also very good. We found other
trees which I think bear nutmegs, because the bark tastes and
smells like that spice, but at present there is no fruit on them;
I saw one root of ginger, which an Indian wore hanging
round his neck. There are also aloes; not like those which
we have hitherto seen in Spain, but no doubt they are of the

---

sido poco se han visto cosas bien de maravillar, que se han visto
árboles que llevan lana y harto fina, tal que los que saben del arte
dicen que podrán hacer buenos paños dellas. Destos árboles hay
tantos que se podrán cargar las carabelas de la lana, aunque es tra-
bajosa de coger, porque los árboles son muy espinosos; pero bien
se puede hallar ingenio para la coger. Hay infinito algodon de árboles perpetuos tan grandes como duraznos. Hay árboles que
llevan cera en color y en sabor é en arder tan buena como la de
abejas, tal que no hay diferencia mucha de la una á la otra. Hay
infinitos árboles de trementina muy singular é muy fina. Hay
mucho alquitira, tambien muy buena. Hay árboles que pienso que
llevan nueces moscadas, salvo que agora estan sin fruto, é digo que
lo pienso porque el sabor y olor de la corteza es como de nueces
moscadas. Vi una raiz de gengibre que la traia un indio colgada
al cuello. Hay tambien linaloe, aunque no es de la manera del que

[33] A spices of the *N. O. Bombaceœ*; perhaps the *Eriodendron an-
fractuosum*.

same kind as those used by us doctors. A sort of cinnamon also has been found; but, to speak the truth, it is not so fine as that with which we are already acquainted in Spain. I do not know whether this arises from ignorance of the proper season to gather it, or whether the soil does not produce better. We have also seen some yellow mirabolans; at this season they are all lying under the trees, and have a bitter flavour, arising, I think, from the rottenness occasioned by the moisture of the ground; but the taste of such parts as have remained sound, is that of the genuine mirabolan. There is also very good mastic. None of the natives of these islands, as far as we have yet seen, possess any iron; they have, however, many tools, such as hatchets and axes, made of stone, which are so handsome and well finished, that it is wonderful how they contrive to make them without the use of iron. Their food consists of bread, made of the roots of a vegetable which is between a tree and a vegetable, and the *age*, which I have already described as being like the turnip, and very good food; they use, to season it, a spice

---

fasta agora se ha visto en nuestras partes; pero no es de dudar que sea una de las especias de linaloes que los dotores ponemos. Tambien se ha hallado una manera de canela, verdad es que no es tan fina como la que allá se ha visto, no sabemos si por ventura lo hace el defeto de saberla coger en sus tiempos como se ha de coger, ó si por ventura la tierra no la lleva mejor. Tambien se ha hallado mirabolanos cetrinos, salvo que agora no estan sino debajo del árbol, como la tierra es muy humida estan podridos, tienen el sabor mucho amargo, yo creo sea del podrimiento; pero todo lo otro, salvo el sabor que está corrompido, es de mirabolanos verdaderos. Hay tambien almástica muy buena. Todas estas gentes destas islas, que fasta agora se han visto, no poseen fierro ninguno. Tienen muchas ferramientas, ansi como hachas é azuelas hechas de piedra tan gentiles é tan labradas que es maravilla como sin fierro se pueden hacer. El mantenimiento suyo es pan hecho de raices de una yerba que es entre árbol é yerba, é el age, de que ya tengo dicho que es como nabos, que es muy buen mantenimiento: tienen por

called *agi*, which they also eat with fish, and such birds as
they can catch of the many kinds which abound in the
island. They have, besides, a kind of grain like hazel-nuts,
very good to eat. They eat all the snakes, and lizards, and
spiders, and worms, that they find upon the ground; so that,
to my fancy, their bestiality is greater than that of any beast
upon the face of the earth. The admiral had at one time
determined to leave the search for the mines until he had
first despatched the ships which were to return to Spain[34] on
account of the great sickness which had prevailed among the
men, but afterwards he resolved upon sending two bands
under the command of two captains, the one to Cibao,[35] and
the other to Niti, where, as I have already said, Caonabó
lived. These parties went, one of them returning on the
twentieth, and the other on the twenty-first of January. The
party that went to Cibao saw gold in so many places as to
seem almost incredible, for in truth they found it in more

---

especia, por lo adobar, una especia que se llama *agi*, con la cual
comen tambien el pescado, como aves cuando las pueden haber, que
hay infinitas de muchas maneras. Tienen otrosí unos granos como
avellanas, muy buenos de comer. Comen cuantas culebras é lagartos é arañas é cuantos gusanos se hallan por el suelo ; ansi que
me parece es mayor su bestialidad que de ninguna bestia del mundo. Despues de una vez haber determinado el Almirante de dejar
el descobrir las minas fasta primero enviar los navíos que se habian
de partir á Castilla, por la mucha enfermedad que habia seido en
la gente, acordó de enviar dos cuadrillas con dos Capitanes, el uno
á Cibao y el otro á Niti, donde está Caonabó, de que ya he dicho,
los cuales fueron é vinieron el uno á veinte dias de Enero, é el otro
á veinte é uno : el que fue á Cibao halló oro en tantas partes que

[34] In fact he sent twelve vessels under the command of Antonio de
Torres, who set sail from the port of Navidad, on the second of February,
1494, charged with an account of all that had occurred. (Navarrete.)

[35] This was Alonzo de Ojeda, who went out with fifteen men, in the
month of January 1494, to seek the mines of Cibao, and returned a few
days after with good news, having been well received everywhere by the
natives. (Navarrete.)

than fifty streamlets and rivers, as well as upon their banks ; so that, the captain said they had only to seek throughout that province, and they would find as much as they wished. He brought specimens from the different parts, namely, from the sand of the rivers and small springs.   It is thought, that by digging, it will be found in greater pieces, for the Indians neither know how to dig nor have the means of digging more than a hand's depth.   The other captain, who went to Niti, returned also with news of a great quantity of gold in three or four places ; of which he likewise brought specimens.

Thus, surely, their Highnesses the King and Queen may henceforth regard themselves as the most prosperous and wealthy Sovereigns in the world; never yet, since the creation, has such a thing been seen or read of; for on the return of the ships from their next voyage, they will be able to carry back such a quantity of gold as will fill with amazement all who hear of it.   Here I think I shall do well to break off my narrative.   I think those who do not know me will consider me prolix, and somewhat an exaggerator, but

---

no lo osa hombre decir, que de verdad en mas de cincuenta arroyos é rios hallaban oro, é fuera de los rios por tierra ; de manera que en toda aquella provincia dice que do quiera que lo quieran buscar lo hallarán.   Trajo muestra de muchas partes como en la arena de los rios é en las hontizuelas, que estan sobre tierra, creese que cabando, como sabemos hacer, se hallará en mayores pedazos, porque los indios no saben cabar ni tienen con que puedan cabar de un palmo arriba.   El otro que fue á Niti trajo tambien nueva de mucho oro en tres ó cuatro partes; ansi mesmo trajo la muestra dello. Ansi que de cierto los Reyes nuestros Señores desde agora se pueden tener por los mas prósperos é mas ricos Príncipes del mundo, porque tal cosa hasta agora no se ha visto ni leido de ninguno en el mundo, porque verdaderamente á otro camino que los navíos vuelvan pueden llevar tanta cantidad de oro que se puedan maravillar cualesquiera que lo supieren.   Aquí me parece será bien cesar el cuento : creo los que no me conocen que oyeren éstas cosas, me ternán por prolijo é por hombre que ha alargado algo ;

God is my witness, that I have not exceeded, by one tittle, the bounds of truth.

The preceding is the translation of that part of Doctor Chanca's letter, which refers to intelligence respecting the Indies.[36] The remainder of the letter does not bear upon the subject, but treats of private matters, in which Doctor Chanca requests the interference and support of the Chapter of Seville (of which city he was a native), in behalf of his family and property, which he had left in the said city. This letter reached Seville in the month of[37] in the year fourteen hundred and ninety-three.

---

pero Dios es testigo que yo no he traspasado una jota los términos de la verdad.

Hasta aquí es el treslado de lo que conviene á nuevas de aquellas partes é Indias. Lo demas que venia en la carta no hace al caso, porque son cosas particulares que el dicho Dotor Chanca, como natural de Sevilla, suplicaba y encomendaba á los del Cabildo de Sevilla que tocaba á su hacienda y á los suyos, que en la dicha cibdad habia dejado, y llegó esta á Sevilla en el mes de

año de mil é cuatrocientos énoventa y tres años.

[36] It is to be regretted, Navarrete here justly remarks, that Dr. Chanca should not have described the subsequent occurrences in Hispaniola, which are very important, and which have been related by cotemporary historians.

[37] A similar gap in the original. The date of the year is a mistake. This letter must have been brought by the ships commanded by Torres, and consequently must have been written at the end of January 1494, after the first expedition of Ojeda. (Navarrete.)

MEMORIAL.

Memorial of the results of the Second Voyage of the Admiral, Christopher Columbus, to the Indies, drawn up by him for their Highnesses King Ferdinand and Queen Isabella; and addressed to Antonio de Torres, from the City of Isabella, the 30th of January 1494. The reply of their Highnesses is affixed at the end of each chapter.[1]

THE report which you, Antonio de Torres, captain of the ship Marigalante, and Governor of the city of Isabella, have to make, on my behalf, to the King and Queen our sovereigns, is as follows:

Imprimis: after having delivered the credentials which you bear from me to their Highnesses, you will do homage in my name, and commend me to them as to my natural sovereigns,

MEMORIAL.

Que para los Reyes Católicos dió el Almirante D. Cristobal Colon, en la ciudad Isabela, á 30 de Enero de 1494 á Antonio de Torres, sobre el suceso de su segundo viage á las Indias; y al final de cada capítulo la respuesta de sus Altezas.

Lo que vos Antonio de Torres, capitan de la nao Marigalante, é Alcaide de la ciudad Isabela, habeis de decir é suplicar de mi parte al Rey é la Reina nuestros Señores es lo siguiente:

Primeramente, dadas las cartas de creencia que llevais de mí para sus Altezas, besareis por mi sus reales pies é manos, é me encomendareis en sus Altezas como á Rey é Reina mis señores naturales, en cuyo servicio yo deseo fenecer mis dias, como esto mas

[1] In the original, the replies are affixed in the margin of each chapter. (Navarrete.)

in whose service I desire to continue till death; and you
will furthermore be able to lay before them all that you have
yourself seen and known respecting me.

Their Highnesses accept aud acknowledge the service.

Item. Although, by the letters which I have written to their
Highnesses, as well as to Father Buil and to the Treasurer,
a clear and comprehensive idea may be formed of all that has
transpired since our arrival; you will, notwithstanding, inform
their Highnesses, on my behalf, that God has been pleased to
manifest such favour towards their service, that not only has
nothing hitherto occurred to diminish the importance of
what I have formerly written or said to their Highnesses;
but on the contrary I hope, by God's grace, shortly to prove
it more clearly by facts; because we have found upon the
sea shore, without penetrating into the interior of the country,
some spots showing so many indications of various spices, as
naturally to suggest the hope of the best results for the
future.   The same holds good with respect to the gold mines;
for two parties only, who were sent out in different directions
to discover them, and who, because they had few people with

---

largamente vos podreis decir á sus altezas, segun lo que en mi vistes é supistes.

Sus Altezas se lo tienen en servicio.

Item: Como quiera que por las cartas que á sus altezas escribo
y aun el Padre Fray Buil y el Tesorero, podrán comprender todo
lo que acá despues de nuestra llegada se fizo, y esto harto por me-
nudo y extensamente; con todo direis á sus altezas de mi parte,
que á Dios ha placido darme tal gracia para en su servicio, que
hasta aquí no hallo yo menos ni se ha hallado en cosa alguna de
lo que yo escribí y dije, y afirmé á sus Altezas en los dias pasados,
antes por gracia de Dios espero que aun muy mas claramente y
muy presto por la obra parecerá, porque las cosas de especeria en
solas las orillas de la mar, sin haber entrado dentro en la tierra, se
halla tal rastro é principios della, que es razon que se esperen muy
mejores fines, y esto mismo en las minas del oro, porque con solos
dos que fueron á descubrir cada uno por su parte, sin detenerse

them, remained out but a short time, found, nevertheless, a great number of rivers whose sands contained this precious metal in such quantity, that each man took up a sample of it in his hand; so that our two messengers returned so joyous, and boasted so much of the abundance of gold, that I fear I should weary the attention of their Highnesses, were I to repeat all that they said. But as Gorbalan, who was one of the persons who went on the discovery, is returning to Spain, he will be able to relate all that he has seen and observed; although there remains here another individual,—named Hojeda, formerly servant of the Duke of Medinaceli, and a very discreet and pains-taking youth,—who without doubt discovered, beyond all comparison, more than the other, judging by the account which he gave of the rivers he had seen; for he reported, that each of them contained things that appeared incredible. It results from all this, that their highnesses ought to return thanks to God, for the favour which He thus accords to all their highnesses' enterprises.

Their Highnesses return thanks to God for all that is here recorded, and regard as a very signal service all that the Admiral has already done, and is yet doing; for they are

---

allá porque era poca gente, se han descubierto tantos rios tan poblados de oro, que cualquier de los que lo vieron é cogieron, solamente con las manos por muestra, vinieron tan alegres, y dicen tantas cosas de la abundancia dello, que yo tengo empacho de las decir y escribir á sus altezas; pero porque allá v Gorbalan, que fue uno de los descubridores, el dirá lo que vió aunque acá queda otro que llaman Hojeda, criado del Duque de Medinaceli, muy discreto mozo y de muy gran recabdo, que sin duda y aun sin comparacion, descubrió mucho mas, segun el memorial de los rios que él trajo, diciendo que en cada uno de ellos hay cosa de no creella; por lo cual sus altezas pueden dar gracias á Dios, pues tan favorablemente se ha en todas sus cosas.

Sus Altezas dan muchas gracias a Dios por esto, y tienen en muy senalado servicio al Almirante todo lo que en esto ha fecho y hace,

sensible that, under God, it is he who has procured for them
their present and future possessions in these countries; and as
they are about to write to him on this subject more at length,
they refer to their letter.

Item.   You will repeat to their Highnesses what I have
already written to them, that I should have ardently desired
to have been able to send them, by this occasion, a larger
quantity of gold than what they have any hope of our being
able to collect, but that the greater part of the people we
employed fell suddenly ill.   Moreover, the departure of this
present expedition could not be delayed any longer, for two
reasons: namely, on account of the heavy expense which their
stay here occasioned; and because the weather was favourable for their departure, and for the return of those who
should bring back the articles of which we stand in the most
pressing need.   If the former were to be put off the time of
their starting, and the latter were to delay their departure,
they would not be able to reach here by the month of
May.   Besides, if I wished now to undertake a journey to
the rivers with those who are well,—whether with those who

---

porque conocen que despues de Dios á él son en cargo de todo lo que
en esto han habido y hobieren; y porque cerca desto le escriben mas
largo, á su carta se remiten.

Item: Direis á sus Altezas, como quier que ya se les escribe, que yo
deseaba mucho en esta armada poderles enviar mayor cuantidad de
oro del que acá seespera poder coger, si la gente que acá está nuestra, la mayor parte subitamente no cayera doliente; pero porque
ya esta armada non se podia detener acá mas, siquiera por la costa
grande que hace, siquiera porque el tiempo es este propio para ir y
poder volver los que han de traer acá las cosas que aquí hacen mucha mengua, porque si tardasen de irse de aquí non podrian vol-
verse para Mayo los que han de volver, y allende desto si con los
sanos que acá se hallan, así en mar como en tierra en la poblacion,
yo quisiera emprender de ir á las minas ó rios agora, habia muchas
dificultades é aun peligros, porque de aquí á veinte y tres ó veinte
y cuatro leguas, en donde hay puertos é rios para pasar y para tan

are at sea, or those who are on land in the huts,—I should experience great difficulties, and even dangers; because, in traversing three or four-and-twenty leagues, where there are bays and rivers to pass, we should be obliged to carry, as provision for so long a journey, and for the time necessary for collecting the gold, many articles of food, &c., which could not be carried on our backs, and there are no beasts of burden to be found, to afford the necessary assistance. Moreover, the roads and passes are not in such a condition as I should wish for travelling over; and, first of all, I have turned my attention to this point. It would be also extremely inconvenient to leave the sick men here in the open air, or in huts, with such food and defences as they have on shore; although these Indians appear every day to be more simple and harmless to those who land for the purpose of making investigations. In short, although they come every day to visit us, it would nevertheless be imprudent to risk the loss of our men and our provisions, which might very easily happen, if an Indian were only, with a lighted coal, to set fire to the huts, for they ramble about both night and day; for this reason, we keep sentinels constantly on the watch while the dwellings are exposed and undefended.

----

largo camino, y para estar allá al tiempo que seria menester para coger el oro, habia menester llevar muchos mantenimientos, los cuales non podrian llevar á cuestas, ni hay bestias acá que á esto pudiesen suplir, ni los caminos é pasos non estan tan aparejados, como quier que se han comenzado á adobar para que se podiesen pasar; y tambien era grande inconveniente dejar acá los dolientes en lugar abierto y chozas, y las provisiones y mantenimientos que estan en tierra, que como quier que estos indios se hayan mostrado á los descubridores, y se muestran cada dia muy simples y sin malicia; con todo, porque cada dia vienen acá entre nosotros non pareció que fuera buen consejo meter á riesgo y á ventura de perderse esta gente y los mantenimientos, lo que un indio con un tizon podria hacer poniendo huego á las chozas, porque de noche y de dia siempre van y vienen: á causa dellos tenemos guardas en el campo mientras la poblacion está abierta y sin defension.

L

He has done well.

Further, as we have remarked that the greatest part of those who have gone out to make discoveries, have fallen sick on their return, and that some have even been obliged to abandon the undertaking in the middle of their journey, and return, it was equally to be feared that the same would occur to those who were at the time enjoying good health, if they were also to go. There were two evils to fear:—one, the chance of falling ill in undertaking the same work, in a place where there were no houses nor any kind of protection, and of being exposed to the attacks of the cacique called Caonabo, who, by all accounts, is a badly-disposed man, and extremely daring; who, if he were to find us in a dispirited condition and sick, might venture upon what he would not dare to do if we were well. The other evil consisted in the difficulty of carrying the gold; for, either we should have to carry it in small quantities, and go and return every day, and thus daily expose ourselves to the chance of sickness; or we should have to send it under the escort of a party of our people, and equally run the risk of losing them.

He has done well.

These are the reasons, you will tell their Highnesses, why

Que lo hizo bien.

Otrosí : Como habemos visto en los que fueron por tierra á descobrir que los mas cayeron dolientes despues de vueltos, y aun algunos se hobieron de volver del camino, era tambien razon de temer que otro tal conteciese á los que agora irian destos sanos que se hallan, y seguirse hian dos peligros de allí, el uno de adolecer allá en la misma obra dó no hay casa ni reparo alguno de aquel Cacique que llaman Caonabó, que es hombre, segun relacion de todos, muy malo y muy mas atrevido, el cual viéndonos allá así desbaratados y dolientes, podria emprender lo que non osaria si fuesemos sanos : y con esto mismo se allega otra dificultad de traer acá lo que llegasemos de oro, porque ó habiamos de traer poco y ir y venir cada dia, y meterse en el riesgo de las dolencias, ó se habia de enviar con alguna parte de la gente con el mismo peligro de perderlo.

Lo hizo bien.

the departure of the expedition has not been delayed, and why only a sample of the gold is sent to them; but I trust in the mercy of God, who in all things and in every place has guided us hitherto, that all our men will be soon restored to health, as, indeed, they are already beginning to be; for there are but a few places which agree with them, but when they are in these places, they speedily recover their health. One thing is certain, that if they could have fresh meat, they would very quickly, by the help of God, be up and doing; and those who are most sickly, would speedily recover. I hope that they may be restored. The small number of those who continue well, are employed every day in barricading our dwelling, so as to put it in a state of defence, and in taking necessary measures for the safety of our ammunition; which will be finished now in a few days, for all our fortifications will consist simply of stone walls.² These precautions will be sufficient, as the Indians are not a people to be much afraid of; and, unless they should find us asleep, they would not dare to undertake any hostile movement against us, even if they should entertain the idea of so doing. The misfortune which happened to those who remained here, must be

---

Así que, direis á sus Altezas, que estas son las cabsas porque de presente non se ha detenido el armada, ni se les envia oro mas de las muestras; pero confiando en la misericordia de Dios, que en todo y por todo nos ha guiado hasta aquí, esta gente convalescerá presto, como ya lo hace, porque solamente les prueba la tierra de algunas ceciones, y luego se levantan; y es cierto que si toviesen algunas carnes frescas para convalescer muy presto serian todos en pie con ayuda de Dios, é aun los mas estarian ya convalescidos en este tiempo, espero que ellos convalescerán : con estos pocos sanos que acá quedan, cada dia se entiende en cerrar la poblacion y meterla en alguna defensa, y los mantenimientos en seguro, que será fecho en breves dias, porque nón ha de ser sino albarradas que non son gente los indios, que si dormiendo non nos fallasen para emprender cosa ninguna, aunque la toviesen pensada, que así hicieron á los otros

² *Albarrada*—an Arabic word implying a stone wall without mortar.

attributed to their want of vigilance; for however few they were in number,—however favourable the opportunities that the Indians had for doing what they did,—they would never have ventured to do them any injury, if they had only seen that they took proper precautions against an attack. As soon as that object is gained, I will undertake to go in search of these rivers; either by going by land from hence, and employing the best means we can devise, or else by sea, rounding the island, until we come to the place which is described as being only six or seven leagues from where these rivers that I speak of are situated; so that we may collect the gold in safety, and put it in security against all attacks in some stronghold or tower, which may be quickly built for that purpose : and thus, when the two caravels shall return thither, the gold may be taken away and finally sent home in safety at the first favourable season for making the voyage.

This is well, and exactly as he should have done.

Item. You will inform their Highnesses (as indeed has been already done), that the cause of the sickness so general among us, is the change of air and water, for we find that all

---

que acá quedaron por su mal recabdo, los cuales por pocos que fuesen, y por mayores ocasiones que dieran á los indios de haber é de hacer lo que hicieron, nunca ellos osaran emprender de dañarles si los vieran á buen recabdo : y esto fecho luego se entenderá en ir á los dichos rios, ó desde aquí tomando el camino, y buscando los mejores expedientes que se puedan, ó por la mar rodeando la isla fasta aquella parte de donde se dice que no debe haber mas de seis ó siete leguas hasta los dichos rios ; por forma que con seguridad se pueda cojer el oro y ponerlo en recabdo de alguna fortaleza ó torre que allí se haga luego, para tenerlo cogido al tiempo que las dos carabelas volverán acá, é para que luego con el primer tiempo que sea para navegar este camino se envie á buen recabdo.

Que está bien, y así lo debe hacer.

Item : Direis á sus altezas, como dicho es, que las causas de las dolencias tan general de todos es de mudamiento de aguas y aires, of us are affected, though few dangerously; consequently, the preservation of the health of the people will depend, under God, on their being provided with the same food that they are accustomed to in Spain: without this precaution, neither those who are here now, nor those that shall come, will be in a position to be of service to their Highnesses, unless they enjoy good health. We ought to have fresh supplies of provisions until the time that we may be able to gather a sufficient crop from what we shall have sown or planted here: I speak of wheat, barley, and grapes, towards the cultivation of which not much has been done this year, from our being unable earlier to choose a convenient settlement. When we had chosen it, the small number of labourers that were with us fell sick; and, even when they recovered, we had so few cattle, and these cattle were so lean and weak, that the utmost they could do was very little; however, they have sown a few plots of ground, rather for the sake of trying the soil, which seems excellent, than with any other object, and the result of our attempt makes us look forward to a remedy for our necessities. We are very certain, as the fact has shown, that wheat and grapes will grow very well in this

---

porque vemos que á todos arreo se extiende y peligran pocos; por consiguiente la conservacion de la sanidad, despues de Dios, está que esta gente sea proveida de los mantenimientos que en España acostumbrada, porque dellos, ni de otros que viniesen de nuevo sus Altezas se podrián servir si no estan sanos; y esta provision ha de durar hasta que acá se haya fecho cimiento de lo que acá se sembrare é plantare, digo de trigos y cebadas, é viñas, de lo cual para este año se ha fecho poco, porque no se pudo de antes tomar asiento, y luego que se tomó adolescieron aquellos poquitos labradores que acá estaban, los cuales aunque estovieran sanos tenian tan pocas bestias y tan magras y flacas, que poco es lo que pudieran hacer: con todo, alguna cosa han sembrado, mas para probar la tierra, que parece muy maravillosa, para que de alli se puede esperar remedio alguno en nuestras necesidades. Somos bien ciertos, como la obra lo muestra, que en esta tierra así el trigo como el vino nacerá muy country. We must, however, wait for the fruit; and if it grows as quickly and well as the corn, in proportion to the number of vines that have been planted, we shall certainly not sigh for these productions as the produce of Andalusia and Sicily. There are also sugar-canes, of which the small quantity that we have planted has succeeded very well. The beauty of the country in these islands,—the mountains, the valleys, the streams, the fields watered by broad rivers,—in short, everything is so wonderful, that there is no country on which the sun sheds his beams that can present such an appearance, together with so productive a soil.

Since the land is so fertile, it is desirable to sow as much as possible; and Don Juan de Fonseca has been desired to send over immediately everything requisite for that purpose.

Item. You will say, that as a large portion of the wine that we brought with us has run away, and that, as all the men say, in consequence of the bad cooperage of the butts made at Seville, the article that fails us most at this moment, and yet which we most want, is wine; and although we have biscuit and corn for some time longer, it is nevertheless

---

bien; pero hase de esperar el fruto, el cual si tal será como muestra la presteza del nacer del trigo, y de algunos poquitos de sarmientos que se pusieron, es cierto que non fará mengua el Andalucía ni Secilia aquí, ni en las cañas de azucar, segun unas poquitas que se pusieron han prendido; porque es cierto que la hermosura de la tierra de estas islas, así de montes é sierras y aguas, como de vegas donde hay rios cabdales, es tal la vista que ninguna otra tierra que sol escaliente puede ser mejor al parecer ni tan fermosa.

Pues la tierra es tal, que debe procurar que se siembre lo mas que ser pudiere de todas cosas, y á D. Juan de Fonseca se escribe que envie de contino todo lo que fuere menester para esto.

Item: Direis que á cabsa de haberse derramado mucho vino en este camino del que la flota traia, y esto, segun dicen los mas, á culpa de la mala obra que los toneleros ficieron en Sevilla, la mayor mengua que agora tenemos aquí, ó esperamos por esto tener, es de vinos, y como quier que tengamos para mas tiempo así vizcocho necessary that a reasonable quantity of these be sent to us, for the voyage is a long one, and it is impossible to make a calculation for every day; the same holds good with respect to pork and salt meat, which should be better than what we have had on our voyage hitherto; sheep, lambs, both male and female, young calves and heifers, also are necessary. Consequently it would be expedient that every caravel that may be dispatched hither, should bring a stock of these necessaries; and at the same time some asses, both male and female, and some mares that can be put to work; for here there are no beasts that can be employed to assist man in his labour. As I fear that their Highnesses may not be at Seville, and that their officers or ministers will not, without their express instructions, make any movement towards the carrying out of the necessary arrangements for the return voyage; and that, in the interval between the report and the reply, the favourable moment for the departure of the vessels which are to return hither (and which should be in all the month of May) may elapse, you will tell their Highnesses that I have given strict orders that the gold that you carry

---

como trigo, con todo es necesario que tambien se envie alguna cuantidad razonable, porque el camino es largo y cada dia no se puede proveer, é asimismo algunas canales, digo tocinos, y otra cecina que sea mejor que la que habemos traido este camino. De carneros vivos y aun antes corderos y cordericas, mas fembras que machos, y algunos becerras pequeños son menester, que cada vez vengan en cualquier carabela que acá se enviare, y algunas asnas y asnos, y yeguas para trabajo y simiente, que acá ninguna de estas animalias hay de que hombre se pueda ayudar ni valer. Y porque recelo que sus Altezas no se fallarán en Sevilla, ni los Oficiales ó Ministros suyos sin expreso mandamiento non proveerían en lo porque agora con este primero camino es necesario que venga, porque en la consulta y en la respuesta se pasaria la sazon del partir los navíos que acá por todo Mayo es necesario que sean; direis á sus Altezas, como yo vos dí cargo y mandé, que del oro que allá llevais empeñándolo, ó poniéndolo en poder de algun mercader en with you be placed in the hands of some merchant in Seville, in order that he may therefrom disburse the sums that shall be necessary for loading the two caravels with wine, corn, and the other articles detailed in this memorial; and this merchant shall convey or send the said gold to their Highnesses, that they may see it, receive it, and from it cause to be defrayed the expenses that may arise from the fitting-up and loading of the said two caravels. It is necessary, for the encouragement of the men who remain here, and for the support of their spirits, that an effort should be made to let the expedition arrive in the course of the month of May, so that they may have the fresh provisions, and other necessaries, before summer, especially for the sick people. We particularly stand in need of raisins, sugar, almonds, honey, and rice, of which we ought to have had a great quantity, but brought very little with us, and what we had is now consumed. It is the same with the greater part of the medicines that we brought from Spain; which is not to be wondered at, when it is considered how many of our number have been sick. For all these articles, which are intended as much for

---

Sevilla, el cual distraya y ponga los maravedis que serán menester para cargar dos carabelas de vino y de trigo, y de las otras cosas que llevais por memorial, el cual mercader lleve ó envie el dicho oro para sus Altezas, que le vean, resciban y hagan pagar lo que hobiere distraido é puesto para el despacho y cargazon de las dichas dos carabelas, las cuales por consolar y esforzar esta gente que acá queda, cumple que fagan mas de poder de ser ac vueltas por todo el mes de Mayo, porque la gente antes de entrar en el verano vea é tengan algun refrescamiento destas cosas, en especial para las dolencias ; de las cuales cosas acá ya tenemos gran mengua, como son pasas, azucar, almendras, miel é arroz, que debiera venir en gran cuantidad y vino muy poca, é aquello que vino es ya consumido é gastado, y aun la mayor parte de las medecinas que de allá trojieron, por la muchedumbre de los muchos dolientes ; de las cuales cosas, como dicho es, vos llevais memoriales así para sanos, como para dolientes, fermados de mi mano, los cuales cumplidamente si the sick as for those who are in good health, you carry, as I have already said, memorials signed by my hand; you will execute my orders to the full, if there be sufficient money wherewith to do so, or you will at least procure what is more immediately necessary, and which ought, consequently, to come as speedily as possible by the two vessels. With respect to such articles as cannot be sent off by them, you will, in submission to their Highnesses' pleasure, look to it that they be sent by other vessels without loss of time.

Their Highnesses will give instructions to Don Juan de Fonseca to make immediate inquiry respecting the imposition in the construction of the casks, in order that a sufficient levy be made on the makers to cover the losses occasioned by the waste of the wine, as well as all the other expenses. He will have to see that sugar-canes of good quality be sent, and will immediately look to the despatch of the other articles herein required.

Item. You will tell their Highnesses, that as we are not acquainted with the language of these people, so as to make them acquainted with our holy faith, as their Highnesses and we ourselves desire, and as we will do so soon as we are able, we send by these two vessels some of these cannibal men and women, as well as some children, both male and female.

---

el dinero bastare, ó á lo menos lo que mas necesario sea para agora despachar, es para que lo puedan luego traer los dichos dos navíos, y lo que quedare procurareis con sus Altezas que con otros navíos venga lo mas presto que ser pudiere.

Sus Altezas enviaron á mandar á D. Juan de Fonseca que luego haya informacion de los que hicieron ese engano en los toneles, y de sus bienes haga que se cobre todo el dano que vino en el vino, con las costas; y en lo de las canas vea como las que se enviaren sean buenas, y en las otras cosas que aquí dice que las provea luego.

Item: Direis á sus Altezas que á cabsa que acá no hay lengua por medio de la cual á esta gente se pueda dar á entender nuestra santa Fé, como sus Altezas desean, y aun los que acá estamos, como quiere que se trabajará cuanto pudieren, se envian de presente con estos navíos así de los canibales, hombres y mugeres y niños y

Their Highnesses can order them to be placed under the care of the most competent persons to teach them the language, giving instructions, at the same time, that they may be employed in useful occupations; and that by degrees more care be bestowed upon them than would be given to other slaves, in order that afterwards one may learn from the other. By not seeing or speaking to each other for a long time, they will learn much sooner in Spain than they will here, and become much better interpreters. We will, however, do what we can; it is true, that as there is but little communication between one of these islands and another, there is some difference in their mode of expressing themselves, which mainly depends on the distance between them. But as amongst all these islands, those inhabited by the cannibals are the largest and the most populous, I have thought it expedient to send to Spain men and women from the islands which they inhabit, in the hope that they may one day be led to abandon their barbarous custom of eating their fellow-creatures. By learning the Spanish language in Spain, they will much earlier receive baptism and ensure the salvation of their souls; moreover, it will be a great happiness to the

---

niñas, los cuales sus Altezas pueden mandar poner en poder de personas con quien puedan mejor aprender la lengua, ejercitándolos en cosas de servicio, y poco á poco mandando poner en ellos algun mas cuidado que en otros esclavos para que deprendan unos de otros, que no se hablen ni se vean sino muy tarde, que mas presto deprenderán allá que no acá, y serán mejores intérpretes, como quier que acá non se dejará de hacer lo que se pueda; es verdad que como esta gente platican poco los de la una isla con los de la otra, en las lenguas hay alguna diferencia entre ellos, segun como estan mas cerca ó mas lejos; y porque entre las otras islas las de los canibales son mucho grandes, y mucho bien pobladas, parecerá acá que tomar dellos y dellas y enviarlos allá á Castilla non seria sino bien, porque quitarse hian una vez de aquella inhumana costumbre que tienen de comer hombres, y allá en Castilla entendiendo la lengua muy mas presto rescibirian el Bautismo, y farian el provecho de sus animas: aun entre estos pueblos que non son de esas cos-

Indians who do not practise the above-mentioned cruel custom, when they see that we have seized and led captive those who injure them, whom they dread so much, that their name alone fills them with horror. You will assure their Highnesses, that our arrival in this country, and the sight of so fine a fleet, have produced the most desirable effect and ensured our future safety; for all the inhabitants of this great island, and of those around it, when they see the good treatment that we shall shew to those who do well, and the punishment that we shall inflict on those who do wrong, will hasten to submit, and their Highnesses will shortly be able to reckon them among the number of their subjects. And as even now they not only readily comply with every wish that we express, but also spontaneously endeavour to do what they think will prove agreeable to us; I think that their Highnesses may rest certain, that on many accounts, both for the present and the future, the arrival of this fleet has secured for them a wide renown amongst all Christian Princes; but they themselves will be able to form a much better judgment on this subject than it is in my power to put into language.

---

tumbres, se ganaria gran crédito por nosotros viendo que aquellos prendiesemos y cativasemos, de quien ellos suelen rescibir daños, y tienen tamaño miedo que del hombre solo se espantan; certificando á sus Altezas que la venida é vista de esta flota acá en esta tierra así junta y hermosa, ha dado muy grande autoridad á esto y muy grande seguridad para las cosas venideras, por que toda esta gente de esta grande isla y de las otras, viendo el buen tratamiento que á los bueno se fará, y el castigo que á los malos se dará, verná á obediencia prestamente para poderlos mandar como vasallos de sus Altezas. Y como quier que ellos agora donde quier que hombre se halle non solo hacen de grado lo que hombre quiere que fagan mas ellos de su voluntad se ponen á todo lo que entienden que nos puede placer, y tambien pueden ser ciertos sus Altezas que non menos allá, entre los cristianos Principes haber dado gran reputacion la venida desta armada por muchos respetos, así presentes como venideros, los cuales sus Altezas podrán mejor pensar y entender que non sabria decir.

Let him be informed of what has transpired respecting the cannibals that came over to Spain.   He has done well and his suggestions are good; but let him endeavour by all possible means to convert them to our holy Catholic religion, and do the same with respect to the inhabitants of all the islands to which he may go.

Item.   You will tell their Highnesses, that for the good of the souls of the said cannibals, and even of the inhabitants of this island, the thought has suggested itself to us, that the greater the number that are sent over to Spain the better, and thus good service may result to their Highnesses in the following manner : considering what great need we have of cattle and of beasts of burthen, both for food and to assist the settlers in their work, their Highnesses will be able to authorize a suitable number of caravels to come here every year to bring over the said cattle, etc., in order that the fields may become covered with people and cultivation; these cattle, etc., might be sold at moderate prices for account of the bearers, and the latter might be paid with slaves, taken from among the Caribbees, who are a wild people, fit for any work, well proportioned and very intelligent, and who, when

---

Decirle heis lo que acá habido en lo de los canibales que acá vinieron.

Que está muy bien, y así lo debe hacer ; pero que procure allá, como si ser pudiere, se reduzgan á nuestra santa Fé católica, y asimismo lo procure con los de las islas donde está.

Item : Direis á sus Altezas, que el provecho de las almas de los dichos canibales, y aun destos de acá, ha traido el pensamiento que cuantos mas allá se llevasen seria mejor, y en ello podrian sus Altezas ser servidos desta manera : que visto cuanto son acá menester los ganados y bestias de trabajo para el sostenimiento de la gente que acá ha de estar, y bien de todas estas islas, sus Altezas podrán dar licencia e permiso á un número de carabelas suficiente que vengan acá cada año, y trayan de los dichos ganados y otros mantenimientos y cosas para poblar el campo y aprovechar la tierra, y esto en precios razonables á sus costas de los que las trugieren, las cuales cosas se les podrian pagar en esclavos de estos canibales, gente tan they have got rid of the cruel habits to which they have become accustomed, will be better than any other kind of slaves. When they lose sight of their country, they will forget their cruel customs; and it will be easy to obtain plenty of these savages by means of row-boats that we propose to build. It is taken for granted, that each of the caravels sent by their Highnesses, will have on board a confidential man, who will take care that the vessels do not stop anywhere else than here, where they are to unload and reload their vessels. Their Highnesses might fix duties on the slaves that may be taken over, upon their arrival in Spain. You will ask for a reply upon this point, and bring it to me, in order that I may be able to take the necessary measures, should the proposition merit the approbation of their Highnesses.

The consideration of this subject has been suspended for a time, until some other measure may be suggested with reference to the island: the Admiral will do well to write what further he thinks upon the subject.

Item. You will also tell their Highnesses, that freighting the ships by the ton, as the Flemish merchants do, will be

---

fiera y dispuesta, y bien proporcionada y de muy buen entendimiento, los cuales quitados de aquella inhumanidad creemos que serán mejores que otros ningunos esclavos, la cual luego perderán que sean fuera de su tierra, y de estos podrán haber muchos con las fustas de remos que acá se entienden de hacer, fecho empero presupuesto que cada una de las carabelas que viniesen de sus Altezas pusiesen una persona fiable, la cual defendiese las dichas carabelas que non descendiesen á ninguna otra parte ni isla salvo aquí donde ha de estar la carga y descarga de toda la mercaduría; y aun destos esclavos que se llevaren, sus Altezas podrian haber sus derechos allá; y desto traeres ó enviareis respuesta, porque acá se hagan los aparejos que son menester con mas confianza, si á sus Altezas pareciere bien.

En esto se ha suspendido por agora hasta que venga otro camino de allá, y escriba el Almirante lo que en esto le paresciere.

Item: Tambien direis á sus Altezas que mas provechoso es, y

more advantageous and less expensive than any other mode, and for this reason I have given instructions to freight the caravels in this manner that you have to send off. It will be well to adopt this plan with all the others that their Highnesses may send if it meets their approbation; but I do not mean to say that this measure should be applied to the vessels that shall come over licensed for the traffic of slaves.

Their Highnesses have given directions to Don Juan de Fonseca, to have the caravels freighted in the manner described, if it can be done.

Item. You will tell their Highnesses, that in order to save any extra expense, I have purchased the caravels mentioned in the memorial of which you are the bearer, in order to keep them here with the two vessels, the "Gallega" and the "Capitana", of which, by advice of the pilot its commander, I purchased the three-eighths for the price declared in the said memorial, signed by my hand. These vessels will not only afford strength and security to those who will have to remain on shore and whose duty it will be to make arrangements with the Indians for collecting the gold; but they will be also very useful to ward off any attack that may be made

---

menos costa, fletar los navíos como los fletan los mercaderes para Flandes por toneladas que non de otra manera; por ende que yo vos dí cargo de fletar á este respecto las dos carabelas que habeis luego de enviar: y así se podrá hacer de todas las otras que sus Altezas enviaren, si de aquella forma se ternán por servidos; pero non entiendo decir esto de las que han devenir con su licencia por la mercaduría de los esclavos.

Sus Altezas mandan á D. Juan de Fonseca que en el fletar de las carabelas tenga esta forma si ser pudiere.

Item: Direis á sus Altezas que á causa de escusar alguna mas costa, yo merqué estas carabelas que llevais por memorial para retenerlas acá con estas dos naos, conviene á saber, la Gallega y esa otra Capitana, de la cual merqué por semejante del Maestre della los tres ochavos por el precio que en el dicho memorial destas copias llevais firmado de mi mano, los cuales navíos non solo darán upon them by strangers; moreover, the caravels will be required for the task of making the discovery of terra firma, and of the islands which lie scattered about in this vicinity. You will therefore beg their Highnesses to pay, at the term of credit arranged with the sellers, the sums which these vessels shall cost, for without doubt their Highnesses will be very soon reimbursed for what they may expend; at least, such is my belief and hope in the mercy of God.

The Admiral has done well. You will tell him that the sum mentioned has been paid to the seller of the vessels, and that Don Juan de Fonseca has been ordered to pay the cost of the caravels purchased by the Admiral.

Item. You will speak to their Highnesses, and beseech them on my behalf, in the most humble manner possible, to be pleased to give mature reflection to the observations I make (and which I have most at heart) with reference to the peacefulness, harmony, and good feeling of those who come hither; and you will beg them to make choice of persons in whom they can place full confidence for all matters connected with their service. You will beseech them to hold in view

---

autoridad y gran seguridad á la gente que ha de estar dentro y conversar con los indios para cojer el oro, mas aun para otra cualquier cosa de peligro que de gente estraña pudiese acontescer, allende que las carabelas son necesarias para el descubrir de la tierra firme y otras islas que entre aquí é allá estan; y suplicareis á sus Altezas que los maravedis que estos navíos cuestan manden pager en los tiempos que se les ha prometido, porque sin dubda ellos ganará bien su costa, segun yo creo y espero en la misericordia de Dios.

El Almirante lo hizo bien, y decirle heis como acá se pago al que venidó la nao, y mandaron á D. Juan de Fonseca que pague lo de las carabelas que el Almirante compró.

Item: Direis á sus Altezas y suplicareis de mi parte cuanto mas humilmente pueda, que les plega mucho mirar en lo que por las cartas y otras escripturas verán mas largamente tocante á la paz é sosiego e concordia de los que acá estan, y que para las cosas del servicio de sus Altezas escojan tales personas que non se tenga recelo dellas y the purpose for which these men are sent, rather than their own interest; and since you yourself have seen and are acquainted with these matters, you will speak to their Highnesses upon this subject, and will tell them the truth on every point exactly as you have understood it; you will also take care that the orders which their Highnesses shall give on this point be put into effect, if possible, by the first vessels, in order that no further injury occur here in the matters that affect their service.

Their Highnesses are well informed of all that takes place, and will see to it that everything is done as it should be.

Item. You will describe to their Highnesses the position of this city, the beauty of the province in which it is situated, as you have seen it, and as you can honestly speak of it; and you can inform them, that in virtue of the powers which I have received from them, I have made you governor of the said city; and you will tell them also that I humbly beseech them, out of consideration for your services, to receive your nomination favourably, which I sincerely hope they may do.

Their Highnesses are pleased to sanction your appointment as governor.

---

que miren mas á lo por que se envian que non á sus propios intereses; y en esto, pues que todas las cosas vistes é supistes, hablareis é direis á sus Altezas la verdad de todas las cosas como las comprendistes, y que la provision de sus Altezas que sobre ello mandaren facer venga con los primeros navíos si posible fuere, á fin que acá non se hagan escándalos en cosa que tanto va en el servicio de sus Altezas.

Sus Altezas estan bien informados desto, y en todo se proveerá como conviene.

Item: Direis á sus Altezas el asiento de esta ciudad, é la fermosura de la provincia alderedor como lo vistes y compreendistes, y como yo vos hice Alcayde della por los poderes que de sus Altezas tengo para ello, á las cuales humilmente suplico que en alguna parte de satisfaccion de vuestros servicios tengan por bien la dicha provision, como de sus Altezas yo espero.

A sus Altezas plaze que vos seais Alcayde.

Item. As Moses Pedro Margarite, an officer of the household to their Highnesses, has done good service, and will, I hope, continue to do so for the future in all matters which may be entrusted to him, I have felt great pleasure in his continuing his stay in this country; and. I have been much pleased to find that Gaspar and Beltran also remain : and as they are all three well known to their Highnesses as faithful servants, I shall place them in posts or employments of trust. You will beg their Highnesses especially to have regard to the situation of the said Moses Pedro Margarite, who is married and the father of a family, and beseech them to give him some vacant command in the order of St. James, of which he is a knight, in order that his wife and children may thus have a competence to live upon. You will also make mention of Juan Aguado, a servant of their Highnesses ; you will inform them of the zeal and activity with which he has served them in all matters that have been entrusted to him ; and also that I beseech their Highnesses on his behalf, as well as on behalf of those above mentioned, not to forget my recommendation, but to give it full consideration.

Their Highnesses grant an annual pension of thirty thousand maravedis to Moses Pedro Margarite, and pensions of

---

Item : Porque Mosen Pedro Margarité, criado de sus Altezas, há bien servido, y espero que así lo hara adelante en las cosas que le fueren encomendadas, he habido placer de su quedada aqui, y tambien de Gaspar y de Beltran por ser conocidos criados de sus Altezas pàra los poner en cosas de confianza : suplicareis á sus Altezas que especial al dicho Mosen Pedro, que es casado y tiene hijos le provean de alguna encomienda en la Orden de Santiago, de la cual él tiene el hábito, porque su muger é hijos tengan en que vivir. Asimismo hareis relacion de Juan Aguado, criado de sus Altezas, cuan bien é diligentemente ha servido en todo lo que le ha seido mandado ; que suplico á sus Altezas á él é á los sobredichos los hayan por encomendados é por presentes.

Sus Altezas mandan asentar á Mosen Pedro 30000 maravedis cada ano, y á Gaspar y Beltran á cada uno 15000 maravedis cada año

N

fifteen thousand maravedis to Gaspard and Beltran, which will be reckoned from this day, the 15th of August 1494. They give orders that the said pensions be paid by the Admiral out of the sums to be paid in the Indies, and by Don Juan de Fonseca out of the sums to be paid in Spain. With respect to the matter of Juan Aguado, their Highnesses will not be forgetful.

Item. You will inform their Highnesses of the continual labour that Doctor Chanca has undergone, from the prodigious number of sick and the scarcity of provisions: and that, in spite of all this, he exhibits the greatest zeal and benevolence in everything that relates to his profession. As their Highnesses have entrusted me with the charge of fixing the salary that is to be paid to him while out here (although it is certain that he neither receives, nor can receive anything from any one, and does not receive anything from his position, equal to what he did, and could still do in Spain, where he lived peaceably and at ease, in a very different style from what he does here ; and, although he declares that he earned more in Spain, exclusive of the pay which he received from their Highnesses), I have, nevertheless, not ventured to place to the credit of his account more than fifty thousand mara-

---

desde hoy 15 de Ayosto de 94 en adelante, y así les hagar pagar el Almirante en lo que allá se hobiere de pagar, y D. Juan de Fonseca en lo que acá se hobiere de pagar : y en lo de Juan Aguado sus Altezas habrán memoria de él.

Item : Direis á sus Altezas el trabajo que el Doctor Chanca tiene con el afruenta de tantos dolientes, y aun la estrechura de los mantenimientos, é aun con todo ello se dispone con gran diligencia y caridad en todo lo que cumple á su oficio, y porque sus Altezas remitieron á mí el salario que acá se le habia de dar, porque estando acá es cierto quel non toma ni puede haber nada de ninguno, ni ganar de su oficio como en Castilla ganaba, ó podria ganar estando á su reposo é viviendo de otra manera que acá no vive ; y así que como quiera que él jura que es mas lo que allá ganaba allende el salario que sus Altezas le dan, y non me quise estender mas de vedis per annum, as the sum which he is to receive for his yearly labour during the time of his stay in this country. I beg their Highnesses to give their sanction to this salary, exclusive of his maintenance while here; and I do so, because he asserts that all the medical men who attend their Highnesses in the royal yachts, or in any of their expeditions, are accustomed to receive by right the day's pay out of the annual salary of each individual. Let this be as it may, I am informed for certain, that on whatever service they are engaged, it is the custom to give them a certain fixed sum, settled at the will and by order of their Highnesses, in compensation for the said day's pay. You will, therefore, beg their Highnesses to decide this matter, as well with respect to the annual pay as to the above-mentioned usage, so that the said doctor may be reasonably satisfied.

Their Highnesses acknowledge the justice of Doctor Chanca's observations, and it is their wish that the Admiral shall pay him the sum which he has allowed him, exclusive of his fixed annual salary. With respect to the day's pay allowed to medical men, it is not the custom to authorize them to receive it, except when they are in personal attendance upon the King.

---

cincuenta mil maravedis por el trabajo que acá pasa cada un año mientras acá estoviere ; los cuales suplico á sus Altezas le manden librar con el sueldo de acá y eso mismo, porque él dice y afirma que todos los fisicos de vuestras Altezas, que andan en reales ó semejantes cosas que estas, suelen haber de derecho un dia de sueldo en todo el año de toda la gente : con todo he seido informado, y dicenme, que como quier que esto sea, la costumbre es de darles cierta suma tasada á voluntad y mandamiento de sus Altezas en compensa de aquel dia de sueldo. Suplicareis á sus Altezas que en ello manden proveer, así en lo del salario como de esta costumbre, por forma que el dicho Doctor tenga razon de ser contento.

A sus Altezas place desto del Doctor Chanca, y que se le pague esto desde quel Almirante gelo asentó, y que gelos pague con lo del sueldo.

En esto del dia del sueldo de los fisicos, non lo acostumbran haber sino donde el Rey nuestro Senor esté en persona.

Item.   You will tell their Highnesses what great devotion Coronel has shown to the service in many respects, and what great proofs he has given of it in every important matter that has been trusted to him, and how much we feel his loss now that he is sick.   You will represent to them how just it is that he should receive the recompense of such good and loyal services, not only in the favours which may hereafter be shown to him, but also in his present pay, in order that he, and all those that are with us, may see what profit will accrue to them from their zeal in the service; for the importance and difficulty of exploring the mines should call for great consideration towards those to whom such extensive interests are entrusted ; and, as the talents of the said Coronel have made me determine upon appointing him principal constable of this portion of the Indies,—and, as I have given him *carte blanche* for fixing the salaries of those who come under his charge,—I beg their Highnesses to condescend to sanction these grants as fully as they may think proper, upon consideration of his services, and to confirm his nomination to the service which I have allotted to him, by giving him an official appointment thereto.

Their Highnesses grant him, besides his salary, an annnal

Item : Direis á sus Altezas de Coronel cuanto es hombre para servir, á sus Altezas en muchas cosas, y cuanto ha servido hasta aquí en todo lo mas necesario, y la mengua que dél sentimos agora que está doliente, y que sirviendo de tal manera es razon quel sienta el fruto de su servicio, non solo en las mercedes para despues mas en lo de su salario en lo presente, en manera quél é los que acá estan sientan que les aprovecha el servicio, y porque segun el ejercicio que acá se ha de tener en cojer este oro, no son de tener en poco las personas en quien tanta diligencia hay : porque por su habilidad se proveyó acá por mí del oficio de Alguacil mayor destas Indias, y en la provision va el salario en blanco, que suplico á sus Altezas gelo manden henchir como mas sea su servicio, mirando sus servicios, confirmándole la provision que acá se le dió, e proveyéndole de él de juro.

pension of fifteen thousand maravedis; the same to be paid him at the same time as the said salary.

Item.   You will, at the same time, tell their Highnesses that the bachelor, Gil Garcia, came out here in quality of principal alcalde, without having any salary fixed or allowed to him: that he is a good man, well-informed, correct in his conduct, and one that is very necessary to us; and that I beg their Highnesses to be pleased to give him such appointments as shall enable him to support himself honourably; and that such may be granted to him extra the funds due to the appointments given to him beyond the sea.

Their Highnesses grant him an annual pension of twenty thousand maravedis during his stay in the Indies, and that over and above his fixed appointments; and it is their order that this pension be paid to him at the same time as his salary.

Item.   You will tell their Highnesses, as I have already told them in writing, that I think it will be impossible to go this year to make discoveries until arrangements have been made to work the two rivers in which the gold has been found in the most profitable manner for their Highnesses' interest; and this may be done more effectively hereafter, because it is

---

Sus Altezas mandan que le asienten quince mil maravedis cada año mas de su sueldo, é que se le paguen cuando le pagaren su sueldo.

Asimismo direis á sus Altezas como aquí vino el Bachiller Gil García por Alcalde mayor é non se le ha consignado ni nombrado salario, y es persona de bien y de buenas letras, é diligente, é es acá bien necesario; que suplico á sus Altezas le manden nombrar é consignar su salario, por manera que él se pueda sostener, é le sea librado con el dinero del sueldo de acá.

Sus Altezas le mandan asentar cada año veinte mil maravedis en tanto que allá estoviere y mas su sueldo, y que gelo paguen cuando pagaren el sueldo.

Item: Direis á sus Altezas como quier que ya se lo escribo por las cartas, que para este año non entiendo que sea posible ir á descobrir hasta que esto destos rios que se hallaron de oro sea puesto en el asiento debido á servicio de sus Altezas, que despues mucho mejor not a thing that every one can do to my satisfaction, or with advantage to their Highnesses' service, unless I be present; for whatever is to be done always turns out best under the eye of the party interested.

Let him continue to carry on his operations, as well as he is able, and let him try to discover the places where the gold is hidden.

Item. You will tell their Highnesses, that the horse-soldiers that came from Grenada to the review which took place at Seville, offered good horses, but that at the time of their being sent on board, they took advantage of my absence (for I was somewhat indisposed), and changed them for others, the best of which does not seem worth two thousand maravedis, for they sold the first and bought these; and this deception on the part of the horse soldiers, is very like what I have known to occur to many gentlemen in Seville of my acquaintance. It seems that Juan de Sorias, after having settled an advantageous price for himself, put other horses in the place of those that I expected to find, and when I came to see them, there were horses there that had never been

---

se podrá facer, porque no es cosa que nadie la podiese facer sin mi presencia á mi grado, ni á servicio de sus Altezas, por muy bien que lo ficiese, como es en dubda segun lo que hombre vee por su presencia.

Trabaje como lo mas preciso que ser pueda se sepa lo adito de ese oro.

Item: Direis á sus Altezas como los escuderos de caballo que vinieron de Granada, en el alarde que ficieron en Sevilla mostraron buenos caballos, é despues al embarcar, yo no lo vi porque estaba un poco doliente, y metiéronlos tales quel mejor dellos non parece que vale dos mil maravedis, porque vendieron los otros y compraron estos, y esto fue de la suerte que se hizo lo de mucha gente que allá en los alardes de Sevilla yo vi muy buena; parece que Juan de Soria, despues de dado el dinero del sueldo, por algun interese suyo puso otros en lugar de aquellos que yo acá pensaba fallar, y fallo gente que yo nunca habia visto: en esto ha habido gran maldad, de offered to me for sale. In all this the greatest dishonesty has been shown, so that I do not know whether I ought to complain of him alone, since these horse-soldiers have been paid their expenses up to the present day, besides their salary and the hire of their horses, and when they are ill, they will not allow their horses to be used, because they are not present. Their Highnesses did not wish the horses to be purchased, but desired that the men should be taken into their service, but only to be employed in work which required them to ride on horse-back, which is not the case at present. All these considerations lead me to think, that it would be more convenient to buy their horses, which are worth but little, and thus avoid being exposed daily to new disputes ; finally, their Highnesses will decide on what plan is best for their own interests.

Their Highnesses order Don Juan de Fonseca to make enquiries respecting the matter of the horses, and if it be true that such a deception has been practised, to send up the culprits to be punished as they deserve ; also to gain information respecting the other people that the admiral speaks of, and to send the result of the information to their Highnesses. With respect

---

tal manera que yo no sé si me queje del solo : por esto, visto que á estos escuderos se ha fecho la costa hasta aquí, allende de sus sueldos y tambien á sus caballos, y se hace de presente y son personas que cuando ellos estan dolientes, ó non se les antoja, non quieren que sus caballos sirvan sin ellos mismos ; sus Altezas no quieren que se les compren estos caballos sino que sirvan á sus Altezas, y esto mismo no les paresce que deban servir ni cosa ninguna sino á caballo ; lo cual agora de presente non face mucho al caso, é por esto parece que seria mejor comprarles los caballos, pues que tan poco valen, y non estar cada dia con ellos en estas pendencias ; por ende que sus Altezas determinen esto como fuere su servicio.

Sus Altezas mandan á D. Juan de Fonseca, que se informe de esto de estos caballos, y si se hallare que es verdad que hicieron ese engano, lo envien á sus Altezas porque lo mandarán castigar; tambien se informe deso que dice de la otra gente, y envie la pesquisa á sus Altezas : y

to the horse soldiers, it is their Highnesses' wish and command,
that they continue where they are, and remain in service, because
they belong to the guards and to the class of their Highnesses'
servants. Their Highnesses also command the said horse
soldiers to give up their horses into the charge of the Admiral
on all occasions when they shall be required, and if the use of
the horses should occasion any loss, their Highnesses direct that
compensation shall be made for the amount of the injury, through
the medium of the Admiral.

Item.   You will mention to their Highnesses, that more
than two hundred persons have come here without fixed salaries, and that some of them are very useful to the service;
and in order to preserve system and uniformity, the others
have been ordered to imitate them. For the three first years,
it is desirable that we should have here a thousand men, in
order to keep a safeguard upon the island and upon the rivers
that supply the gold : and even when we are able to mount
a hundred men on horse-back, so far from being an evil, it
will be a very necessary thing for us; but their Highnesses
might pass by the question of the horse-men until gold shall
be sent.   In short, their Highnesses should give instructions

---

en lo destos escuderos sus Altezas mandan que esten allá y sirvan, pues
son de las guardas y criados de sus Altezas; y á los escuderos man-
dan sus Altezas qne den los caballos cada vez que fueren menester y el
Almirante lo mandare, y si algun dano recibieren los caballos yendo
otros en ellos, por medio del Almirante mandan sus Altezas que gelo
paguen.

Item : Direis á sus Altezas como aquí han venido mas de doscientas personas sin sueldo, y hay algunos dellos que sirven bien, y
aun los otros por semejante se mandan que lo hagan así y porque
para estos primeros tres años será gran bien que aqui esten mil
hombres para asentar y poner en muy gran seguridad esta Isla y
rios de oro, y aunque hobiese ciento de caballo non se perderia nada,
antes parece necesario, aunque en estos de caballo fasta que oro se
envie sus Altezas podrán sobreceer : con todo á estas doscientas
personas, que vienen sin sueldo, sus Altezas deben enviar á decir si

as to whether the two hundred people who have come over without pay, should receive pay like the others, if they do their work well; for we certainly have great need of them to commence our labours, as I have already shown.

It is their Highnesses' wish and command, that the two hundred persons without pay shall replace such of those who are paid as have failed, or as shall hereafter fail, in their duty, provided they are fit for the service and please the Admiral; and their Highnesses order the Accomptant to enter their names in the place of those who shall fail in their duty, as the Admiral shall determine.

Item. As there are means of diminishing the expenses that these people occasion, and of saving a considerable portion of the expenditure, by imitating the plans which other princes have been able to employ with great effect, it would be desirable that we should do likewise.

I think it would be well that all ships that come here should be ordered to bring, besides the ordinary stores and medicines, shoes, and leather for making shoes, shirts, both of common and superior quality, doublets, laces, some peasants' clothing, breeches, and cloth for making clothes, all at moderate prices;

---

se les pagará sueldo como á los otros sirviendo bien, porque cierto son necesarios como dicho tengo para este comienzo.

De estas doscientas personas que aquî dice que fueron sin sueldo, mandan sus Altezas que entren en lugar de los que han faltado y faltaren de los que iban á sueldo, seyendo habiles y á contentamiento del Almirante, y sus Altezas mandan al Contador que los asiente en lugar de los que faltaren como el Almirante lo dijere.

Item : Porque en algo la costa de esta gente se puede aliviar con industria y formas que otros Principes suelen tener en otras, lo gastado mejor que acá se podria escusar, paresce que seria bien mandar traer en los navíos que vinieren allende de las otras cosas que son para los mantenimientos comunes, y de la botica, zapatos y cueras para los mandar facer; camisas comunes y de otras, jubones, lienzo, sayos, calzas. paños para vestir en razonables precios; y otras cosas, como son conservas, que son fuera de racion, y para conservacion de la they might also bring other articles, such as sweetmeats, which do not enter into the daily ration, nor are absolutely necessary to health. The Spaniards that are here would always be happy to receive such articles as these in lieu of part of their pay; and if they were purchased by men who were selected for their known loyalty, and who take an interest in the service of their Highnesses, great economy would result from this arrangement. If their Highnesses find that this plan is expedient for the service, it is desirable that it should be adopted immediately.

It would have been desirable that the Admiral had entered more fully into the details of this subject; meanwhile, Don Juan de Fonseca shall be ordered to instruct Don Ximenes de Bribiesca to make the necessary arrangements for the execution of the proposed plans.

Item. You will tell their Highnesses that, in a review that was holden yesterday, it was remarked that a great number of the people were without arms, which I think must be attributed partly to the exchange made at Seville, or in the harbour, when those who presented themselves armed were left for a while, and for a trifle exchanged their arms for others of an inferior quality. I think it would be desirable that two

---

salud, las cuales cosas todas la gente de ac rescibiria de grado en descuento de su sueldo, y si allá esto se mercase por Ministros leales y que mirasen el servicio de sus Altezas, se ahorraria algo: por ende sabreis la voluntad de sus Altezas cerca desto, y si les pareciere ser su servicio luego se debe poner en obra.

Por este camino se solia ser fasta que mas escriba el Almirante, y ya enviarán á mandar á D. Juan de Fonseca con Jimeno de Bribiesca que provea en esto.

Item : Tambien direis á sus Altezas, que por cuanto ayer en el alarde que se tomó se falló la gente muy desarmada, lo cual pienso que en parte contesció por aquel trocar que allá se fizo en Sevilla ó en el puerto cuando se dejaron los que se mostraron armados, y tomaron otros que daban algo á quien los trocaba, paresce que seria bien que se mandasen traer doscientas corazas, y cien espingardas hundred cuirasses, a hundred arquebuses, a hundred arbalists, and many other articles of defensive armour, should be sent over to us; for we have great need of them to arm those who are at present without them.

Don Juan de Fonseca has already been written to, to provide them.

Item. Many married persons have come over here, and are engaged in regular duties, such as masons and other tradesmen, who have left their wives in Spain, and wish that the pay that falls due to them may be paid to their wives, or whomsoever they may appoint, in order that they may purchase for them such articles as they may need. I therefore beseech their Highnesses to take such measures as they may deem expedient on this subject; for it is of importance to their interests that these people be well provided for.

Their Highnesses have already ordered Don Juan de Fonseca to attend to this matter.

Item. Besides the other articles which I have begged from their Highnesses in the memorial which you bear, signed by my hand, and which articles consist of provisions and other stores, both for those who are well and for those who are sick,

---

y cien ballestas, y mucho almacen, que es la cosa que mas menester habemos, y de todas estas armas se podrán dar á los desarmados.

Ya se escribe á D. Juan de Fonseca que provea en esto.

Item: Por cuanto algunos oficiales que acá vinieron como son albañies y de otros oficios, que son casados y tienen sus mugeres allá, y querrian que allá lo que se les debe de su sueldo se diese á sus mugeres ó á las personas á quien ellos enviaren sus recabdos, para que les compren las cosas que acá han menester; que á sus Altezas suplico les mande librar, porque su servicio es que estos esten proveidos acá.

Ya enviaron á mandar sus Altezas á D. Juan, de Fonseca que provea en esto.

Item: Porque allende las otras cosas que allá se envian á pedir por los memoriales que llevais de mi mano firmados, así para mantenimiento de los sanos como para los dolientes, seria muy bien que it would be very serviceable that fifty pipes of molasses should be sent hither from the island of Madeira; for it is the most nutritious food in the world, and the most wholesome. A pipe of it does not ordinarily cost more than two ducats, exclusive of the casks; and if their Highnesses would order one of the caravels to call at the said island on the return voyage, the purchase might be made, and they might, at the same time, buy ten casks of sugar, of which we stand greatly in need. It is the most favourable season of the year to obtain it at a cheap rate, that is to say, between this and the month of April. The necessary orders might be given, if their Highnesses think proper, and yet the place of destination be carefully concealed.

Don Juan de Fonseca will see to it.

Item. You will tell their Highnesses that, although the rivers contain in their beds the quantity of gold described by those who have seen it, there is no doubt that this metal is produced in the bosom of the earth; and that the water happening to come in contact with the mines, washes it away mingled with the sand. And as among the great number of rivers that have been already discovered

---

se hobiesen de la isla de la Madera cincuenta pipas de miel de azúcar, porque es el mejor mantenimiento del mundo y mas sano, y non suele costar cada pipa sino á dos ducados sin el casco, y si sus Altezas mandan que á la vuelta pase por allí alguna carabela las podrá mercar, y tambien diez cajas de azúcar que es mucho menester, que esta es la mejor sazon del año, digo entre aquí é el mes de Abril para fallarlo, é haber dello buena razon y podriase dar orden mandándolo sus Altezas, é que non supiesen allá para donde lo quieren.

D. Juan de Fonseca que provea en esto.

Item : Direis á sus Altezas, por cuanto aunque los rios tengan en la cuantidad que se dice por los que lo han visto, pero que lo cierto dello es quel oro non se engendra en los rios mas en la tierra, quel agua topando con las minas lo trae envuelto en las arenas, y porque en estos tantos rios se han descubierto, como quiera que hay there are some of considerable magnitude, there are also some so small that they might rather be called brooks than rivers, only two fingers' breadth deep, and very short in their course; there will, therefore, be some men wanted to wash the gold from the sand, and others to seek for it in the bosom of the earth. This latter operation will be the principal and the most productive; it will be expedient, therefore, that their Highnesses send men both for the washing and for the mining, from among those who are employed in Spain in the mines at Almaden,[4] so that, by one means or another, the work may be managed. We shall not, however, wait for the arrival of these workmen, but hope, with the aid of God and with the washers that we have here with us, when they shall be restored to health, to send a good quantity of gold by the first caravels that shall leave for Spain.

This shall be completely provided for by other means; meanwhile, Don Juan de Fonseca has their Highnesses' orders to send the best miners that he can find. Their Highnesses write also to Almaden, with instructions to select the greatest number that can be spared, and to send them up.

---

algunos grandecitos hay otros tan pequeños que son mas fuentes que no rios, que non llevan de dos dedos de agua, y se falla luego el cabo doede nasce; para lo cual non solo serán provechosos los lavadores para cogerlo en el arena, mas los otros para cavarlo en la tierra, que será lo mas especial é de mayor cuantidad; é por esto será bien que sus Altezas envien lavadores, é de los que andan en las minas allá en Almaden, porque en la una manera y en la otra se faga el ejercicio, como quier que acá non esperaremos á ellos, que con los lavadores que aquí tenemos, esperamos con la ayuda de Dios, si una vez la gente está sana, allegar un buen golpe de oro para las primeras carabelas que fueren.

A otro camino se proveerá en esto cumplidamente; en tanto mandan sus Altezas á D. Juan de Fonseca que envie luego los mas minadores que pudiere haber, y escriben al Almaden, que de allí tomen los que mas pudieren y los envien.

[4] In La Mancha, New Castile, famous for mines of quicksilver.

Item.   You will beseech their Highnesses very humbly in my name, to condescend to pay regard to my strong recommendation of Villacorta, who, as their Highnesses are in some degree aware, has been extremely useful, and has shown the greatest possible zeal in this affair.   From all that I have observed in him, I consider him a man of strict integrity,— zealous and devoted to their Highnesses' service.   I shall feel very grateful if they would deign to grant him some confidential employment adapted to his qualifications, and in which he might evince his industry and warm desire to serve their Highnesses : and you will take care that Villacorta shall have practical evidence that none of this work which he has done for me, or under my orders, has remained without recompense.

This shall be done as he wishes.

Item. That the said Moses Pedro, Gaspar, Beltran, and others remaining here, came to command caravels which have already gone back, and are in receipt of no salary whatever : as these are people who should be employed in matters of principal importance, and requiring the greatest confidence, their pay has not been fixed, because it ought to be different

---

Item : Suplicareis á sus Altezas de mi parte muy humildemente, que quieran tener por muy encomendado á Villacorta, el cual, como sus Altezas saben, ha mucho servido en esta negociacion, y con muy buena voluntad, y segun le conozco persona diligente y afecionada á su servicio ; rescebiré merced que se le dé algun cargo de confianza, para lo cual él ser suficiente, y pueda mostrar su deseo de servir y diligencia, y esto procurareis por forma que el Villacorta conozca por la obra que lo que ha trabajado por mí en lo que yo le hobe menester le aprovecha en esto.

Así se hará.

Item : Que los dichos Mosen Pedro y Gaspar y Beltran, y otros que han quedado acá, trajieron capitanías de carabelas, que son agora vueltas, y non gozan del sueldo ; pero porque son tales personas, que se han de poner en cosas principales y de confianza, non se les ha determinado el sueldo que sea diferenciado de los otros:

from that of the rest. You will beg their Highnesses, on my behalf, to settle what ought to be given them either yearly or monthly, with respect to their Highnesses' service.

Given in the City of Isabella, the thirtieth of January, in the year fourteen hundred and ninety-four.

This point has been already replied to above; but as in the said clause it is said that they should receive their pay, it is their Highnesses' command that their salary shall be paid to them from the time that the command was issued.

---

suplicareis de mi parte á sus Altezas determinen lo que se les ha de dar en cada un año, ó por meses, como mas fueren servidos. Fecho en la ciudad Isabela á treinta dias de Enero de mil cuatrocientos y noventa y cuatro años.

Ya está respondido arriba, pero porque en el dicho capitulo que en esto habia dice que gozan del salario, desde agora mandan sus Altezas que se les cuenten á todos sus salarios desde que dejaron las capitanias.

THIRD VOYAGE OF COLUMBUS.

The History of a Voyage which Don Christopher Columbus made the third time that he came to the Indies, when he discovered terra firma, and which he sent to their Majesties from the Island of Hispaniola.

MOST serene and most exalted and powerful Princes, the King and Queen, our Sovereigns. The Blessed Trinity moved your Highnesses to the encouragement of this enterprise to the Indies; and of its infinite goodness has made me your messenger therein; as ambassador for which undertaking I approached your royal presence, moved by the consideration that I was appealing to the most exalted monarchs in Christendom, who exercised so great an influence over the Christian faith, and its advancement in the world : those who heard of it looked upon it as impossible, for they fixed

TERCER VIAGE DE COLON.

La historia del viage quel Almirante D. Cristobal Colon hizo la tercera vez que vino á las Indias cuando descubrió la tierra firme, como lo envió á los Reyes desde la Isla Espanola.

SERENÍSIMOS é muy altos é muy poderosos Príncipes Rey é Reina nuestros Señores : La Santa Trinidad movió á vuestras Altezas á esta empresa de las Indias, y por su infinita bondad hizo á mí mensagero dello, al cual vine con el embajada á su Real conspetu, movido como á los mas altos Príncipes de cristianos y que tanto se ejercisaban en la fé y acrecentamiento della ; las personas que entendieron en ello lo tuvieron por imposible, y el caudal hacian sobre bienes de fortuna, y allí echaron el clavo. Puse en esto seis ó siete all their hopes on the favours of fortune, and pinned their faith solely upon chance. I gave to the subject six or seven years of great anxiety, explaining, to the best of my ability, how great service might be done to our Lord, by this undertaking, in promulgating His sacred name and our holy faith among so many nations ;—an enterprise so exalted in itself, and so calculated to enhance the glory and immortalize the renown of the greatest sovereigns. It was also requisite to refer to the temporal prosperity which was foretold in the writings of so many trustworthy and wise historians, who related that great riches were to be found in these parts. And at the same time I thought it desirable to bring to bear upon the subject, the sayings and opinions of those who have written upon the geography of the world. And finally, your Highnesses came to the determination that the undertaking should be entered upon. In this your Highnesses exhibited the noble spirit which has been always manifested by you on every great subject ; for all others who had thought of the matter or heard it spoken of, unanimously treated it with contempt, with the exception of two friars,[1] who always

---

años de grave pena, amostrando lo mejor que yo sabia cuanto servicio se podia hacer á nuestro Señor en esto en divulgar su santo nombre y Fé á tantos pueblos ; lo cual todo era cosa de tanta excelencia y buena fama y gran memoria para grandes Príncipes fue tambien necesario de hablar del temporal adonde se les amostró el escrebir de tantos sabios dignos de fé, los cuales escribieron historias. Los cuales contaban que en estas partes habia muchas riquezas, y asimismo fue necesario traer á esto el decir é opinion de aquellos que escribieron é situaron el mundo : en fin vuestras Altezas determinaron questo se pusiese en obra. Aquí mostraron el grande corazon que siempre ficieron en toda cosa grande, porque todos los que habian entendido en ello y oido esta platica todos á una mano lo tenian á burla, salvo dos frailes que siempre fueron

---

[1] These were Fray Juan Perez de Marchena, a Franciscan, keeper of the Convent de la Rabida, and Fray Diejo de Deza, a Dominican, afterwards Archbishop of Seville.

remained constant in their belief of its practicability.   I, my-self, in spite of fatiguing opposition, felt sure that the enter-prise would nevertheless prosper, and continue equally con-fident of it to this day, because it is a truth, that though everything will pass away, the Word of God will not; and I believe, that every prospect which I hold out will be accom-plished; for it was clearly predicted concerning these lands, by the mouth of the prophet Isaiah, in many places in Scrip-ture, that from Spain the holy name of God was to be spread abroad.   Thus I departed in the name of the Holy Trinity, and returned very soon, bringing with me an account of the practical fulfilment of everything I had said.   Your Highnesses again sent me out, and in a short space of time, by God's mercy, not by[2]   I discovered three hundred and thirty-three leagues of terra firma on the eastern side, and seven hundred islands,[3] besides those which I discovered on the first voyage;

---

constantes.   Yo, bien que llevase fatiga, estaba bien seguro que esto no vernia á menos, y estoy de contino, porque es verdad que todo pasará, y no la palabra de Dios, y se complirá todo lo que dijo; el cual tan claro habló de estas tierras por la boca de Isaías en tantos lugares de su Escriptura, afirmando que de España les seria divulgado su santo nombre.   E partí en nombre de la Santa Trinidad, y volví muy presto con la experiencia de todo cuanto yo habia dicho en la mano : tornáronme á enviar vuestras Altezas, y en poco espacio digo, no de   le descubri por virtud divinal trescientas y treinta y tres leguas de la tierra firme, fin de Oriente, y setcentas islas de nombre, allende de lo descubierto en el primero

[2] A similar gap in the original.

[3] He did not discover terra firma in the second voyage as he here says, but imagined the island of Cuba to be terra firma, because he was unable to explore it fully ; nor did he ascertain that it was an island, until, by order of the king, the Comendador Mayor Nicolas Ovando gave Sebastian de Ocampo a commission to circumnavigate the island, and he explored the whole coast in the year 1508.   (See Herrera, Dec. i, lib. 7, cap. i.) Amongst the number of these islands, Columbus doubtless included many of those to the south of Cuba, lying in the part which he called the *Queen's Gardens*.

I also succeeded in circumnavigating the island of Española, which is larger in circumference than all Spain, the
inhabitants of which are countless, and all of whom may be
laid under tribute. It was then that complaints arose, dis-
paraging the enterprise that I had undertaken, because, for-
sooth, I had not immediately sent the ships home laden with
gold,—no allowance being made for the shortness of the
time, and all the other impediments of which I have already
spoken. On this account (either as a punishment for my
sins, or, as I trust, for my salvation), I was held in detesta-
tion, and had obstacles placed in the way of every thing I
said or for which I petitioned. I therefore resolved to apply
to your Highnesses, to inform you of all the wonderful events
that I had experienced, and to explain the reason of every
proposition that I made, making reference to the nations
that I had seen, among whom, and by whose instrumentality,
many souls may be saved. I related how the natives of
Española had been laid under tribute to your Highnesses,
and regarded you as their sovereigns. And I laid before
your Highnesses abundant samples of gold and copper,—
proving the existence of extensive mines of those metals. I
also laid before your Highnesses many sorts of spices, too

---

víage, y le allané la Isla Española que boja mas que España, en
que la gente della es sin cuento, y que todos le pagasen tributo.
Nació allí mal decir y menosprecio de la empresa comenzada en
ello, porque no habia yo enviado luego los navíos cargados de oro,
sin considerar la brevedad del tiempo, y lo otro que yo dije de tantos inconvenientes ; y en esto por mis pecados ó por mi salvacion
creo que será, fue puesto en aborrecimiento y dado impedimento á
cuanto yo decia y demandaba ; por lo cual acordé de venir á vuestras Altezas, y maravillarme de todo, y mostrarles la razon que en
todo habia, y les dige de los pueblos que yo habia vesto, en qué ó de
qué se podrian salvar muchas animas, y les truje las obligaciones
de la gente de la Isla Española, de como se obligaban á pagar tributo é les tenian por sos Reyes y Señores, y les truje abastante
muestra de oro, y que hay mineros y granos muy grandes, y asi-

numerous to detail; and I spoke of the great quantity of bra-
zil-wood, and numberless other articles found in those lands.
All this was of no avail with some persons; who began, with
determined hatred, to speak ill of the enterprise, not taking
into account the service done to our Lord in the salvation of
so many souls, nor the enhancement of your Highnesses'
greatness to a higher pitch than any earthly prince has yet
enjoyed; nor considering, that from the exercise of your
Highnesses' goodness, and the expense incurred, both spiritual
and temporal advantage was to be expected, and that Spain
must in the process of time derive from thence, beyond all
doubt, an unspeakable increase of wealth. This might be
manifestly seen by the evidences already given in writing in
the descriptions of the voyages already made, which also
prove that the fulfilment of every other hope may be reasonably expected. Nor were they affected by the consideration
of what great princes throughout the world have done to increase their fame: as, for example, Solomon, who sent from
Jerusalem, to the uttermost parts of the east, to see Mount
Sopora, in which expedition his ships were detained three
years; and which mountain your Highnesses now possess in

---

mismo de cobre ; y les truje de muchas maneras de especerias, de
que seria largo de escrebir, y les dije de la gran cantidad de brasil,
y otras infinitas cosas. Todo no aprovechó para con algunas personas que tenian gana y dado comienzo á mal decir del negocio, ni
entrar con fabla del servicio de nuestro Señor con se salvar tantas
animas, ni á decir questo era grandeza de vuestras Altezas, de la
mejor calidad que hasta hoy haya usado Príncipe, por quel ejercicio
é gasto era para el espiritual y temporal, y que no podiá ser que
andando el tiempo no hobiese la España de aquí grandes provechos,
pues que se veian las señales que escribieron de lo de estas partidas
tan manifiestas : que tambien se llegaria á ver todo el otro complimi-
ento, ni á decir cosas que usaron grandes Principes en el mundo
para crecer su fama, así como de Salomon que envió desde Hierusalem en fin de Oriente á ver el monte Sopora, en que se detovieron
los navíos tres años, el cual tienen vuestras Altezas agora en la Isla

the island of Española. Nor, as in the case of Alexander, who sent to observe the mode of government in the island of Taprobana,[4] in India; and Cæsar Nero, to explore the sources of the Nile,[5] and to learn the causes of its increase in the spring,[6] when water is needed; and many other mighty deeds that princes have done, and which it is allotted to princes to achieve. Nor was it of any avail that no prince of Spain, as far as I have read, has ever hitherto gained possession of land out of Spain; and that the world of which I speak is different from that in which the Romans, and Alexander, and the Greeks, made mighty efforts with great armies to gain the possession of. Nor have they been affected by the recent noble example of the kings of Portugal, who have had the courage to explore as far as Guinea, and to make the discovery of it, expending so much gold and so many lives in the undertaking, that a calculation of the population of the kingdom would show, that one half of them have died in Guinea: and though it is now a long time since they com-

---

Española; ni de Alejandre, que envió á ver el regimiento de la Isla de Trapobana en India, y Nero Cesar á ver las fuentes del Nilo, y la razon porque crecian en el verano, cuando las aguas son pocas, y otras muchas grandezas que hicieron Príncipes, y que á Príncipes son estas cosas dadas de hacer; ni valia decir que yo nunca habia leido que Príncipes de Castilla jamas hobiesen ganado tierra fuera della, y que esta de acá es otro mundo en que se trabajaron Romanos y Alejandre y Griegos, para la haber con grandes ejercicios, ni decir del presente de los Reyes de Portugal, que tovieron corazon para sostener á Guinea, y del descobrir della, y que gastaron oro y gente á tanta, que quien contase toda la del Reino se hallaria que otra tanta como la mitad son muertos en Guinea, y todavia la continuaron hasta que les salió dello lo que parece, lo cual todo comen-

[4] Ceylon.

[5] These examples quoted by the admiral from ancient history, are commented upon very learnedly, and at considerable length, by his historian, Las Casas, in the hundred and twenty-eighth and hundred and twenty-ninth chapters of his unpublished history. (Navarrete.)

[6] Columbus should have said summer.

menced these great exertions, the return for their labour and expense has hitherto been but trifling ; this people has also dared to make conquests in Africa, and to carry on their exploits to Ceuta, Tangier, Algiers, and Alcazar, repeatedly giving battle to the Moors; and all this at great expense; simply because it was an exploit worthy of a prince, undertaken for the service of God, and to advance the enlargement of His kingdom.   The more I said on the subject, the more two-fold was reproach cast upon it, even to the expression of abhorrence, no consideration being given to the honour and fame that accrued to your Highnesses throughout all Christendom, from your Highnesses having undertaken this enterprise; so that there was neither great nor small who did not desire to hear tidings of it.   Your Highnesses replied to me encouragingly, and desired that I should pay no regard to those who spoke ill of the undertaking, inasmuch as they had received no authority or countenance whatever from your Highnesses.

I started from San Lucar, in the name of the most Holy Trinity, on Wednesday the 30th of May,[7] much fatigued with

---

zaron de largo tiempo, y ha muy poco que les da renta ; los cuales tambien osaron conquistar en Africa, y sostener la empresa á Cepta, Tanjar y Arcilla, é Alcazar, y de contino dar guerra á los moros, y todo esto con grande gasto, solo por hacer cosa de Príncipe servir á Dios y acrecentar su Señorío.

Cuanto yo mas decia tanto mas se doblaba á poner esto á vituperio, amostrando en ello aborrecimiento, sin considerar cuánto bien parecio en todo el mundo, y cuánto bien se dijo en todos los cristianos de vuestras Altezas por haber tomado esta empresa, que no hobo grande ni pequeño que no quisiese dello carta.   Respondiéronme vuestras Altezas riéndose y diciendo que yo no curase de nada porque no daban autoridad ni creencia á quien les mal decia de esta empresa.

Partí en nombre de la santísima Trinidad, Miercoles 30 de Mayo de la villa de S. Lúcar, bien fatigado de mi viage, que adonde es-

---

[7] Of the year 1498.

my voyage, for I had hoped, when I left the Indies, to find repose in Spain; whereas, on the contrary, I experienced nothing but opposition and vexation. I sailed to the island of Madeira by a circuitous route, in order to avoid any encounter with an armed fleet from France,[8] which was on the look out for me off Cape St. Vincent. Thence I went to the Canaries,[9] from which islands I sailed with but one ship and two caravels, having dispatched the other ships to Española by the direct road to the Indies;[10] while I myself moved southward, with the view of reaching the equinoctial line, and of then proceeding westward, so as to leave the island of Española to the north. But having reached the Cape Verde islands[11] (an incorrect name, for they are so barren that nothing

---

peraba descanso, cuando yo partí de estas Indias, se me dobló la pena, y navegué á la Isla de la Madera por camino no acostumbrado, por evitar escándalo que pudiera tener con un armada de Francia, que me aguardaba al Cabo de S. Vicente, y de allí á las Islas de Canaria, de adonde me partí con una nao y dos carabelas, y envié los otros navíos á derecho camino á las Indias á la Isla Española, y yo navegué al Austro con propósito de llegar á la línea equinocial, y de allí seguir al Poniente hasta que la Isla Española me quedase al Septentrion, y llegado á las Islas de Cabo Verde, falso nombre, porque son atan secas que no ví cosa verde en ellas,

[8] Herrera says (Dec. i, lib. 3, cap. 9) that it was a Portuguese squadron; but Las Casas (cap. 30) distinctly states it to have been French. (Navarrete.)

[9] Herrera and Don Ferdinand Columbus say that he reached the island of Puerto Santo on the seventh of June, from which island he sailed directly for Madeira, and thence to Gomera, which he reached on the nineteenth, and put to sea again on the twenty-first.

[10] The commanders of the three ships which the admiral despatched to Española, were Pedro de Arana, native of Cordova, brother to the mother of Ferdinand Columbus; Alonzo Sanchez de Carabajal, magistrate of Raeza; and Juan Antonio Columbus, a relative of the admiral; all of whom were known to and are spoken of by F. Bartolomé de Las Casas, in the hundred and thirtieth chapter of his history. (Navarrete.)

[11] This was on the twenty-seventh of June. He anchored in the island of Sal, and on the thirtieth proceeded to the island of Santiago, from whence he put to sea again on the fourth of July. (Navarrete.)

green was to be seen there, and the people so sickly that I did not venture to remain among them), I sailed away four hundred and eighty miles, which is equivalent to a hundred and twenty leagues, towards the south-west, where, when it grew dark, I found the north star to be in the fifth degree. The wind then failed me, and I entered a climate where the intensity of the heat was such, that I thought both ships and men would have been burnt up, and everything suddenly got into such a state of confusion, that no man dared go below deck to attend to the securing of the water-cask and the provisions. This heat lasted eight days; on the first day the weather was fine, but on the seven other days it rained and was cloudy, yet we found no alleviation of our distress; so that I certainly believe, that if the sun had shone as on the first day, we should not have been able to escape in any way.

I recollect, that in sailing towards the Indies, as soon as I passed a hundred leagues to the westward of the Azores, I found the temperature change : and this is so all along from north to south. I determined, therefore, if it should please the Lord to give me a favourable wind and good weather, so that I might leave the part where I then was, that I would

y toda la gente enferma, que no osé detenerme en ellas, y navegué al Sudueste cuatrocientas y ochenta millas, que son ciento y veinte leguas, adonde en anocheciendo tenia la estrella del norte en cinco grados ; allí me desamparó el viento y entré en tanto ardor y tan grande que creí que se me quemasen los navíos y gente, que todo de un golpe vino á tan desordenado, que no habia persona que osase descender debajo de cubierta á remediar la vasija y mantenimientos ; duró este ardor ocho dias ; al primer dia fue claro, y los siete dias siguientes llovió é hizo ñumblado, y con todo no fallamos remedio, que cierto si así fuera de sol como el primero, yo creo que no pudiera escapar en ninguna manera.

Acórdome que navegando á las Indias siempre que yo paso al Poniente de las Islas de los Azores cien leguas, allí fallo mudar la temperanza, y esto es todo de Septentrion en Austro, y determiné que si á nuestro Señor le pluguiese de me dar viento y buen tiempo give up pursuing the southward course, yet not turn backwards, but sail towards the west, moving in that direction in the hope of finding the same temperature that I had experienced when I sailed in the parallel of the Canaries,—and then, if it proved so, I should still be able to proceed more to the south. At the end of these eight days it pleased our Lord to give me a favourable east wind, and I steered to the west, but did not venture to move lower down towards the south, because I discovered a very great change in the sky and the stars, although I found no alteration in the temperature. I resolved, therefore, to keep on the direct westward course, in a line from Sierra Leone, and not to change it until the chance offered of more speedily reaching land on another tack, which I was very desirous to do, for the purpose of repairing the vessels, and of renewing, if possible, our stock of provisions, and taking in what water we wanted. At the end of seventeen days, during which our Lord gave me a propitious wind, we saw land at noon of Tuesday the 31st of July.[12] This I had expected on the Monday before,

---

que pudiese salir de adonde estaba, de dejar de ir mas al Austro, ni volver tampoco atrás, salvo de navegar al Poniente, á tanto que ya llegase á estar con esta raya con esperanza que yo fallaria alli así temperamiento, como habia fallado cuando yo navegaba en el paralelo de Canaria. E que si así fuese que entonces yo podria ir mas al Austro, y plugó á nuestro Señor que al cabo de estos ocho dias de me dar buen viento Levante, y yo seguí al Poniente, mas no osé declinar abajo al Austro porque fallé grandísimo mudamiento en el cielo y en las estrellas, mas non fallé mudamiento en la temperancia; así acordé de proseguir delante siempre justo al Poniente, en aquel derecho de la Sierra Lioa, con propósito de non mudar derrota fasta adonde yo habia pensado que fallaria tierra, y allí adobar los navíos, y remediar si pudiese los mantenimientos y tomar agua que no tenia; y al cabo de diez y siete dias, los cuales nuestro Señor me dió de próspero viento, Martes 31 de Julio á medio dia

[12] It was first seen by a mariner of Huelva, a servant of the admiral, named Alonzo Perez. (Navarrete.)

and held that route up to this point; but as the sun's strength increased, and our supply of water was failing, I resolved to make for the Carribee Islands, and set sail in that direction; when, by the mercy of God, which He has always extended to me, one of the sailors went up to the main-top and saw to the westward a range of three mountains. Upon this we repeated the "Salve Regina", and other prayers, and all of us gave many thanks to our Lord. I then gave up our northward course, and put in for the land: at the hour of complines we reached a cape, which I called Cape Galea,[13] having already given to the island the name of Trinidad, and here we found a harbour, which would have been excellent but that there was no good anchorage. We saw houses and people on the spot, and the country around was very beautiful, and as fresh and green as the gardens of Valencia in the month of March. I was disappointed at not being able to put into the harbour, and ran along the coast to the westward. After sailing five leagues I found very good bottom, and anchored. The next day I set sail in the same direction,

---

nos amostró tierra, é yo la esperaba el Lunes antes, y tuve aquel camino fasta entonces, que en saliendo el sol, por defecto del agua que no tenia, determiné de andar á las Islas de los Caribales, y tomé esa vuelta ; y como su alta Magestad haya siempre usado de misericordia conmigo, por acertamiento subió un marinero á la gavia, y vido al Poniente tres montañas juntas : dijimos la Salve Regina y otras prosas, y dimos todos muchas gracias á nuestro Señor, y despues dejé el camino de Septentrion, y volví hácia la tierra, adonde yo llegué á hora de completas á un Cabo á que dije de la Galea despues de haber nombrado á la Isla de la Trinidad, y allí hobiera muy buen puerto si fuera fondo, y habia casas y gente, y muy lindas tierras, atan fermosas y verdes como las huertas de Valencia en Marzo. Pesóme cuando no puede entrar en el puerto, y corri la costa de esta tierra del luengo fasta el poniente, y andadas cinco leguas fallé muy buen fondo y surgí, y en el otro dia dí la vela á este

---

[13] It is now called Cape Galeota, and is the most south-eastern point of the island of Trinidad.

in search of a harbour where I might repair the vessels and take in water, as well as improve the stock of provisions which I had brought out with me. When we had taken in a pipe of water, we proceeded onwards till we reached the cape, and there finding good anchorage and protection from the east wind, I ordered the anchors to be dropped, the water-cask to be repaired, a supply of water and wood to be taken in, and the people to rest themselves from the fatigues which they had endured for so long a time. I gave to this point the name of Sandy Point (Punta del Arenal). All the ground in the neighbourhood was filled with foot-marks of animals, like the impression of the foot of a goat; but although it would have appeared from this circumstance that they were very numerous, only one was seen, and that was dead. On the following day a large canoe came from the eastward, containing twenty-four men, all in the prime of life, and well provided with arms, such as bows, arrows, and wooden shields; they were all, as I have said, young, well-proportioned, and not dark black, but whiter than any other Indians that I had seen,—of very graceful gesture and handsome forms, wearing their hair long and straight, and cut in the

---

camino buscando puerto para adobar los navíos y tomar agua, y remediar el trigo y los bastimentos que llevaba solamente. Allí tomé una pipa de agua, y con ella anduve ansi hasta llegar al cabo, y allí fallé abrigo de Levante y buen fondo, y así mandé surgir y adobar la vasija y tomar agua y leña, y descendir la gente á descansar de tanto tiempo que andaban penando.

A esta punta llamé del Arenal, y allí se falló toda la tierra follada de unas animalías que tenian la pata como de cabra, y bien que segun parece ser allí haya muchas, no se vido sino una muerta. El dia siguiente vino de hácia oriente una grande canoa con veinte y cuatro hombres, todos mancebos é muy ataviados de armas, arcos y flechas y tablachinas, y ellos, como dije, todos mancebos, de buena disposicion y no negros, salvo mas blancos que otros que haya visto en las Indias, y de muy lindo gesto, y fermosos cuerpos, y los cabellos largos y llanos, cortados á la guisa de Castilla, y traian la

Spanish style. Their heads were bound round with cotton scarfs elaborately worked in colours, which resembled the Moorish head-dresses. Some of these scarfs were worn round the body and used as a covering in lieu of trousers. The natives spoke to us from the canoe while it was yet at a considerable distance, but none of us could understand them; I made signs to them, however, to come nearer to us, and more than two hours were spent in this manner,—but if by any chance they moved a little nearer, they soon pushed off again. I caused basins and other shining objects to be shewn to them to tempt them to come near; and after a long time, they came somewhat nearer than they had hitherto done,— upon which, as I was very anxious to speak with them, and had nothing else to shew them to induce them to approach, I ordered a drum to be played upon the quarter-deck, and some of our young men to dance, believing the Indians would come to see the amusement. No sooner, however, did they perceive the beating of the drum and the dancing, than they all left their oars, and strung their bows, and each man laying hold of his shield, they commenced discharging their arrows at us; upon this, the music and dancing soon ceased,

---

cabeza atada con un pañuelo de algodon tejido á labores y colores, el cual creia yo que era almaizar. Otro de estos pañuelos traían ceñido é se cobijaban con él en lugar de pañetes. Cuando llegó esta canoa habló de muy lejos, é yo ni otro ninguno no los entendiamos, salvo que yo les mandaba hacer señas que se allegasen, y en esto se pasó mas de dos horas, y si se llegaban un poco luego se desviaban. Yo les hacia mostrer bacines y otras cosas que lucian por enamorarlos porque viniesen, y á cabo de buen rato se allegaron mas que hasta entonces no habian, y yo deseaba mucho haber lengua, y no tenia ya cosa que me pareciese que era de mostrarles para que viniesen; salvo que hice sobir un tamborin en el castillo de popa que tañesen, é unos mancebos que danzasen, creyendo que se allegarian á ver la fiesta; y luego que vieron tañer y danzar todos dejaron los remos y echaron mano á los arcos y los encordaron, y embrazo cada uno su tablachina, y comenzaron á tirarnos flechas:

and I ordered a charge to be made from some of our cross-
bows; they then left us, and went rapidly to the other caravel, and placed themselves under its poop. The pilot of
that vessel received them courteously, and gave to the man
who appeared to be their chief, a coat and hat; and it was
then arranged between them, that he should go to speak with
him on shore. Upon this the Indians immediately went
thither and waited for him; but as he would not go without
my permission, he came to my ship in the boat, whereupon
the Indians got into their canoe again and went away, and I
never saw any more of them or of any of the other inhabitants of the island. When I reached the point of Arenal,
I found that the island of Trinidad formed with the land of
Gracia[14] a strait of two leagues' width from east to west, and
as we had to pass through it to go to the north, we found
some strong currents which crossed the strait, and which
made a great roaring, so that I concluded there must be a
reef of sand or rocks, which would preclude our entrance;
and behind this current was another and another, all making

cesó luego el tañer y danzar, y mandé luego sacar unas ballestas, y
ellos dejáronme y fueren á mas andar á otra carabela, y de golpe
se fueron debajo la popa della, y el piloto entró con ellos, y dió un
sayo é un bonete á un hombre principal que le pareció dellos, y
quedó concertado que le iria hablar allí en la playa, adonde ellos
luego fueron con la canoa esperándole, y él como no quiso ir sin mi
licencia, como ellos le vieron venir á la nao con la barca, tornaron
á entrar en la canoa é se fueron, é nunca mas los vide ni á otros de
esta isla.

Cuando yo llegué á esta punta del Arenal, allí se hace una boca
grande de dos leguas de Poniente á Levante, la Isla de la Trinidad
con la tierra de Gracia, y que para haber de entrar dentro para
pasar al Septentrion habia unos hileros de corrientes que atrave-
saban aquella boca y traían un rugir muy grande, y creí yo que
sería un arrecife de bajos é peñas, por el cual no se podria entrar
dentro en ella, y detras de este hilero habia otro y otro que todos

14 Coast of Cumaná.

a roaring noise like the sound of breakers against the rocks. I anchored there, under the said point of Arenal, outside of the strait, and found the water rush from east to west with as much impetuosity as that of the Guadalquivir at its conflux with the sea; and this continued constantly day and night, so that it appeared to be impossible to move backwards for the current or forwards for the shoals. In the dead of night, while I was on deck, I heard an awful roaring that came from the south towards the ship; I stopped to observe what it might be, and I saw the sea rolling from west to east like a mountain as high as the ship, and approaching by little and little; on the top of this rolling sea came a mighty wave roaring with a frightful noise, and with all this terrific uproar were other conflicting currents, producing, as I have already said, a sound as of breakers upon the rocks.[15] To this day I have a vivid recollection of the dread I then felt, lest the ship might founder under the force of that tremendous sea; but it passed by, and reached the mouth of the beforementioned passage, where the uproar lasted for a considerable

---

traian un rugir grande como ola de la mar que va á romper y dar en peñas. Surgí allí á la dicha punta del Arenal, fuera de la dicha boca, y fallé que venia el agua del Oriente fasta el Poniente con tanta furia como hace Guadalquivir en tiempo de avenida, y esto de contino noche y dia, que creí que no podria volver atrás por la corriente, ni ir adelante por los bajos; y en la noche ya muy tarde, estando al bordo de la nao, oí un rugir muy terrible que venia de la parte del Austro hácia la nao, y me paré á mirar, y ví levantando la mar de Poniente á Levante, en manera de una loma tan alta como la nao, y todavia venia hácia mi poco á poco, y encima della venia un filero de corriente que venia rugiendo con muy grande estrépito con aquella furia de aquel rugir que de los otros hileros que yo dije que me parecian ondas de mar que daban en peñas, que hoy en dia tengo el miedo en el cuerpo que no me trabucasen la nao cuando llegasen debajo della, y passó y llegó fasta la boca adonde allí se

[15] Produced by the confluence of the Orinoco with the sea. See Rapin, Hist. Phil. vol. iv, p. 272.

time. On the following day I sent out boats to take soundings, and found that in the strait, at the deepest part of the
embouchure, there were six or seven fathoms of water, and
that there were constant contrary currents, one running in-
wards, and the other outwards. It pleased the Lord, however, to give us a favourable wind, and I passed through the
middle of the strait, after which I recovered my tranquillity.
The men happened at this time to draw up some water from
the sea, which, strange to say, proved to be fresh. I then
sailed northwards till I came to a very high mountain, at
about twenty-six leagues from the Punta del Arenal; here
two lofty headlands appeared, one towards the east, and
forming part of the island of Trinidad,[16] and the other, on
the west, being part of the land which I have already called
Gracia;[17] we found here a channel still narrower than that of
Arenal,[18] with similar currents, and a tremendous roaring of
water; the water here also was fresh. Hitherto I had held
no communication with any of the people of this country,
although I very earnestly desired it; I therefore sailed along
the coast westwards, and the further I advanced, the fresher

---

detuvo grande espacio. Y el otro dia siguiente envie las barcas á
sondar y fallé en el mas bajo de la boca, que habia seis ó siete brazas de fondo, y de contino andaban aquellos hileros unos por entrar
y otros por salir, y plugo á nuestro Señor de me dar buen viento, y
atravesé por esa boca adentro, y luego hallé tranquilidad, y por
acertamiento se sacó del agua de la mar y la hallé dulce. Navegué
al Septentrion fasta una sierra muy alta, adonde serian veinte y seis
leguas de esta punta del Arenal, y allí habia dos cabos de tierra muy
alta, el uno de la parte del Oriente, y era de la misma Isla de la
Trinidad, y el otro del Occidente de la tierra que dije de Gracia, y
allí hacia una boca muy angosta mas que aquella de la punta del
Arenal, y allí habia los mismos hileros y aquel rugir fuerte del agua
como era en la punta del Arenal, y asimismo allí la mar era agua
dulce; y fasta entonces yo no habia habido lengua con ninguna
gente de estas tierras, y lo descaba en gran manera, y por esto na-

[16] Point Peña Blanca.   [17] Point Peña.   [18] Boca Grande.

and more wholesome I found the water; and when I had proceeded a considerable distance, I reached a spot where the land appeared to be cultivated. There I anchored, and sent the boats ashore, and the men who went in them found the natives had recently left the place; they also observed that the mountain was covered with monkeys. They came back, and as the coast at that part presented nothing but a chain of mountains, I concluded that further west we should find the land flatter, and consequently in all probability inhabited. Actuated by this thought I weighed anchor, and ran along the coast until we came to the end of the cordillera; I then anchored at the mouth of a river, and we were soon visited by a great number of the inhabitants, who informed us, that the country was called Paria, and that further westward it was more fully peopled. I took four of these natives, and proceeded on my westward voyage; and when I had gone eight leagues further, I found on the other side of a point which I called the Needle,[19] one of the most lovely countries in the world, and very thickly peopled: it

vegué al luengo de la costa de esta tierra hácia el Poniente, y cuanto mas andaba hallaba el agua de la mar mas dulce y mas sabrosa, y andando una gran parte llegué á un lugar donde me parecian las tierras labradas y surgí y envié las barcas á tierra, y fallaron que de fresco se habia ido de allí gente, y fallaron todo el monte cubierto de gatos paules: volviéronse, y como esta fuese sierra me pareció que mas allá al Poniente las tierras eran mas llanas, y que allí seria poblado, y por esto seria poblado, y mandé levantar las anclas y corrí esta costa fasta el cabo de esta sierra, y allí á un rio surgi, y luego vino mucha gente, y me dijeron como llamaron á esta tierra Paria, y que de allí mas al Poniente era mas poblada; tomé dellos cuatro, y despues navegué al Poniente, y andadas ocho leguas mas al Poniente allende una punta á que yo llamé del Aguja: hallé unas tierras las mas hermosas del mundo, y muy pobladas: llegué allí una mañana á hora de tercia, y por ver esta verdura y esta hermosura acordé surgir y ver esta gente, de los cuales luego vinieron en

[19] It is now called Point Alcatraz, or Point Pelican.

was three o'clock in the morning when I reached it, and seeing its verdure and beauty, I resolved to anchor there and communicate with the inhabitants. Some of the natives soon came out to the ship, in canoes, to beg me, in the name of their king, to go on shore; and when they saw that I paid no attention to them, they came to the ship in their canoes in countless numbers, many of them wearing pieces of gold on their breasts, and some with bracelets of pearls on their arms; on seeing which I was much delighted, and made many inquiries with the view of learning where they found them. They informed me, that they were to be procured in their own neighbourhood, and also at a spot to the northward of that place. I would have remained here, but the provisions of corn, and wine, and meats, which I had brought out with so much care, for the people whom I had left behind, were nearly wasted, so that all my anxiety was to get them into a place of safety, and not to stop for any thing. I wished, however, to get some of the pearls that I had seen, and with that view sent the boats on shore. The natives are very numerous, and for the most part handsome in person, and of the same colour as the Indians we had already seen; they

---

canoas á la nao á rogarme, de partes de su Rey, que descendiese en tierra; é cuando vieron que no curé dellos vinieron á la nao infinitísimos en canoas, y muchos traían piezas de oro al pescuezo, y algunos atados á los brazos algunas perlas: holgué mucho cuando las ví é procuré mucho de saber donde las hallaban, y me dijeron que allí, y de la parte del Norte de aquella tierra.

Quisiera detenerme, mas estos bastimentos, que yo traía, trigo y vino é carne para esta gente que acá esta se me acababan de perder, los cuales hobe allá con tanta fatiga, y por esto yo no buscaba sino á mas andar á venir á poner en ellos cobro, y no me detener para cosa alguna: procuré de haber de aquellas perlas, y envié las barcas á tierra: esta gente es muy mucha, y toda de muy buen parecer, de la misma color que los otros de antes, y muy tratables: la gente nuestra que fue á tierra los hallaron tan convenibles, y los recibieron muy honradamente: dicen que luego que llegaron las barcas

R

are, moreover, very tractable, and received our men who went
on shore most courteously, seeming very well disposed towards us. These men relate, that when the boats reached
shore, two of the chiefs, whom they took to be father and
son, came forward in advance of the mass of the people, and
conducted them to a very large house with façades, and not
round and tent-shaped as the other houses were; in this
house were many seats, on which they made our men sit
down, they themselves sitting on other seats. They then
caused bread to be brought, with many kinds of fruits, and
various sorts of wine, both white and red, not made of grapes,
but apparently produced from different fruits. The most
reasonable inference is, that they use maize, which is a plant
that bears a spine like an ear of wheat, some of which I took
with me from Spain, where it grows abundantly; this they
seemed to regard as most excellent, and set a great value
upon it. The men remained together at one end of the house,
and the women at the other. Great vexation was felt by both
parties that they could not understand each other, for they
were mutually anxious to make inquiries respecting each
other's country. After our men had been entertained at the

á tierra que vinieron dos personas principales cón todo el pueblo,
creen que el uno el padre y el otro era su hijo, y los llevaron á una
casa muy grande hecha á dos aguas, y no redonda, como tienda de
campo, como son estas otras, y allí tenian muchas sillas á donde los
ficieron asentar, y otras donde ellos se asentaron ; y hicieron traer
pan, y de muchas maneras frutas é vino de muchas maneras blanco
é tinto, mas no de uvas : debe él de ser de diversas maneras uno
de una fruta y otro de otra ; y asimismo debe de ser dello de maiz,
que es una simiente que hace una espiga como una mazorca de que
llevé yo allá, y hay ya mucho en Castilla, y parece que aquel que
lo tenia mejor lo traia por mayor excelencia, y lo daba en gran precio : los hombres todos estaban juntos á un cabo de la casa, y las
mugeres en otro. Recibieron ambas las partes gran pena porque
no se entendian, ellos para preguntar á los otros de nuestra patria,
y los nuestros por saber de la suya. E despues que hobieron resce-

house of the elder Indian, the younger took them to his
house, and gave them an equally cordial reception; after
which they returned to their boats and came on board. I
weighed anchor forthwith, for I was hastened by my anxiety
to save the provisions which were becoming spoiled, and which
I had procured and preserved with so much care and trouble,
as well as to attend to my own health, which had been affected
by long watching; and although on my former voyage, when I
discovered terra firma, I passed thirty-three days without
natural rest, and was all that time deprived of sight, yet
never were my eyes so much affected or so painful as at this
period. These people, as I have already said, are very graceful in form,—tall, and elegant in their movements, wearing
their hair very long and smooth, they also bind their heads
with handsome worked handkerchiefs, which from a distance
look like silk or gauze; others use the same material in a
longer form, wound round them so as to cover them like
trousers, and this is done by both the men and the women.
These people are of a whiter skin than any that I have seen
in the Indies. It is the fashion among all classes to wear
something at the breast, and on the arms, and many wear

---

bido colacion allí en casa del mas viejo, los llevó el mozo á la suya,
e fizo otro tanto, é despues se pusieron en las barcas é se vinieron
á la nao, é yo luego levanté las anclas porque andaba mucho de
priesa por remediar los mantenimientos que se me perdian que yo
habia habido con tanta fatiga, y tambien por remediarme é mí que
habia adolescido por el desvelar de los ojos, que bien quel viage que
yo fuí á descubrir la tierra firme estuviese treinta y tres dias sin
concebir sueño, y estoviese tauto tiempo sin vista, non se me da-
ñaron los ojos, ni se me rompieron de sangre y con tantos dolcres
como agora.

Esta gente, como ya dije, son todos de muy linda estatura, altos
de cuerpos, é de muy lindos gestos, los cabellos muy largos é llanos,
y traen las cabezas atadas con unos pañuelos labrados, como ya dije,
hermosos, que parecen de lejos de seda y almaizares: otro traen
ceñido mas largo que se cobijan con él en lugar de pañetes, ansi

pieces of gold hanging low on the bosom.   Their canoes are
larger, lighter, and of better build than those of the islands
which I have hitherto seen, and in the middle of each they
have a cabin or room, which I found was occupied by the
chiefs and their wives.   I called this place " Jardines", that
is, "the Gardens", for the place and the people corresponded
with that appellation.   I made many inquiries as to where
they found the gold, in reply to which, all of them directed
me to an elevated tract of land at no great distance, on the
confines of their own country, lying to the westward; but
they all advised me not to go there, for fear of being eaten,
and at the time, I imagined that by their description they
wished to imply, that they were cannibals who dwelt there,
but I have since thought it possible, that they meant merely
to express, that the country was filled with beasts of prey.   I
also inquired of them where they obtained the pearls? and in
reply to this question likewise, they directed me to the westward, and also to the north, behind the country they occupied.
I did not put this information to the test, on account of the
provisions, and the weakness of my eyes, and because the

-----

hombres como mugeres.   La color de esta gente es mas blanca que
otra que haya visto en las Indias ; todos traían al pescuezo y á los
brazos algo á la guisa de estas tierras, y muchos traían piezas de oro
bajo colgado al pescuezo.   Las canoas de ellos son muy grandes y
de mejor hechura que no son estas otras, y mas livianas, y en el
medio de cada una tienen un apartamiento como cámara en que ví
que andaban los principales con sus mugeres.   Llamé allí á este lugar
Jardines, porque así conforman por el nombre.   Procuré mucho de
saber donde cogian aquel oro, y todos me aseñalaban una tierra
frontera dellos al Poniente, que era muy alta, mas no lejos ; mas
todos me decian que no fuese allá porque allí comian los hombres,
y entendí entonces que decian que eran hombres caribales, é que
serian como los otros, y despues he pensado que podria ser que lo
decian porque allí habria animalias.   Tambien les pregunté adonde
cogian las perlas, y me señalaron tambien que al Poniente, y al
Norte detrás de esta tierra donde estaban.   Dejélo de probar por

large ship that I had with me was not calculated for such an undertaking. The short time that I spent with them was all passed in putting questions; and at evening, as I have already said, we returned to the ships, upon which I weighed anchor and sailed to the westward. I proceeded onwards on the following day, until I found that we were only in three fathoms water; at this time I was still under the idea that it was but an island, and that I should be able to make my exit by the north. Upon which I sent a light caravel in advance of us, to see whether there was any exit, or whether the passage was closed; the caravel proceeded a great distance, until it reached a very large gulf, in which there appeared to be four smaller gulfs, from one of which debouched a large river; they invariably found ground at five fathoms, and a great quantity of very fresh water, indeed, I never tasted any equal to it. I felt great anxiety when I found that I could make no exit, either by the north, south, or west, but that I was enclosed on all three sides by land; I therefore weighed anchor, and sailed in a backward direction, with the hope of finding a passage to the north by the strait, which I have al-

---

esto de los mantenimientos, y del mal de mis ojos, y por una nao grande que traigo que no es para semejante hecho.

Y como el tiempo fue breve se pasó todo en preguntas, y se volvieron á los navíos, que seria hora de visperas, como ya dije, y luego levanté las anclas y navegué al Poniente; y asimesmo el dia siguiente fasta que me fallé que no habia si non tres brazas de fondo, con creencia que todavía esta seria isla, y que yo podria salir al Norte; y así visto envié una carabela sotil adelante á ver si habia salida ó si estaba cerrado, y ansi anduvo mucho camino fasta un golfo muy grande en el cual parecia que habia otros cuatro medianos, y del uno salia un rio grandisimo: fallaron siempre cinco brazas de fondo y el agua muy dulce, en tanta cantidad que yo jamas bebíla pareja della. Fuí yo muy descontento della cuando ví que no podia salir al Norte ni podia andar ya al Austro ni al Poniente porque yo estaba cercado por todas partes de la tierra, y así levanté las anclas, y torne atrás para salir al Norte por la boca que yo arriba dije, y ready described; but I could not return along the inhabited part where I had already been, on account of the currents, which drove me entirely out of my course. But constantly, at every headland, I found the water sweet and clear, and we were carried eastwards very powerfully towards the two straits already mentioned; I then conjectured, that the currents and the overwhelming mountains of water which rushed into these straits with such an awful roaring, arose from the contest between the fresh water and the sea. The fresh water struggled with the salt to oppose its entrance, and the salt contended against the fresh in its efforts to gain a passage outwards. And I formed the conjecture, that at one time there was a continuous neck of land from the island of Trinidad and with the land of Garcia, where the two straits now are, as your Highnesses will see, by the drawing which accompanies this letter. I passed out by this northern strait, and found the fresh water come even there; and when, by the aid of the wind, I was enabled to proceed, I remarked, while on one of the watery billows which I have described, that in the channel, the water on the inner side of the current was fresh, and on the outside salt.

---

no pude volver por la poblacion adonde yo habia estado, por causa de las corrientes que me habian desviado della, y siempre en todo cabo hallaba el agua dulce y clara, y que me llevaba al Oriente muy recio fácia las dos bocas que arriba dije, y entonces conjeture que los hilos de la corriente, y aquellas lomas que salian y entraban en estas bocas con aquel rugir tan fuerte que era pelea del agua dulce con la salada. La dulce empujaba á la otra porque no entrase, y la salada porque la otra no saliese; y conjeturé que allí donde son estas dos bocas que algun tiempo seria tierra continua á la Isla de la Trinidad con la tierra de Gracia, como podrán ver vuestras Altezas por la pintura de lo que con esta les envio. Salí yo por esta boca del Norte y hallé quel agua dulce siempre vencia, y cuando pasé, que fue con fuerza de viento, estando en una de aquellas lomas, hallé en aquellos hilos de la parte de dentro el agua dulce, y de fuera salada.

When I sailed from Spain to the Indies, I found, that as soon as I had passed a hundred leagues westward of the Azores, there was a very great change in the sky and the stars, in the temperature of the air, and in the water of the sea; and I have been very diligent in observing these things. I remarked, that from north to south, in traversing these hundred leagues from the said islands, the needle of the compass, which hitherto had turned towards the north-east, turned a full quarter of the wind to the north-west, and this took place from the time when we reached that line. At the same time an appearance was presented, as if the sea shore had been transplanted thither, for we found the sea covered all over with a sort of weed, resembling pine branches, and with fruits like that of the mastic tree, so thick, that on my first voyage I thought it was a reef, and that the ships could not avoid running aground; but until I reached this line, I did not meet with a single bough. I also observed, that at this point the sea was very smooth, and that though the wind was rough, the ships never rolled. I likewise found, that within the same line, towards the west, the temperature was always mild, and that it did not vary summer or winter.

Cuando yo navegué de España á las Indias fallo luego en pasando cien leguas á Poniente de los Azores grandísimo mudamiento en el cielo é en las estrellas, y en la temperancia del aire, y en las aguas de la mar, y en esto he tenido mucha diligencia en la experiencia.

Fallo que de Septentrion en Austro, pasando las dichas cien leguas de las dichas islas, que luego en las agujas de marear, que fasta entonces nordesteaban, noruestean una cuarta de viento todo entero, y esto es en allegando allí á aquella línea, como quien traspone una cuesta, asimesmo fallo la mar toda llena de yerba de una calidad que parece ramitos de pino y muy cargada de fruta como de lantisco, y es tan espesa que al primer viage pensé que era bajo, y que daria en seco con los navíos, y hasta llegar con esta raya no se falla un solo ramito : fallo tambien en llegando allí la muy suave y llana, y bien que vente recio nunca se levanta. Asimismo hallo dentro de la dicha raya hácia Poniente la temperancia del cielo muy suave, y

While I was there, I observed that the north star described a circle five degrees in diameter; that when its satellites[20] are on the right side, then the star was at its lowest point, and from this point it continues rising until it reaches the left side, where it is also at five degrees, and then again it sinks until it at length returns to the right side. In this voyage I proceeded immediately from Spain to the island of Madeira, thence to the Canaries, and then to the Cape Verde isles, and from the Cape Verde isles I sailed southwards, even below the equinoctial line, as I have already described. When I reached the parallel of Sierra Leone, in Guinea, I found the heat so intense, and the rays of the sun so fierce, that I thought that we should have been burnt; and although it rained and the sky was heavy with clouds, I still suffered the same oppression, until our Lord was pleased to grant me a favourable wind, giving me an opportunity of sailing to the west, so that I reached a latitude where I experienced, as I have already said, a change in the temperature. Immediately upon my reaching this line, the temperature of the sky became very mild, and the more I advanced, the more this mildness in-

---

no discrepa de la cantidad quier sea invierno, quier sea en verano. Cuando allí estoy hallo que la estrella del Norte escribe un círculo el cualo tiene en el diámetro cinco grados, y estando las guardas en el brazo derecho estonces está la estrella en el mas bajo, y se vá alzando fasta que llega albrazo izquierdo, y estonces está cinco grados, y de allí se vá abajando fasta llegar á volver otra vez al brazo derecho.

Yo allegué agora de España á la Isla de la Madera, y de allí á Canaria, y dende á las Islas de Cabo Verde, de adonde cometí el viage para navegar al Austro fasta debajo la linea equinocial, como ya dije : allegado á estar en derecho con el paralelo que pasa por la Sierra Leoa en Guinea, fallo tan grande ardor, y los rayos del sol tan calientes que pensaba de quemar, y bien que lloviese y el cielo fuese muy turbado siempre yo estaba en esta fatiga, fasta que nuestro Señor proveyó de buen viento y á mi puso en voluntad que yo

[20] He doubtless alludes to the constellation of Ursa Minor.

ffortort632

creased; but I did not find the positions of the stars correspond with these effects. I remarked at this place, that when night came on, the polar star was five degrees high, and then the satellites were over head; afterwards, at midnight, I found the north star elevated ten degrees, and when morning was advancing, the satellites were fifteen feet below. I found the smoothness of the sea continue, but not so the weeds; as to the polar star, I watched it with great wonder, and devoted many nights to a careful examination of it with the quadrant, and I always found that the lead and line fell to the same point. I look upon this as something new, and I think my opinion will be supported by that of others, that it is a short distance for so great a change to take place in the temperature. I have always read, that the world comprising the land and the water was spherical, as is testified by the investigations of Ptolemy, and others, who have proved it by the eclipses of the moon, and other observations made from east to west, as well as by the elevation of the pole from north to south. But I have now seen so much irregularity, as I have

navegase al Occidente con este esfuerzo, que en llegando á la raya de que yo dije que allí fallaria mudamiento en la temperancia. Despues que yo emparejé á estar en derecho de esta raya luego falle la temperancia del cielo muy suave, y cuanto mas andaba adelante mas multiplicaba; mas no hallé conforme á esto las estrellas.

Fallé allí que en anocheciendo tenia yo la estrella del Norte alta cinco grados, y estonces las guardas estaban encima de la cabeza, y despues á la media noche fallaba la estrella alta diez grados, y en amaneciendo que las guardas estaban en los pies quince.

La suavelidad de la mar fallé conforme, mas no en la yerba: en esto de la estrella del Norte tomé grande admiracion, y por esto muchas noches con mucha diligencia tornaba yo á repricar la vista della con el cuadrante, y siempre fallé que caía el plomo y hilo á un punto.

Por cosa nueva tengo yo esto, y podrá ser que será tenida que en poco espacio haga tanta diferencia el cielo.

Yo siempre lei que el mundo, tierra é agua era esférico é las aualready described, that I have come to another conclusion respecting the earth, namely, that it is not round as they describe, but of the form of a pear, which is very round except where the stalk grows, at which part it is most prominent; or like a round ball, upon one part of which is a prominence like a woman's nipple, this protrusion being the highest and nearest the sky, situated under the equinoctial line, and at the eastern extremity of this sea,—I call that the eastern extremity, where the land and the islands end. In confirmation of my opinion, I revert to the arguments which I have above detailed respecting the line, which passes from north to south, a hundred leagues westward of the Azores; for in sailing thence westward, the ships went on rising smoothly towards the sky, and then the weather was felt to be milder, on account of which mildness, the needle shifted one point of the compass; the further we went, the more the needle moved to the north-west, this elevation producing the variation of the circle, which the north star describes with its satellites; and the nearer I approached the equinoctial line,

---

toridades y esperencias que Tolomeo y todos los otros escribieron de este sitio, daban é amostraban para ello así por eclipses de la luna y otras demostraciones que hacen de Oriente fasta Occidente, como de la elevacion del polo de Septentrion en Austro. Agora ví tanta disformidad, como ya dije, y por esto me puse á tener esto del mundo, y fallé que no era redondo en la forma que escriben; salvo que es de la forma de una pera que sea toda muy redonda, salvo allí donde tiene el pezon que allí tiene mas alto, ó como quien tiene una pelota muy redonda, y en un lugar della fuese como una teta de muger allí puesta, y que esta parte deste pezon sea la mas alta é mas propinca al cielo, y sea debajo la línea equinocial, y en esta mar Océana en fin del Oriente, llamo yo fin de Oriente, adonde acaba toda la tierra é islas, é para esto allego todas las razones sobre-escriptas de la raya que pasa al Occidente delas islas de los Azores cien leguas de Septentrion en Austro, que en pasando de allí al Poniente ya van los navíos alzándose hácia el cielo suavemente, y entonces se goza de mas suave temperancia y se muda the more they rose, and the greater was the difference between these stars and their circles. Ptolemy and the other philosophers, who have written upon the globe, thought that it was spherical, believing that this hemisphere was round as well as that in which they themselves dwelt, the centre of which was in the island of Arin,[21] which is under the equinoctial line between the Arabian Gulf and the Gulf of Persia; and the circle passes over Cape St. Vincent, in Portugal, westward, and eastward, by Cangara and the Seras,[22] in which hemisphere I make no difficulty as to its being a perfect sphere as they describe; but this western half of the world, I maintain, is like the half of a very round pear, having a raised projection for the stalk, as I have already described, or like a woman's nipple on a round ball. Ptolemy and the others who have written upon the globe, had no information respecting this part of the world, which was then unexplored; they only established their arguments with respect to their own hemisphere, which, as I have already said, is half of a

---

el aguja del marear por causa de la suavidad desa cuarta de viento, y cuanto mas va adelante é alzándose mas noruestea, y esta altura causa el desvariar del circulo que escribe la estrella del Norte con las guardas, y cuanto mas pasare junto con la línea equinocial, mas se subirán en alto, y mas diferencia habrá en las dichas estrellas, y en los circulos dellas. Y Tolomeo y los otros sabios que escribieron de este mundo, creyeron que era esférico, creyendo queste hemisferio que fuese redondo como aquel de allá donde ellos estaban, el cual tiene el centro en la Isla de Arin, qués debajo la linea equinocial entre el sino Arabico y aquel de Persia, y el círculo pasa sobre el Cabo de S. Vicente en Portugal por el Poniente, y pasa en Oriente por Cangara y por las Seras, en el cual hemisferio no hago yo que hay ninguna dificultad, salvo que sea esférico redondo como ellos dicen : mas este otro digo que es como sería la mitad de la pera bien redonda, la cual toviese el pezon alto como yo dije, ó como una teta de muger en una pelota redonda, así que desta media parte non hobo noticia Tolomeo ni los otros quo escribieron del mundo por

[21] It is difficult to conjecture what island he alludes to.
[22] Japan and China.

perfect sphere.   And now that your Highnesses have commissioned me to make this voyage of discovery, the truths which I
have stated are evidently proved, because in this voyage, when
I was off the island of Hargin,[23] and its vicinity, which is twenty
degrees to the north of the equinoctial line, I found the people
are black, and the land very much burnt; and when after that
I went to the Cape Verde islands, I found the people there
much darker still, and the more southward we went, the
more they approach the extreme of blackness ; so that when I
reached the parallel of Sierra Leone, where, as night came
on, the north star rose five degrees, the people there were ex-
cessively black ; and as I sailed westward, the heat became
extreme.   But after I had passed the meridian, or line which
I have already described, I found the climate become gradu-
ally more temperate; so that when I reached the island of
Trinidad, where the north star rose five degrees as night
came on, there, and in the land of Gracia, I found the temperature exceedingly mild ; the fields and the foliage likewise
were remarkably fresh and green, and as beautiful as the

---

ser muy ignoto ; solamente hicieron raiz sobre el hemisferio, adonde
ellos estaban ques redondo esférico, como arriba dije. Y agora que
vuestras Altezas lo han mandado navegar y buscar y descobrir, se
amuestra evidentísimo, porque estando yo en este viage al Septentrion veinte grados de la línea equinocial, allí era en derecho de
Hargin, é de aquellas tierras : é allí es la gente negra é la tierra
muy quemada, y despues que fuí á las Islas de Cabo Verde, allí en
aquellas tierras es la gente mucho mas negra, y cuanto mas bajo se
van al Austro tanto mas llegan al extremo, en manera que allí en
derecho donde yo estaba, qués la Sierra Leoa, adonde se me alzaba
la estrella del Norte en anocheciendo cinco grados, allí es la gente
negra en extrema cantidad, y despues que de allí navegue al Occidente tan extremos calores ; y pasada la raya de que yo dije
fallé multiplicar la temperancia, andando en tanta cantidad que
cuando yo llegué á la isla de la Trinidad, adonde la estrella del
Norte en anocheciendo tambien se me alzaba cinco grados, allí y

[23] Arguin, off the west coast of Africa.

gardens of Valencia in April. The people there are very graceful in form, less dark than those whom I had before seen in the Indies, and wear their hair long and smooth; they are also more shrewd, intelligent, and courageous. The sun was then in the sign of Virgo, over our heads and theirs; therefore, all this must proceed from the extreme blandness of the temperature, which arises, as I have said, from this country being the most elevated in the world, and the nearest to the sky. On these grounds, therefore, I affirm, that the globe is not spherical, but that there is the difference in its form which I have described; the which is to be found in this hemisphere, at the point where the Indies meet the ocean, the extremity of the hemisphere being below the equinoctial line. And a great confirmation of this is, that when our Lord made the sun, the first light appeared in the first point of the east, where the most elevated point of the globe is; and although it was the opinion of Aristotle, that the antarctic pole, or the land which is below it, was the highest part of the world, and the nearest to the heavens, other philosophers oppose him, and say, that the highest part was below

---

en la tierra de Gracia hallé temperancia suavísima, y las tierras y árboles muy verdes, y tan hermosos como en Abril en las huertas de Valencia; y la gente de allí de muy linda estatura, y blancos mas que otros que haya visto en las Indias, é los cabellos muy largos é llanos, é gente mas astuta é de mayor ingenio, é no cobardes. Entonces era el sol en Virgen encima de nuestras cabezas é suyas, ansí que todo esto procede por la suavísima temperancia que allí es, la cual procede por estar mas alto en el mundo mas cerca del aire que cuento; y así me afirmo quel mundo no es esférico, salvo que tiene esta diferencia que ya dije: la cual es en este hemisferio adonde caen las Indias é la mar Oceana, y el extremo dello es debajo la línea equinocial, y ayuda mucho á esto que sea ansí, porque el sol cuando nuestro Señor lo hizo fue en el primer punto de Oriente, ó la primera luz fue aquí en Oriente, allí donde es el extremo de la altura deste mundo; y bien quel parecer de Aristotel fuese que el Polo antártico ó la tierra ques debajo dél sea la mas alta parte en el the arctic pole, by which reasoning it appears, that they understood, that one part of the world ought to be loftier, and nearer the sky, than the other; but it never struck them that it might be under the equinoctial, in the way that I have said, which is not to be wondered at, because they had no certain knowledge respecting this hemisphere, but merely vague suppositions, for no one has ever gone or been sent to investigate the matter, until your Highnesses sent me to explore both the sea and the land. I found that between the two straits, which, as I have said, face each other in a line from north to south, is a distance of twenty-six leagues; and there can be no mistake in this calculation, because it was made with the quadrant. I also find, that from these two straits on the west up to the above-mentioned gulf, to which I gave the name of the Gulf of Pearls,[24] there are sixty-eight leagues of four miles to the league, which is the reckoning we are accustomed to make at sea; from this gulf the water runs constantly with great impetuosity towards the east, and this is the cause why, in these two straits, there is so fierce a tur-

---

mundo, y mas propincua al cielo, otros sabios le impugnan diciendo que es esta ques debajo del ártico, por las cuales razones parece que entendian que una parte deste mundo debia de ser mas propincua y noble al cielo que otra, y no cayeron en esto que sea debajo del equinocial por la forma que ye dijo, y no es maravilla porque deste hemisferio non se hobiese noticia cierta, salvo muy liviana y por argumento, porque nadie nunca lo ha andado ni enviado á buscar, hasta agora que vuestras Altezas le mandaron explorar é descubrir la mar y la tierra.

Fallo que de allí de estas dos bocas, las cuales como yo dije estan frontero por línea de Septentrion en Austro, que haya de la una á la otra veinte y seis leguas, y no pudo haber en ello yerro porque se midieron con cuadrante, y destas dos bocas de occidente fasta el golfo que yo dije, al cual llamé de las Perlas, que son sesenta é ocho leguas de cuatro millas dada una como acostumbramos en la mar, y que de allá de este golfo corre de contino el agua muy fuerte

[24] The innermost gulf within the Gulf of Paria.

moil from the fresh water encountering the water of the sea. In the southern strait, which I named the Serpent's Mouth, I found that towards evening the polar star was nearly at five degrees elevation; and in the northern, which I called the Dragon's Mouth, it was at an elevation of nearly seven degrees. The before-mentioned Gulf of Pearls is to the west of the[25]   of Ptolemy, nearly three thousand nine hundred miles, which make nearly seventy equinoctial degrees, reckoning fifty-six miles and two thirds to a degree. The Holy Scriptures record, that our Lord made the earthly paradise, and planted in it the tree of life, and thence springs a fountain from which the four principal rivers in the world take their source; namely, the Ganges in India, the Tigris, and Euphrates in[26]   which rivers divide a chain of mountains, and forming Mesopotamia, flow thence into Persia,—and the Nile, which rises in Ethiopia, and falls into the sea at Alexandria.

---

hácia el oriente ; y que por esto tienen aquel combate estas dos bocas con la salada. En esta boca de Austro, á que yo llamé de la Sierpe, fallé en anocheciendo que yo tenia la estrella del Norte alta cuasi cinco grados, y en aquella otra del Septentrion, á que yo llamé del Drago, eran cuasi siete, y fallo quel dicho Golfo de las Perlas está occidental al Occidente de el   de Tolomeo cuasi tres mil é novecientas millas, que son cuasi setenta grados equinociales, contando por cada uno cincuenta y seis millas é dos tercios.

La Sacra Escriptura testifica que nuestro Señor hizo al Paraiso terrenal, y en él puso el Arbol de la vida, y del sale una fuente de donde resultan en este mundo cuatro rios principales : Ganges en India, Tigris y Eufrates en   los cuales apartan la sierra y hacen la Mesopotamia y van á tener en Persia, y el Nilo que nace en Etiopa y va en la mar en Alejandría.

[25] A similar gap in the original. In all probability " first meridian" or some such words, are omitted.

[26] A similar gap in the original, which would seem to want the words " Asiatic Turkey."

I do not find, nor have ever found, any account by the
Romans or Greeks, which fixes in a positive manner the
site of the terrestrial paradise, neither have I seen it given
in any mappe-monde, laid down from authentic sources.
Some placed it in Ethiopia, at the sources of the Nile,
but others, traversing all these countries, found neither
the temperature nor the altitude of the sun correspond with
their ideas respecting it; nor did it appear that the overwhelming waters of the deluge had been there.   Some pagans
pretended to adduce arguments to establish that it was in the
Fortunate Islands, now called the Canaries, etc.

St. Isidore, Bede, Strabo,[27] and the master of scholastic
history,[28] with St. Ambrose, and Scotus, and all the learned
theologians, agree that the earthly paradise is in the east, etc.

I have already described my ideas concerning this hemisphere and its form, and I have no doubt, that if I could
pass below the equinoctial line, after reaching the highest
point of which I have spoken, I should find a much milder

Yo no hallo ni jamas he hallado escriptura de Latinos ni de
Griegos que certificadamente diga el sitio en este mundo del Paraiso
terrenal, ni visto en ningun mapamundo, salvo, situado con autoridad de argumento.   Algunos le ponian allí donde son las fuentes
del Nilo en Etiopia ; mas otros anduvieron todas estas tierras y no
hallaron conformidad dello en la temperancia del cielo, en la altura
hácia el cielo, porque se pudiese comprehender que el era allí, ni
que las aguas del diluvio hobiesen llegado allí, las cuales subieron
encima, &c.   Algunos gentiles quisieron decir por argumentos, que
el era en las islas Fortunatas que son las Canarias, &c.

S. Isidro y Beda y Strabo, y el Maestro de la historia escolástica, y San Ambrosio, y Scoto, y todos los sanos teólogos conciertan
quel Paraiso terrenal es en el Oriente, &c.

Ya dije lo que yo hallaba deste hemisferio y de la hechura, y
creo que si yo pasara por debajo de la línea equinocial que en
llegando allí en esto mas alto que fallara muy mayor temperancia,

[27] Walafried Strabus, Abbé of Reichenau, in Baden.
[28] Petrus Comestor, who wrote the " Historia Scholastica."

temperature, and a variation in the stars and in the water; not that I suppose that elevated point to be navigable, nor even that there is water there; indeed, I believe it is impossible to ascend thither, because I am convinced that it is the spot of the earthly paradise, whither no one can go but by God's permission; but this land which your Highnesses have now sent me to explore, is very extensive, and I think there are many other countries in the south, of which the world has never had any knowledge.

I do not suppose that the earthly paradise is in the form of a rugged mountain, as the descriptions of it have made it appear, but that it is on the summit of the spot, which I have described as being in the form of the stalk of a pear; the approach to it from a distance must be by a constant and gradual ascent; but I believe that, as I have already said, no one could ever reach the top; I think also, that the water I have described may proceed from it, though it be far off, and that stopping at the place which I have just left, it forms this lake. There are great indications of this being the terrestrial paradise, for its site coincides with the opinion of the holy and wise theologians whom I have mentioned;

---

y diversidad en las estrellas y en las aguas ; no porque yo crea que allí donde es el altura del extremo sea navegable ni agua, ni que se pueda subir allá, porque creo que allí es el Paraiso terrenal adonde no puede llegar nadie, salvo por voluntad Divina ; y creo que esta tierra que agora mandaron descubrir vuestras Altezas sea grandísima y haya otras muchas en el Austro de que jamas se hobo noticia.

Yo no tomo quel Paraise terrenal sea en forma de montaña aspera como el escrebir dello nos amuestra, salvo quel sea en el colmo allí donde dije la figura del pezon de la pera, y que poco á poco andando hácía allí desde muy lejos se va subiendo á él ; y creo que nadie no podria llegar al colmo como yo dije, y creo que pueda salir de allí esa agua, bien que sea lejos y venga á parar allí donde yo vengo, y faga este lago. Grandes indicios son estos del Paraiso terrenal, porquel sitio es conforme á la opinion de estos santos é and moreover, the other evidences agree with the supposition, for I have never either read or heard of fresh water coming in so large a quantity, in close conjunction with the water of the sea; the idea is also corroborated by the blandness of the temperature; and if the water of which I speak, does not proceed from the earthly paradise, it appears to be still more marvellous, for I do not believe that there is any river in the world so large or so deep.

When I left the Dragon's Mouth, which is the northernmost of the two straits which I have described, and which I so named on the day of our Lady of August, I found that the sea ran so strongly to the westward, that between the hour of mass, when I weighed anchor, and the hour of complines, I made sixty-five leagues of four miles each; and not only was the wind not violent, but on the contrary very gentle, which confirmed me in the conclnsion, that in sailing southward, there is a continuous ascent, while there is a corresponding descent towards the north.

I hold it for certain, that the waters of the sea move from east to west with the sky, and that in passing this track, they

sanos teólogos, y asimismo las señales son muy conformes, que yo jamas leí ni oí que tanta cantidad de agua dulce fuese así adentro é vecina con la salada; y en ello ayuda asimismo la suavísimà temperancia, y si de allí del Paraiso no sale, parece aun mayor maravilla, porque no creo que se sepa en el mundo de rio tan grande y tan fondo.

Despues que yo salí de la boca del Dragon, ques la una de las dos aquella del Septentrion, á la cual así puse nombre, el dia siguiente, que fue dia de Nuestra Señora de Agosto, fallé que corria tanto la mar al Poniente, que despues de hora de misa que entré en camino, anduve fasta hora de completas sesenta y cinco leguas de cuatro millas cada una, y el viento no era demasiado, salvo muy suave; y esto ayuda el cognoscimiento que de allí yendo al Austro se va mas alto, y andando hácia el Septentrion, como entonces, se va descendiendo.

Muy conoscido tengo que las aguas de la mar llevan su curso de hold a more rapid course, and have thus carried away large tracts of land, and that from hence has resulted this great number of islands; indeed, these islands themselves afford an additional proof of it, for all of them, without exception, run lengthwise from west to east, and from the north west to the south east, which is in a directly contrary direction to the said winds; furthermore, that these islands should possess the most costly productions, is to be accounted for by the mild temperature, which comes to them from heaven, since these are the most elevated parts of the world. It is true, that in some parts, the waters do not appear to take this course, but this occurs in certain spots, where they are obstructed by land, and hence they appear to take different directions.

Pliny writes that the sea and land together form a sphere, but that the ocean forms the greatest mass, and lies uppermost, while the earth is below and supports the ocean, and that the two afford a mutual support to each other, as the kernel of a nut is confined by its shell. The master of scholastic history, in commenting upon Genesis, says, that the waters are not very extensive; and that although

---

Oriente á Occidente con los cielos, y que allí en esta comarca cuando pasan llevan mas veloce camino, y por esto han comido tanta parte de la tierra, porque por eso son acá tantas islas, y ellas mismas hacen desto testimonio, porque todas á una mano son largas de Poniente á Levante, y Norueste é Sueste ques un poco mas alto é bajo, y angostas de Norte á Sur, y Nordeste Sudueste, que son en contrario de los otros dichos vientos, y aquí en ellas todas nascen cosas preciosas por la suave temperancia que les procede del cielo por estar hácia el mas alto del mundo. Verdad es que parece en algunos lugares que las aguas no hagan este curso; mas esto no es, salvo particularmente en algunos lugares donde alguna tierra le está al encuentro, y hace parecer que andan diversos caminos.

Plinio escribe que la mar é la tierra hace todo una esfera, y pone questa mar Oceana sea la mayor cantidad del agua, y está hácia el cielo, y que la tierra sea debajo y que le sostenga, y mezclado es uno con otro como el amago de la nuez con una tela gorda que va abrawhen they were first created they covered the earth, they were yet vaporous like a cloud, and that afterwards they became condensed, and occupied but small space, and in this notion Nicolas de Lira agrees. Aristotle says that the world is small, and the water very limited in extent, and that it is easy to pass from Spain to the Indies; and this is confirmed by Avenruyz,[29] and by the Cardinal Pedro de Aliaco, who, in supporting this opinion, shows that it agrees with that of Seneca, and says that Aristotle had been enabled to gain information respecting the world by means of Alexander the Great, and Seneca by means of Nero, and Pliny through the Romans; all of them having expended large sums of money, and employed a vast number of people, in diligent inquiry concerning the secrets of the world, and in spreading abroad the knowledge thus obtained. The said cardinal allows to these writers greater authority than to Ptolemy, and other Greeks and Arabs; and in confirmation of their opinion concerning the small quantity of water on the surface of the globe,

---

zado en ello. El Maestro de la Historia escolástica sobre el Genesis dice que las aguas son muy pocas, que bien que cuando fueron criadas que cobijasen toda la tierra que entonces eran vaporables en manera de niebla, y que despues que fueron sólidas é juntadas que ocuparon muy poco lugar, y en esto concierta Nicolao de Lira. El Aristotel dice que este mundo es pequeño y es el agua muy poca, y que facilmente se puede pasar de España á las Indias, y esto confirma el Avenruyz y le alega el Cardenal Pedro de Aliaco, autorizando este decir y aquel de Séneca, el cual conforma con estos diciendo que Aristoteles pudo saber muchos secretos del mundo á causa de Alejandro Magno, y Séneca á causa de Cesar Nero y Plinio por respecto de los Romanos, los cuales todos gastaron dineros é gente, y pusieron mucha diligencia en saber los secretos del mundo y darlos á entender á los pueblos ; el cual Cardenal da á estos grande autoridad mas que á Tolomeo ni á otros Griegos ni Arabes, y á confirmacion de decir quel agua sea poca y quel cubi-

[29] Averrhóes, an Arabian philosopher of the twelfth century.

and the limited amount of land covered by that water, in comparison of what had been related on the authority of Ptolemy and his disciples, he finds a passage in the third book of Esdras, where that sacred writer says, that of seven parts of the world six are discovered, and the other is covered with water. The authority of the third and fourth books of Esdras is also confirmed by holy persons, such as St. Augustin, and St. Ambrose in his *Exameron*, where he says,—" Here my son Jesus shall first come, and here my son Christ shall die !" These holy men say that Esdras was a prophet as well as Zacharias, the father of St. John, and *El Braso*[30] Simon; authorities which are also quoted by Francis de Mairones.[31] With respect to the dryness of the land, experience has shown that it is greater than is commonly believed; and this is no wonder, for the further one goes the more one learns. I now return to my subject of the land of Gracia, and of the river and lake found there, which latter might more properly be called a sea; for a lake is but a small expanse of water, which,

---

erto del mundo della sea poco, al respecto de lo que se decia por autoridad de Tolomeo y de sus secuaces : á esto trae una autoridad de Esdras del 3º. libro suyo, adonde dice que de siete partes del mundo las seis son descubiertas y la una es cubierta de agua, la cual autoridad es aprobada por Santos, los cuales dan autoridad al 3º. é 4º. libro de Esdras, ansí como es S. Agustin é S. Ambrosio en su exameron, adonde alega allí vendrá mi hijo Jesus é morira mi hijo Cristo, y dicen que Esdrás fue Profeta, y asimismo Zacarías, padre de S. Juan, y el braso Simon ; las cuales autoridades tambien alega Francisco de Mairones: en cuanto en esto del enjuto de la tierra mucho se ha experimentado ques mucho mas de lo quel vulgo crea; y no es maravilla, porque andando mas mas se sabe.

Torno á mi propósito de la tierra de Gracia y rio y lago que allí fallé, atan grande que mas se le puede llamar mar que lago, porque

[30] This expression is described by the ancient copyist of the letter as being " badly written."

[31] A Scotist of the fourteenth century, surnamed " Doctor illuminatus et acutus."

when it becomes great, deserves the name of a sea, just as we speak of the Sea of Galilee and the Dead Sea; and I think that if the river mentioned does not proceed from the terrestrial paradise, it comes from an immense tract of land situated in the south, of which no knowledge has been hitherto obtained. But the more I reason on the subject, the more satisfied I become that the terrestrial paradise is situated in the spot I have described; and I ground my opinion upon the arguments and authorities already quoted. May it please the Lord to grant your Highnesses a long life, and health and peace to follow out so noble an investigation; in which I think our Lord will receive great service, Spain considerable increase of its greatness, and all Christians much consolation and pleasure, because by this means the name of our Lord will be published abroad.

In all the countries visited by your Highnesses' ships, I have caused a high cross to be fixed upon every headland, and have proclaimed, to every nation that I have discovered, the lofty estate of your Hignesses, and of your court in Spain. I also tell them all I can respecting our holy faith and of the belief in the holy mother Church, which has its members in

---

lago es lugar de agua, y en seyendo grande se dice mar, como se dijo á la mar de Galilea y al mar Muerto, y digo que sino procede del Paraiso terrenal que viene este rio y procede de tierra infinita pues al Austro, de la cual fasta agora no se ha habido noticia, mas yo muy asentado tengo en el anima que allí adonde dije es el Paraiso terrenal, y descanso sobre las razones y autoridades sobre-escriptas.

Plega á nuestro Señor de dar mucha vida y salud y descanso á vuestras Altezas para que puedan proseguir esta tan noble empresa, en la cual me parece que rescibe nuestro Señor mucho servicio, y la España crece de mucha grandeza, y todos los Cristianos mucha consolacion y placer, porque aquí se divulgará el nombre de nuestro Señor ; y en todas las tierras adonde los navíos de vuestras Altezas van, y en todo cabo mando plantar una alta cruz, y á toda la gente que hallo notifico el estado de vuestras Altezas y como su asiento es en España, y les digo de nuestra santa fe todo lo que yo puedo, y all the world; and I speak to them also of the courtesy and nobleness of all Christians, and of the faith they have in the Holy Trinity. May it please the Lord to forgive those who have calumniated and still calumniate this excellent enterprise, and oppose and have opposed its advancement, without considering how much glory and greatness will accrue from it to your Highnesses throughout all the world. They cannot state anything in disparagement of it, except its expense, and that I have not immediately sent back the ships loaded with gold. They speak this without considering the shortness of the time, and how many difficulties there are to contend with; and that every year there are individuals who singly earn by their deserts out of your Majesties' own household, more revenue than would cover the whole of this expense. Nor do they remember that the princes of Spain have never gained possession of any land out of their own country, until now that your Highnesses have become the masters of another world, where our holy faith may become so much increased, and whence such stores of wealth may be derived; for although we have not sent home ships laden with gold, we have, nevertheless,

---

de la creencia de la Santa Madre Iglesia, la cual tiene sus miembros en todo el mundo, y les digo la policia y nobleza de todos los Cristianos, y la fe que en la Santa Trinidad tienen; y plega á nuestro Señor de tirar de memoria á las personas que han impugnado y impugnan tan excelente empresa, y impiden y impidieron porque no vaya adelante, sin considerar cuanta honra y grandeza es del Real Estado da vuestras Altezas en todo el mundo ; no saben que entreponer á maldecir de esto, salvo que se hace gasto en ello, y porque luego no enviaron los navíos cargados de oro sin considerar la brevedad del tiempo y tantos inconvenientes como acá se han habido, y no considerar que en Castilla en casa de vuestras Altezas salen cada año personas que por su merecimiento ganaron en ella mas de renta cada uno dellos mas de lo ques necesario que se gaste en esto ; ansimesmo sin considerar que ningunos Príncipes de España jamas ganaron tierra alguna fuera della, salvo agora que vuestras Altezas tienen acá otro mundo, de adonde puede ser tan sent satisfactory samples, both of gold and of other valuable commodities, by which it may be judged that in a short time large profit may be derived. Neither do they take into consideration the noble spirit of the princes of Portugal, who so long ago carried into execution the exploration of Guinea, and still follow it up along the coast of Africa, in which one-half of the population of the country has been employed, and yet the King is more determined on the enterprise than ever. The Lord grant all that I have said, and lead them to think deeply upon what I have written; which is not the thousandth part of what might be written of the deeds of princes who have set their minds upon gaining knowledge, and upon obtaining territory and keeping it.

I say all this, not because I doubt the inclination of your Highnesses to pursue the enterprise while you live,—for I rely confidently on the answers your Highnesses once gave me by word of mouth,—nor because I have seen any change in your Highnesses, but from the fear of what I have heard from those of whom I have been speaking; for I know that water dropping on a stone will at length make a hole. Your

---

acrescentada nuestra santa fe, y de donde se podrán sacar tantos provechos, que bien que no se hayan enviado los navíos cargados de oro, se han enviado suficientes muestras dello y de otras cosas de valor, por donde se puede juzgar que en breve tiempo se podrá haber mucho provecho, y sin mirar el gran corazon de los Príncipes de Portugal que há tanto tiempo que prosiguen la impresa de Guinea, y prosiguen aquella de Africa, adonde han gastado la mitad de la gente de su Reino, y agora está el Rey mas determinado á ello que nunca. Nuestro Señor provea en esto como yo dije, y les ponga en memoria de considerar de todo esto que va escripto, que no es de mil partes la una de lo que yo podria escrebir de cosas de Príncipes que se ocuparon á saber y conquistar y sostener.

Todo esto dije, y no porque crea que la voluntad de vuestras Altezas sea salvo proseguir en ello en cuanto vivan, y tengo por muy firme lo que me respondió vuestras Altezas una vez que por palabra le decir desto, no porque yo hobiese visto mudamiento nin-

Highnesses responded to me with that nobleness of feeling which all the world knows you to possess, and told me to pay no attention to these calumniations; for that your intention was to follow up and support the undertaking, even if nothing were gained by it but stones and sand. Your Highnesses also desired me to be in no way anxious about the expense, for that much greater cost had been incurred on much more trifling matters, and that you considered all the past and future expense as well laid out; for that your Highnesses believed that our holy faith would be increased, and your royal dignity enhanced, and that they were no friends of the royal estate who spoke ill of the enterprise.

And now, during the despatch of the information respecting these lands which I have recently discovered, and where I believe in my soul that the earthly paradise is situated, the "Adelantado" will proceed with three ships, well stocked with provisions, on a further investigation, and will make all the discoveries he can about these parts. Meanwhile, I shall send your Highnesses this letter, accompanied by a drawing

---

guno en vuestras Altezas salvo por temor de lo que yo oia destos que yo digo, y tanto da una gotera de agua en una piedra que le hace un agujero; y vuestras Altezas me respondió con aquel corazon que se sabe en todo el mundo que tienen, y me dijo que no curase de nada de eso, porque su voluntad era de proseguir esta empresa y sostenerla, aunque no fuese sino piedras y peñas, y quel gasto que en ello se hacia que lo tenia en nada, que en otras cosas no tan grandes gastaban mucho mas, y que lo tenian todo por muy bien gastado lo del pasado y lo que se gastase en adelante, porque creian que nuestra santa fe sería acrecentada y su Real Señorío ensanchado, y que no eran amigos de su Real Estado aquellos que les maldecian de esta empresa: y agora entre tanto que vengan á noticia desto destas tierras que agora nuevamente he descubierto, en que tengo asentado en el ánima que allí es el Pàraiso terrenal, irá el Adelantado con tres navíos bien ataviados para ello á ver mas adelante, y descubrirán todo lo que pudieren haciá aquellas partes. Entretanto yo enviaré á vuestras Altezas esta escriptura y la pin-

of the country, and your Majesties will determine on what is
to be done, and give your orders as to how it is your pleasure
that I should proceed: the which, by the aid of the Holy
Trinity, shall be carried into execution with all possible dili-
gence, in the faithful service and to the entire satisfaction of
your Majesties.   Deo Gratias.

---

tura de la tierra, y acordarán lo que en ello se deba facer, y me
enviarán á mandar, y se cumplirá con ayuda de la Santa Trinidad
con toda diligencia en manera que vuestras Altezas sean servidos
y hayan placer.   Deo gracias.

LETTER

Of the Admiral to the (quondam) nurse[1] of the Prince John, written near the end of the year 1500.

MOST virtuous lady: Although it is a novelty for me to complain of the ill-usage of the world, it is, nevertheless, no novelty for the world to practise ill-usage. Innumerable are the contests which I have had with it, and I have resisted all its attacks until now, when I find, that neither strength nor prudence is of any avail to me: it has cruelly reduced me to the lowest ebb. Hope in Him who has created us all is my support: His assistance I have always found near at hand. On one occasion, not long since, He supported me with His Divine arm, saying: " O man of little faith, arise, it is I, be

---

CARTA

Del Almirante al ama (que habia sido) del Principe D. Juan, escrita hacia fines del año 1500.

MUY virtuosa Señora: Si mi queja del mundo es nueva, su uso de maltratar es de muy antiguo. Mil combates me ha dado y á todos resistí fasta agora que no me aprovechó armas ni avisos. Con crueldad me tiene echado al fondo. La esperanza de aquel que crio á todos me sostiene: su socorro fue siempre muy presto. Otra vez, y no de lejos estando yo mas bajo, me levantó con su brazo divino, diciendo: *ó hombre de poca fe, levantate que yo soy, no hayas miedo.* Yo vine con amor tan entrañable á servir á estos Principes, y hé

---

[1] Although Zuñiga says that Doña Maria de Guzman was appointed nurse by Queen Isabella at the birth of Prince John, it is nevertheless certain, that this letter was addressed by Columbus to Doña Juana de la Torres, a great favourite of the queen, sister of Antonio de Torres, who was with the admiral in the second voyage, and who bore the memorial to their Highnesses.

not afraid."[2] I offered myself with such earnest devotion to
the service of these princes, and I have served them with a
fidelity hitherto unequalled and unheard of. God made me
the messenger of the new heaven and the new earth, of which
He spoke in the Apocalypse by St. John, after having spoken
of it by the mouth of Isaiah; and He showed me the spot
where to find it. All proved incredulous; except the Queen
my mistress, to whom the Lord gave the spirit of intelligence
and the necessary courage, and made her the heiress of all,
as a dear and well beloved daughter. I went to take possession of it in her royal name. All wished to cover the
ignorance in which they were sunk, by enumerating the in-
conveniences and expense of the proposed enterprise. Her
Highness held the contrary opinion, and supported it with all
her power. Seven years passed away in deliberations, and
nine have been spent in accomplishing things truly memorable, and worthy of being preserved in the history of man.

I have now reached that point, that there is no man so vile
but thinks it his right to insult me. The day will come when

---

servido de servicio de que jamas se oyó ni vido. Del nuevo cielo
y tierra que decia nuestro Señor por S. Juan en el Apocalipse,
despues de dicho por boca de Isaías, me hizo dello mensagero, y
amostró en cual parte. En todos hobo incredulidad, y á la Reina
mi Señora dió dello el espíritu de inteligencia y esfuerzo grande, y
lo hizo de todo heredera como á cara y muy amada hija. La posesion de todo esto fuí yo á tomar en su Real nombre. La igno-
rancia en que habian estado todos quisieron enmendallo traspasando
el poco saber á fablar en inconvenientes y gastos. Su Alteza lo
aprobaba al contrario, y lo sostuvo fasta que pudo. Siete años se
pasaron en la platica y nueve ejecutando cosas muy señaladas y
dignas de memoria se pasaron en este tiempo: de todo no se fizo
concepto. Llegué yo y estoy que non ha nadie tan vil que no pi_

[2] This is related by his son Don Ferdinand, in cap. 84 of his history,
and is more amply described in the letter addressed by Columbus to the
sovereigns, describing his fourth voyage. It took place the day after
Christmas day, 1499.

the world will reckon it a virtue to him who has not given his consent to their abuse. If I had plundered the Indies, even to the country where is the fabled altar of St. Peter's, and had given them all to the Moors, they could not have shown towards me more bitter enmity than they have done in Spain. Who would believe such things in a country where there has always been so much magnanimity? I desire earnestly to clear myself of this affair, if only I had the means of doing so face to face with my queen. The support which I have found in our Lord, and in her Highness, has made me persevere; and I would fain cause her to forget a little the griefs which death has occasioned her.[3] I undertook another voyage to the new heavens and new earth, which had been hidden hitherto; and if these are not appreciated in Spain, like the other parts of the Indies, it is not at all wonderful, since it is to my labours that they are indebted for them. The Holy Spirit encompassed St. Peter, and the rest of the twelve, who all had conflicts here below; they wrought many

---

ense de ultrajarme. Por virtud se contará en el mundo á quien puede no consentillo. Si yo robara las Indias ó tierra que san face* en ello de que agora es la fabla del altar de S. Pedro, y las diera á los moros, no pudieran en España amostrarme mayor enemiga. Quién creyera tal adonde hobo siempre tanta nobleza ? Yo mucho quisiera despedir del negocio si fuera honesto para con mi Reina : el esfuerzo de nuestro Señor y de su Alteza fizo que yo continuase, y por aliviarle algo de los enojos en que á causa de la muerte estaba, cometi viaje nuevo al nuevo cielo é mundo, que fasta entonces estaba en oculto, y sino es tenido allí en estima, así como los otros de las Indias, no es maravilla porque salió á parecer de mi industria. A S. Pedro abrasó el Espíritu Santo y con él otros doce, y todos combatieron acá, y los trabajos y fatigas fueron muchas ; en fin de

---

* There is no sense in this expression, nor as it is given in the "Codice Colombo Americano", where it stands thus : "que jaz hase ellas de que," etc.

[3] He refers to the death of Prince John, which occurred in Salamanca, on the fourth of October 1497.

works, they suffered great fatigues, but at last they obtained the victory. I believed that this voyage to Paria would in some degree pacify them, because of the pearls, and the discovery of gold in the island of Española. I left orders for the people to fish for pearls, and collect them together, and made an agreement with them that I should return for them; and I was given to understand that the supply would be abundant.

If I have not written respecting this to their Highnesses, it is because I wished first to render an equally favourable account of the gold; but it has happened with this as with many other things; I should not have lost them, and with them my honour, if I had been only occupied about my own private interests, and had suffered Española to be lost, or even if they had respected my privileges and the treaties. I say the same with regard to the gold which I had then collected, and which I have brought in safety, by Divine grace, after so much loss of life and such excessive fatigues.

In the voyage which I made by way of Paria, I found nearly half the colonists of Española in a state of revolt, and they have made war upon me until now as if I had been a Moor;[4]

---

todo llevaron la victoria. Este viaje de Paria creí que apaciguara algo por las perlas y la fallada del oro en la Española. Las perlas mandé yo ayuntar y pescar á la gente con quien quedó el concierto de mi vuelta por ellas, y á mi comprender á medida de fanega: si yo non lo escribí á SS. AA. fue porque así quisiera haber fecho del oro antes. Esto me salió como otras cosas muchas; no las perdiera ni mi honra si buscara yo mi bien propio y dejara perder la Española, ó se guardaran mis previlegios é asientos. Y otro tanto digo del oro que yo tenia agora junto, que con tantas muertés y trabajos, por virtud divinal, he llegado á perfecto. Cuando yo fuí á Paria fallé cuasi la mitad de la gente en la Española alzados, y me han guerreado fasta agora como á moro, y los indios por otro cabo gra-

[4] After the admiral had discovered the island of Trinidad, he sailed along the coast of Paria, discovered the island of Margarita, and entered the harbour of San Domingo the thirtieth of August 1498, where he found the colony in rebellion, and the Spaniards embroiled in quarrels, both with each other and with the Indians.

while on the other side, I had to contend with the no less cruel Indians. Then arrived Hojeda,[5] and he attempted to put the seal to all these disorders; he said that their Highnesses had sent him, with promises of presents, of immunities, and treaties; he collected a numerous band, for in the whole island of Española, there were few men who were not vagabonds, and there were none who had either wife or children. This Hojeda troubled me much, but he was obliged to retreat, and at his departure he said, that he would return with more ships and men, and reported also, that he had left the queen at the point of death.[6] In the meanwhile, Vincent Yañez came with four caravels; and there were some tumults and suspicions, but no further evil. The Indians reported many other caravels to the cannibals, and in Paria; and afterwards spread the news of the arrival of six other caravels, commanded by a brother of the alcalde; but this was from pure malice; when at last the hope was lost that their Highnesses would send any more ships to the Indies, and we no longer expected them, and when it

---

vemente. En esto vino Hojeda y probó á echar el sello, y dijo que sus Altezas lo enviaban con promesas de dádivas y franquezas y paga: allegó gran cuadrilla, que en toda la Española muy pocos hay, salvo vagabundos y ninguno con muger y fijos. Este Hojeda me trabajó harto y fuele necesario de se ir, y dejó dicho que luego seria de vuelta con mas navíos y gente, y que dejaba la Real persona de la Reina á la muerte. En esto llegó Viceinte Yañez con cuatro carabelas: hobo alboroto y sospechas, mas no daño. Los indios dijeron de otras muchas á los canibales y en Paria, y despues una nueva de seis otras carabelas que traía un hermano del Alcalde, mas fue con malicia, y esto fue ya á la postre cuando ya estaba muy rota la esperanza que sus Altezas hobiesen jamas de enviar navíos á las Indias, ni nos esperarlos, y que vulgarmente decian que su

[5] Alonzo de Hojeda reached Española on the fifth of September 1498.

[6] Roldan was by this time reconciled to the Admiral, and the rebellion was allayed, when Hojeda arrived, making great boast of his favour with bishop Fonseca, Columbus' enemy, and endeavoured to excite fresh animosity against him; but he had to leave Española completely.

was said openly that her Highness (the queen) was dead. At this time, one Adrian attempted a new revolt, as he had done before;[7] but our Lord did not permit his evil designs to succeed. I had determined not to inflict punishment on any person, but his ingratitude obliged me, however regretfully, to abandon this resolution. I should not have acted otherwise with my own brother, if he had sought to assassinate me, and to rob me of the lordship which my sovereigns had given to my keeping. This Adrian, as is now evident, had sent Don Ferdinand to Xaragua, to assemble some of his partisans, and had some discussions with the alcalde, which ended in violence, but all without any good. The alcalde seized him and a part of his band; and in fact, executed justice without my having ordered it. While they were in prison, they were expecting a caravel, in which they hoped to embark; but the news of what had happened to Hojeda, and which I told them, deprived them of the hope that he would arrive in this ship. It is now six months that I have been ready to leave, to bring to their Highnesses the good news of the gold, and to give up the government of these dissolute people, who fear neither

---

Alteza era muerta. Un Adrian en este tiempo probó alzarse otra vez como de antes, mas nuestro Señor no quiso que llegase á efecto su mal propósito. Yo tenia propuesto en mi de no tocar el cabello á nadie, y á este por su ingratitud con lágrimas no se pudo guardar, así como yo lo tenia pensado. A mi hermano no hiciera menos si me quisiera matar y robar el señorío que mi Rey é Reina me tenian dado en guarda. Este Adrian, segun se muestra, tenia enviado á D. Fernando á Jaragua á allegar á algunos sus secuaces, y allá hobo debate con el Alcalde, adonde nació discordia de muerte; mas no llegó á efecto. El Alcalde le prendió y á parte de su cuadrilla; y el caso era que él los justiciaba sin que yo lo proveyere: estovieren presos esperando carabela en que se fuesen: las nuevas de Hojeda que yo dije ficieron perder la esperanza que ya no venia. Seis meses habia que yo estaba despachado para venir á sus Altezas con las buenas nuevas del oro y fuir de gobernar

---

[7] Adrian Mogica, who had been one of the rebels with Roldan.

their king nor queen, but are full of imbecility and malice.
I should have been able to pay every one with six hundred
thousand maravedis, and for this purpose there were four
millions and more of the tithes, without reckoning the third
part of the gold.

Before my departure (from Spain) I have often entreated
their Highnesses to send to these parts, at my expense, some
one charged to administer justice; and since, when I found
the alcalde in a state of revolt, I have besought them afresh
to send at least one of their servants with letters, because I
myself have had so strange a character given to me, that if I
were to build churches or hospitals, they would call them
caves for robbers. Their Highnesses provided for this at last,
but in a manner quite unequal to the urgency of the circumstances; however, let that point rest, since such is their good
pleasure. I remained two years in Spain without being able
to obtain anything for myself, or those who came with me,[8]
but this man has gained for himself a full purse: God knows

---

gente disoluta que no teme á Dios ni á su Rey ni Reina, llena de
achaques y de malicias. A la gente acabara yo de pagar con
seiscientos mil maravedises : y para ello habia cuatro cuentos de
diezmos é alguno sin el tercio del oro. Antes de mi partida supliqué tantas veces á sus Altezas que enviasen allá á mi costa á quien
tuviese cargo de la justicia, y despues que fallé alzado al Alcalde se
lo supliqué de nuevo ó por alguna gente, ó al menos algun criado
con cartas, porque mi fama es tal que aunque yo faga iglesias y
hospitales siempre serán dichas espeluncas para latrones. Prove-
yeron ya al fin, y fue muy al contrario de lo que la negociacion demandaba : vaya en buena hora, pues que es á su grado. Yo estuve
allá dos años sin poder ganar una provision de favor para mí ni por
los que allá fuesen, y este llevó una arca llena : si pararán todas á
su servicio Dios lo sabe. Ya por comienzos hay franquezas por

[8] Columbus returned to Cadiz from his second voyage, on the 11th of
June, 1496. He was well received by the sovereigns, and they gave orders
for preparing the requisites for a third voyage; but the fulfilment of
these orders was delayed by Bishop Fonseca until the 30th of May, 1498.

if all will be employed for His service. Already, to begin with, there is a revenue for twenty years, which is, according to man's calculation, an age; and they gather gold in such abundance, that there are people who, in four hours, have found the equivalent of five marks; but I will speak on this subject more fully hereafter. If their Highnesses would condescend to silence the popular rumours, which have gained credence among those who know what fatigues I have sustained, it would be a real charity; for calumny has done me more injury than the services which I have rendered to their Highnesses, and the care with which I have preserved their property and their government, have done me good; and, by their so doing, I should be re-established in reputation, and spoken of throughout the universe: for the things which I have accomplished are such, that they must gain, day by day, in the estimation of mankind.

In the meanwhile, the commander Bobadilla arrived at St. Domingo,[9] at which time I was at La Vega, and the Adelantado at Xaragua, where this Adrian had made his attempt; but by that time everything was quiet, the land was thriving, and the people at peace. The second day of his arrival he declared himself governor, created magistrates, or-

---

veinte años, que es la edad de un hombre, y se coge el oro, que hobo persona de cinco marcos en cuatro horas, de que diré despues mas largo. Si pluguiese á sus Altezas de desfacer un vulgo de los que saben mis fatigas, que mayor daño me ha hecho el mal decir de las gentes que no me ha aprovechado el mucho servir y guardar su facienda y señorío, seria limosna, é yo restituido en mi honra, é se fablaria dello en todo el mundo, porquel negocio es de calidad que cada dia ha de ser mas sonado y en alta estima. En esto vino el Comendador Bobadilla á Santo Domingo, yo estaba en la Vega y el Adelantado en Jaragua, donde este Adrian habia hecho cabeza, mas ya todo era llano y la tierra rica, y en paz toda. El segundo dia que llegó se crió Gobernador y fizo oficiales y ejecuciones, y

[9] Francesco de Bobadilla, commander of the order of Calatrava, reached San Domingo on the 23rd of August, 1500.

dered executions, published immunities from the collection of gold and from the paying of tithes; and, in fine, announced a general franchise for twenty years, which is, as I have said, the calculation of an age. He also gave out that he was going to pay every one, although they had not even done the service which was due up to that day; and he further proclaimed, with respect to me, that he would send me back loaded with chains, and my brother also (this he has accomplished);[10] and that neither I, nor any of my family, should return for ever to these lands: and, in addition to this, he made innumerable unjust and disgraceful charges against me. All this took place, as I have said, on the very day after his arrival, at which time I was absent at a secure distance, thinking neither of him nor of his coming. Some letters of their Highnesses, of which he brought a considerable number signed in blank, he filled up with exaggerated language, and sent round to the alcalde and his myrmidons, accompanying them with compliments and flattery. To me he never sent either a letter or a messenger, nor has he done so to this day. Reflect upon this, madam! what could any man in my situation think? That honour and favour should

---

apregonó franquezas del oro y diezmos, y generalmente de toda otra cosa por veinte años, que como digo es la edad de un hombre, y que venia para pagar á todos, bien que no habian servido llenamente hasta ese dia, y publicó que á mi me habia de enviar en fierros, y á mis hermanos, así como lo ha fecho, y que nunca yo volveria mas allí ni otro de mi linage, diciendo de mi mil deshonestidades y descorteses cosas. Esto todo fue el segundo dia quel llegó, como dije, y estando yo lejos absente sin saber dello ni de su venida. Unas cartas de sus Altezas firmadas en blanco, de que él llevaba una cantidad, hinchó y envió al Alcalde y á su compañia con favores y encomiendas. A mi nunca me envió carta ni mensagero, ni me ha dado fasta hoy. Piense vuestra merced qué pensaria quien tuviera

[10] This expression of the Admiral's, makes it appear that he wrote this letter when he was near reaching Cadiz, on the 25th of November, 1500.

be granted to him who had given his sanction to plundering their Highnesses of their sovereignty, and who had done so much injury and caused so much mischief?—that he who had defended and preserved their cause through so many dangers, should be dragged through the mire? When I heard this, I thought he must be like Hojeda, or one of the other rebels; but I held my peace, when I learned for certain from the friars, that he had been sent by their Highnesses. I wrote to him, to salute him on his arrival, to let him know that I was ready to set out to go to court, and that I had put up to sale all that I possessed. I entreated him not to be in haste on the subject of the immunities; and I assured him that I would shortly yield this, and everything else connected with the government, implicitly into his charge. I wrote the same thing to the ecclesiastics, but I received no answer either from the one or the other. On the contrary, he took a hostile position, and obliged those who went to his residence to acknowledge him for governor, as I have been told, for twenty years. As soon as I knew what he had done with regard to the immunities, I believed it needful to repair so great an

---

mi cargo ? honrar y favorecer á quien probó á robar á sus Altezas el señorío, y ha fecho tanto mal y daño ? y arrastrar á quien con tantos peligros se lo sostuvo ? Cuando supe esto, creí que esto seria como lo de Hojeda, ó uno de los otros : templóme que supe de los frailes de cierto que sus Altezas lo enviaban. Escrebile yo que su venida fuese en buena hora, y que yo estaba despachado para ir á la corte, y fecho almoneda de cuanto yo tenia, y que en esto de las franquezas que no se acelerase, que esto y el gobierno yo se lo daria luego tan llano como la palma, y así lo escribí á los religiosos. Ni él ni ellos me dieron respuesta, antes se puso él en son de guerra, y apremiaba á cuantos allí iban que le jurasen por Gobernador, dijeronme que por veinte años. Luego que yo supe de estas franquezas pensé de adobar un yerro tan grande, y que él seria contento, las cuales dió sin necesidad y causa de cosa tan gruesa y á gente vagabunda, que fuera demasiado para quien trujera muger y hijos. Publiqué por palabra y por cartas que él no podia usar de error, and I thought he would himself be glad of it; because he had, without any reason or necessity, bestowed upon vagabonds privileges of such importance, that they would have been excessive even for men with wives and children. I published verbally, and by writings, that he could not make use of these grants, because mine had still more power, and I showed the immunities brought by Juan Aguado. All this I did for the purpose of gaining time, that their Highnesses might be informed as to the state of things, and that they might have opportunity to give fresh orders upon everything touching their interests. It is useless to publish such grants in the Indies,—all is in favour of the settlers who have taken up their abode there, because the best lands are given up to them; and, at a low estimate, they are worth two hundred thousand maravedis a head for the four years, at which they are taken, without their having given one stroke of the spade or the mattock. I should not say so much if these people were married men; but there are not six among them all, whose purpose is not to amass all they can, and then decamp with it. It would be well to send people from Spain, and

---

sus provisiones, porque las mias eran las mas fuertes, y les mostré las franquezas que llevó Juan Aguado. Todo esto que yo fice era por dilatar, porque sus Altezas fuesen sabidores del estado de la tierra, y hobiesen lugar de tornar á mandar en ello lo que fuese su servicio. Tales franquezas escusado es de las apregonar en las Indias. Los vecinos que han tomado vecindad es logro, porque se les dan las mejores tierras y á poco valer valerán docientos mil maravedis al cabo de los cuatro años que la vecindad se acaba, sin que den una azadonada en ellas. No diria yo así si los vecinos fuesen casados, mas no hay seis entre todos que no esten sobre el aviso de ayunta lo que pudieren y se ir en buena hora. De Castilla seria bien que fuesen, y aun saber quién y cómo, y se poblase de gente honrada. Yo tenia asentado con estos vecinos que pagarian el tercio del oro y los diezmos, y esto á su ruego, y lo recibieron en grande merced de sus Altezas. Reprendiles cuando yo oí que se dejaban dello, y esperaban quél conmigo faria otro tanto, mas fue el only to send such as are well known, that the country may be peopled with honest men. I had agreed with these settlers that they should pay the third of the gold and of the tithes; and this they not only assented to, but were very grateful to their Highnesses. I reproached them when I heard they had afterwards refused it; they expected, however, to deal with me on the same terms as with the commander, but I would not consent to it. He meanwhile irritated them against me, saying, that I wished to deprive them of that which their Highnesses had given them; and strove to make me appear their enemy, in which he succeeded to the full. He induced them to write to their Highnesses, that they should send me no more commissioned as governor (truly, I do not desire it any more for myself, or for any who belong to me, while the people remain unchanged); and to conciliate them, he ordered inquiries to be made respecting me with reference to imputed misdeeds, such as were never invented in hell. But God is above, who with so much wisdom and power rescued Daniel and the three children, and who, if he please, can rescue me with a similar manifestation of his power, and to the advancement of his own cause. I should have known well enough how to find a remedy for the evils which I now describe and have been describing as having happened to

---

contrario. Indignólos contra mí diciendo, que yo les queria quitar lo que sus Altezas les daban, y trabajo de me los echar acuestas, y lo hizo, y que escribiesen á sus Altezas que no me enviasen mas al cargo, y así se lo suplico yo por mí y por toda cosa mia, en cuanto no haya otro pueblo, y me ordenó él con ellos pesquisas de maldades que al infierno nunca se supo de las semejantes. Allí está nuestro Señor que escapó á Daniel y á los tres muchachos con tanto saber y fuerza como tenia, y con tanto aparejo si le pluguiere como con su gana. Supiera yo remediar todo esto y lo otro que está dicho y ha pasado despues que estoy en las Indias, si me consintiera la voluntad á procurar por mi bien propio y me fuera honesto. Mas el sostener de la justicia y acrecentar el señorío de sus Altezas fasta agora, me tiene al fondo. Hoy en dia que se falla tanto oro me since I came to the Indies, if I had had the wish or had thought it decent, to busy myself about my personal interest; but now I find myself shipwrecked, because until now, I have maintained the justice and augmented the territorial dominions of their Highnesses. Now that so much gold is found, these people stop to consider whether they can obtain the greatest quantity of it by theft, or by going to the mines. For one woman they give a hundred castellanos,[11] as for a farm; and this sort of trading is very common, and there are already a great number of merchants who go in search of girls; there are at this moment from nine or ten on sale; they fetch a good price, let their age be what it will. In saying that the commander could not confer immunities, I did what he desired, although I told him, that it was in order to gain time until their Highnesses had received information respecting the country, and had given their orders as to the regulations best calculated to advance their interest. I say that the calumnies of injurious men have done me more harm, than my services have done me good: which is a bad example for the present as well as for the future. I aver, that a great number of men have been to the Indies, who did not deserve

---

hay division en que haya mas ganancia, ir robando ó ir á las minas. Por una muger tambien se fallan cien castellanos como por una labranza, y es mucho en uso, y ha ya fartos mercaderes que andan buscando muchacha: de nueve á diez son agora en precio: de todas edades ha de tener un bueno. Digo que en decir yo que el Comendador no podia dar franquezas que hice yo lo que él deseaba; bien que yo á él dijese que era para dilatar fasta que sus Altezas toviesen el aviso de la tierra y tornasen á ver y mandar lo que fuese su servicio. Digo que la fuerza del maldecir de desconcertados me ha hecho mas daño que mis servicios fecho provecho: mal ejemplo es por lo presente y por lo futuro. Fago juramento que cantidad de hombres han ido á las Indias que no merescian el agua para con Dios y con el mundo, y agora vuelven allá. Enemistólos á ellos

[11] An ancient gold coin, varying in value under different kings.

baptism in the eyes of God or men, and who are now returning thither. The governor has made every one hostile to me; and it appears, from the manner of his acting, and the plans that he has adopted, that he was already my enemy, and very virulent against me when he arrived; and it is said, that he has been at great expense to obtain this office : but I know nothing about the matter except what I have heard. I never before heard of any one who was commissioned to make an inquiry, assembling the rebels, and taking as evidence against their governor, wretches without faith, and who are unworthy of belief. If their Highnesses would cause a general inquiry to be made throughout the land, I assure you they would be astonished, that the island has not been swallowed up. I believe that you will recollect, that when I was driven by a tempest into the port of Lisbon (having lost my sails), I was falsely accused of having put in thither with the intention of giving the Indies to the sovereign of that country. Since then, their Highnesses have learned the contrary, and that the report was produced by the malice of certain people. Although I am an ignorant man, I do not imagine that any one supposed me so stupid as not to be aware, that even if the Indies had

---

todos conmigo, y él parece, segun se hobo y segun sus formas, que ya lo venia y bien encendido, ó es que se dice que ha gastado mucho por venir á este negocio ; no se dello mas de lo que oyo. Yo nunca oí que el pesquisidor allegase los rebeldes y los tomase por testigos contra aquel que gobierna á ellos y á otros sin fe, ni dignos della. Si sus Altezas mandasen hacer una pesquisa general allí vos digo yo que verian por gran maravilla como la isla no sé funde. Yo creo que se acordará vuestra merced cuando lo tormenta sin velas me echó en Lisbona, que fuí acusado falsamente que habia ido ya allá al Rey para darle las Indias. Despues supieron sus Altezas al contrario, y que todo fue con malicia. Bien que yo sepa poco : no sé quien me tenga por tan torpe que yo no conozca que aunque las Indias fuesen mias, que yo no me pudiera sostener sin ayuda de Príncipe. Si esto es así adónde pudiera yo tener mejor arrimo y seguridad de no ser echado dellas del todo que en el Rey belonged to me, I could not support myself without the assistance of some prince. Since it is thus, where should I find better support, or more security against expulsion, than in the king and queen our sovereigns? who, from nothing, have raised me to so great an elevation, and who are the greatest princes of the world, on the land and on the sea. These princes know how I have served them, and they uphold my privileges and rewards; and if any one violates them, their Highnesses augment them by ordering great favour to be shown me, and ordain me many honours, as was shown in the affair of Juan Aguado. Yes, as I have said, their Highnesses have received some services from me, and have taken my son into their household, which would not have happened with another prince, because where there is no attachment, all other considerations prove of little weight. If I have now spoken severely of a malicious slander, it is against my will, for it is a subject I would not willingly recall even in my dreams. The governor Bobadilla has maliciously exhibited in open day his character and conduct in this affair; but I will prove without difficulty, that his ignorance, his laziness, and his inordinate cupidity, have frustrated all his undertakings. I have already said that I wrote to him, as well as to the monks, and

---

é Reina nuestros Señores, que de nada me han puesto en tanta honra y son los mas altos Príncipes por la mar y por la tierra del mundo? los cuales tienen que yo les haya servido, é me guardan mis privilegios y mercedes, y si alguien me los quebranta sus Altezas me los acrescientan con aventaja, como se vido en lo de Juan Aguado, y me mandar hacer mucha honra, y como dije ya sus Altezas rescibieron de mí servicios y tienen mis hijos sus criados, lo que en ninguna manera pudiera esto llegar con otro Príncipe, porque adonde no hay amor todo lo otro cesa. Dije yo agora ansi contra un maldecir con malicia y contra mi voluntad, porque es cosa que ni en sueños debiera allegar á memoria, porque las formas y fechos del Comendador Bobadilla, con malicia las quiere alumbrar en esto: mas yo le faré ver con el brazo izquierdo que su poco saber y gran cobardiá con desordenada cudicia le ha fecho caer

I set out almost alone, all our people being with the Adelantado and elsewhere, to remove suspicion; when he heard this, he caused D. Diego to be loaded with irons, and thrown into a caravel; he acted in the same manner towards myself, and towards the Adelantado when he arrived. I have never spoken with him, and to this day he has not permitted any one to hold converse with me, and I make oath that I have no conception for what cause I am made prisoner. His first care was to take the gold that I had, and that without measuring or weighing it, although I was absent; he said he would pay those to whom it was owing, and if I am to believe that which has been reported to me, he reserved to himself the greater part, and sent for strangers to make the bargains. I had put aside certain specimens of this gold, as large as the eggs of a goose or a fowl, and many other sizes, which had been collected in a short space of time, in order to please their Highnesses, and that they might be impressed with the importance of the affair, when they saw a great number of large stones loaded with gold. This gold was the first that, after he had feathered his own nest (which he was in great haste to do), his malice suggested to give away, in order that their Highnesses might have a low

---

en ello. Ya dije como yo le escrebí y á los frailes, y luego partí así como le dije muy solo, porque toda la gente estaba con el Adelantado, y tambien por le quitar de sospecha: él cuando lo supo echó á D. Diego preso en una carabela cargado de fierros, y á mi en llegando fizo otro tanto, y despues al Adelantado cuando vino. Ni le fablé mas á él ni consintió que hasta hoy nadie me haya fablado, y fago juramento que no puedo pensar por qué sea yo preso. La primera diligencia que fizo fue á tomar el oro, el cual hobo sin medida ni peso, é yo absente dijo que queria él pagar dello á la gente, y segun oí para si fizo la primera parte, y enviar por resgate resgatadores nuevos. Deste oro tenia yo apartado ciertas muestras, granos muy gruesos como huevos como de ánsar, de gallina y de pollas, y de otras muchas fechuras, que algunas personas tenian cogido en breve espacio, con que se alegrasen sus Altezas, y por ello comprendiesen el negocio con una cantidad de piedras grandes llenas opinion of the whole affair: the gold which required melting, diminished at the fire, and a chain, weighing nearly twenty marks, disappeared altogether. I have been yet more concerned respecting the affair of the pearls, that I have not brought them to their Highnesses. In every thing that could add to my annoyance, the governor has always shown himself ready to bestir himself. Thus, as I have said, with six hundred thousand maravedis, I should have paid every one, without occasioning loss to any; and I had more than four millions of tithes and constabulary dues, without touching the gold. He made the most absurd gifts, although I believe he began by awarding them to the stronger party; their Highnesses will be able to ascertain the truth on this subject when they demand the account to be rendered them, especially if I may assist at the examination. He is continually saying, that there is a considerable sum owing, while it is only what I have already reported, and even less. I have been wounded extremely by the thought, that a man should have been sent out to make inquiry into my conduct, who knew, that if he sent home a very aggravated account of the result of his investigation, he would remain at the head of the government.   Would

---

de oro. Este fue el primero á se dar con malícia, porque sus Altezas no tuviesen este negocio en algo fasta quel tenga fecho el nido de que se dá buena priesa. El oro que está por fundir mengua al fuego : una cadena que pesaria fasta veinte marcos nunca se ha visto. Yo he sido muy agraviado en esto del oro mas aun que de las perlas, porque no las he traido á sus Altezas. El Comendador en todo lo que le pareció que me dañaria luego fue puesto en obra. Ya dije, con seiscientos mil maravedises pagara á todos sin robar á nadie y habia mas de cuatro cuentos de diezmos y alguacilazgo sin tocar en el oro. Hizo unas larguezas que son de risa, bien que creo que encomenzó en sí la primera parte : allá lo sabran sus Altezas cuando le mandaren tomar cuenta, en especial si yo estuviese á ella. El no face sino decir que se debe gran suma, y es la que yo dije y no tanto. Yo he sido muy mucho agraviado en que se haya enviado pesquisidor sobre mí, que sepa que si la pesquisa to God, their Highnesses had sent either him or some other person two years ago, for then I know that I should have had no cause to fear either scandal or disgrace; they could not then have taken away my honour, and I could not have been in the position to have lost it. God is just, and He will in due time make known all that has taken place and why it has taken place. I am judged in Spain, as a governor who had been sent to a province, or city, under regular government, and where the laws could be executed without fear of endangering the public weal; and in this I receive enormous wrong. I ought to be judged as a captain sent from Spain to the Indies, to conquer a nation numerous and warlike, with customs and religion altogether different to ours; a people who dwell in the mountains, without regular habitations for themselves or for us; and where, by the Divine will, I have subdued another world to the dominion of the King and Queen, our sovereigns; in consequence of which, Spain, that used to be called poor, is now the most wealthy of kingdoms. I ought to be judged as a captain, who for so many years has borne arms, never quitting them for an instant. I ought to be judged by cavaliers who have themselves won the meed of victory;[12]

que él enviare fuere muy grave que él quedará en el gobierno.— Pluguiera á nuestro Señor que sus Altezas le enviaran á él ó á otro dos años há, porque sé que yo fuera ya libre de escándalo y de infamia, y no se me quitara mi honra ni la perdiera: Dios es justo, y ha de hacer que se sepa por que y cómo. Allí me juzgan como Gobernador que fue á Cecilia ó ciudad ó villa puesta en regimiento y adonde las leyes se pueden guardar por entero sin temor de que se pierda todo, y rescibo grande agravio. Yo debo ser juzgado como Capitan que fue de España á conquistar fasta las Indias á gente belicosa y mucha, y de costumbres y seta á nos muy contraria: los cuales viven por sierras y montes, sin pueblo asentado ni nosotros; y adonde por voluntad Divina he puesto só el señorio del Rey é de la Reina nuestros Señores otro mundo; y por donde la España,

[12] The old Spaniards used to give the name of "*caballero de conquista*," to each of the conquerors, among whom the conquered lands were divided.

by gentlemen indeed, and not by the lawyers; as least so it would have been among the Greeks and Romans, or any modern nation in which exists so much nobility as in Spain; for under any other judgment I receive great injury, because in the Indies there is neither civil right nor judgment seat.

Already the road is opened to the gold and pearls, and it may surely be hoped that precious stones, spices, and a thousand other things, will also be found. Would to God that it were as certain that I should suffer no greater wrongs than I have already experienced, as it is that I would, in the name of our Lord, again undertake my first voyage; and that I would undertake to go to Arabia Felix as far as Mecca, as I have said in the letter that I sent to their Highnesses by Antonio de Torres, in answer to the division of the sea and land between Spain and the Portuguese; and I would go afterwards to the North Pole, as I have said and given in writing to the monastery of the Mejorada.

The tidings of the gold which I said I would give, are, that on Christmas-day, being greatly afflicted and tormented by the wicked Spaniards and the Indians, at the moment

---

que era dicha pobre, es la mas rica. Yo debo ser juzgado como Capitan que de tanto tiempo fasta hoy trae las armas á cuestas sin las dejar una hora, y de Caballeros de conquistas y del uso, y no de letras, salvo si fuesen de Griegos ó de Romanos, ó de otros modernos de que hay tantos y tan nobles en España, ca de otra guisa rescibo grande agravio porque en las Indias no hay pueblo ni asiento. Del oro y perlas ya está abierta la puerta y cantidad de todo piedras preciosas y especeria, y de otras mil cosas se pueden esperar firmemente; y nunca mas mal me viniese como con el nombre de Nuestro Señor le daria el primer viage, así como diera la negociacion del Arabia feliz fasta la Meca, como yo escribí á sus Altezas con Antonio de Torres en la respuesta de la reparticion del mar é tierra con los Portogueses: y despues viniera á lo de polo artico, así como lo dije y dí por escripto en el monesterio de la Mejorada. Las nuevas del oro que yo dije que daria son que dia de Navidad, estando yo muy afligido guerreado de los malos Cristianos y de of leaving all to save my life if possible, our Lord comforted me miraculously, saying to me, "Take courage, do not abandon thyself to sadness and fear, I will provide for all; the seven years, the term of the gold, are not yet passed; and in this, as in the rest, I will redress thee." I learned, that same day, that there were twenty-four leagues of land where they found mines at every step, which appear now to form but one. Some of the people collected a hundred and twenty castellanos' worth in one day, others ninety; and there have been those who have gathered the equivalent of nearly two hundred and fifty castellanos. They consider it a good day's work when they collect from fifty to seventy, or even from twenty to fifty, and many continue searching; the mean day's work is from six to twelve, and those who get less are very dissatisfied. It appears that these mines, like all others, do not yield equally every day; the mines are new, and those who collect their produce inexperienced. According to the judgment of everybody here, it seems that, if all Spain were to come over, every individual, however inexpert he might be, would gain the equivalent of at least one or two castellanos in a day; and so it is up to the present time. It is certain that any

---

Indios, en términos de dejar todo y escapar si pudiese la vida; me consoló nuestro Señor milagrosamente y dijo: "Esfuerza, no desmayes ni temas : yo proveeré en todo ; los siete años del término del oro no son pasados, y en ello y en lo otro te daré remedio." Ese dia supe que habia ochenta leguas de tierra, y en todo cabo dellas minas ; el parecer agora es que se toda una. Algunos han cogido ciento y veinte castellanos en un dia, otros noventa, y se ha llegado fasta docientos y cincuenta. De cincuenta fasta setenta, y otros muchos de veínte fasta cincuenta, es tenido por buen jornal y muchos lo continuaban : el comun es seis fasta doce, y quien de aquí abaja no es contento. Parece tambien que estas minas son como las otras que responden en los dias no igualmente ; las minas son nuevas y los cogedores. El parecer de todos es que aunque vaya allá toda Castilla, que por torpe que sea la persona, que no abajará de un castellano ó dos cada dia, y agora es esto así en fresco. Es man who has an Indian to work for him, collects as much, but the working of the traffic depends upon the Spaniard. See, now, what discernment was shown by Bobadilla when he gave up everything for nothing, and four millions of tithes without any reason, and even without being asked to do so, and without first giving notice to their Highnesses of his intention; and this is not the only evil which he has caused. I know, assuredly, that the errors which I may have fallen into, have been done without the intention to do wrong, and I think that their Highnesses will believe me when I say so; but I know and see that they show mercy towards those who intentionally do injury to their service. I, however, feel very certain that the day will come when they will treat me much better; since, if I have been in error, it has been innocently and under the force of circumstances, as they will shortly understand beyond all doubt: I, who am their creature, and whose services and usefulness they will every day be more willing to acknowledge. They will weigh all in the balance, even as, according to the Holy Scripture, it will be with the evil and the good at the day of judgment. If, nevertheless, their Highnesses ordain me another judge, which I hope will not be

---

verdad que el que tiene algun indio coge esto, mas el negocio consiste en el Cristiano. Ved que discrecion fue de Bobadilla dar todo por ninguno y cuatro cuentos de diezmos sin causa ni ser requerido, sin primero lo notificar á sus Altezas; y el daño no es este solo. Yo sé que mis yerros no han sido con fin de facer mal, y creo que sus Altezas lo creen así como yo lo digo; y sé y veo que usan de misericordia con quien maliciosamente los desirve. Yo creo y tengo por muy cierto que muy mejor y mas piedad harán conmigo que caí en ello con inocencia y forzosamente, como sabran despues por entero, y el cual soy su fechura, y mirirán á mis servicios, y cognoscerán de cada dia que son muy aventajados. Todo pornan en una balanza, así como nos cuenta la Santa Escriptura que será el bien con el mal en el dia del juicio. Si todavía mandan que otro me juzgue, lo cual no espero, y que sea por pesquisa de las Indias, humilmente les suplico que envien allá dos personas de consciencia

the case, and if my examination is to be holden in the Indies, I
humbly beseech them to send over two conscientious and re-
spectable persons at my expense, who would readily acknowledge that, at this time, five marks of gold may be found in four
hours: be it however as it may, it is highly necessary that their
Highnesses should have this matter inquired into.   The governor, on his arrival at St. Domingo, took up his abode in my
house, and appropriated to himself all that was therein.   Well
and good; perhaps· he was in want of it: but even a pirate
does not behave in this manner towards the merchants that he
plunders.   That which grieved me most was the seizure of
my papers, of which I have never been able to recover one;
and those that would have been most useful to me in proving
my innocence, are precisely those which he has kept most
carefully concealed.   Behold the just and honest inquisitor!
I am told that he does not at all confine himself to the bounds
of justice, but that he acts in all things despotically.   God our
Saviour retains His power and wisdom as of old; and, above
all things, He punishes ingratitude.

----

y honrados á mi costa, los cuales fallaran de ligero agora que se
halla el oro cinco marcos en cuatro horas, con esto é sin ello es muy
necesario que lo provean.   El Comendador en llegando á Santo
Domingo se aposentó en mi casa ; así como la falló así dió todo por
suyo : vaya en buena hora, quizá lo habia menester : cosario nunca
tal usó con mercader.   De mis escripturas tengo yo mayor queja
que así me las haya tomado, que jamas se le pudo sacar una, y aquellas que mas me habian de aprovechar en mi disculpa esas tenia
mas ocultas.   Ved que justo y honesto pesquisidor.   Cosa de cuantas él haya hecho me dicen que haya seido con término de justicia,
salvo absolutamente.   Dios nuestro Señor está con sus fuerzas y
saber, como solia, y castiga en todo cabo, en especial la ingratitud
de injurias.

FOURTH VOYAGE OF COLUMBUS.

A Letter written by Don Christopher Columbus, Viceroy and Admiral of the Indies, to the most Christian and mighty Sovereigns, the King and Queen of Spain, in which are described the events of his voyage, and the countries, provinces, cities, rivers and other marvellous matters therein discovered, as well as the places where gold and other substances of great richness and value are to be found.

MOST Serene, and very high and mighty Princes, the King and Queen our Sovereigns :—My passage from Cadiz to the Canary occupied four days, and thence to the Indies, from which I wrote, sixteen days. My intention was to expedite my voyage as much as possible while I had good vessels, good crews and stores, and because Jamaica was the place to which I was bound. I wrote this in Dominica : and until now my time has been occupied in gaining information.

Up to the period of my reaching these shores I experienced

CUARTO VIAGE DE COLON.

Que escribió D. Cristóbal Colon, Virey y Almirante de las Indias, á los Cristianísimos y muy poderosos Rey y Reina de España, nuestros Señores, en que les notifica cuanto le ha acontecido en su viage; y las tierras, provincias, ciudades, rios y otras cosas maravillosas, y donde hay minas de oro en mucha cantidad, y otras cosas de gran riqueza y valor.

SERENÍSIMOS y muy altos y poderosos Príncipes Rey é Reina, nuestros Señores : De Caliz pasé á Canaria en cuatro dias, y dende á las Indias en diez y seis dias, donde escribia. Mi intencion era dar prisar á mi viage en cuanto yo tenia los navíos buenos, la gente y los bastimentos, y que mi derrota era en la Isla Jamaica ; y en la Isla Dominica escribí esto : fasta allí truje el tiempo á pedir por la boca.

most excellent weather, but the night of my arrival came on
with a dreadful tempest, and the same bad weather has continued ever since. On reaching the island of Española I
despatched a packet of letters, by which I begged as a favour
that a ship should be supplied me at my own cost in lieu of
one of those that I had brought with me, which had become
un-seaworthy, and could no longer carry sail. The letters
were taken, and your Highnesses will know if a reply has
been given to them. For my part I was forbidden to go on
shore; the hearts of my people failed them lest I should take
them further, and they said that if any danger were to befall
them, they should receive no succour, but, on the contrary,
in all probability have some great affront offered them.
Moreover every man had it in his power to tell me that the
new Governor would have the superintendance of the countries that I might acquire.

The tempest was terrible throughout the night, all the
ships were separated, and each one driven to the last extremity, without hope of anything but death; each of them
also looked upon the loss of the rest as a matter of certainty.
What man was ever born, not even excepting Job, who would
not have been ready to die of despair at finding himself as I

Esa noche que alli entré fué con tormenta y grande, y me persiguió
despues siempre. Cuando llegué sobre la Española invié el envoltorio
de cartas, y á pedir por merced un navío por mis dineros, porque otro
que yo llevaba era inavegable y no sufria velas. Las cartas tomaron,
y sabrán si se las dieron la respuesta. Para mí fue mandarme de
parte de ahí, que yo no pasase ni llegase á la tierra: cayó el corazon á la gente que iba conmigo, por temor de los llevar yo lejos,
diciendo que si algun caso de peligro les viniese que no serian re-
mediados allí, antes les sería fecha alguna grande afrenta. Tambien á quien plugo dijo que el Comendador habia de proveer las
tierras que yo ganase. La tormenta era terrible, y en aquella noche
me desmembró los navíos: á cada uno llevó por su cabo sin espe-
ranzas, salvo de muerte : cada uno de ellos tenia por cierto que los
otros eran perdidos. ¿ Quién nasció, sin quitar á Job, que no mu-

then was, in anxious fear for my own safety, and that of my son, my brother and my friends, and yet refused permission either to land or to put into harbour on the shores which by God's mercy I had gained for Spain with so much toil and danger?

But to return to the ships: although the tempest had so completely separated them from me as to leave me single, yet the Lord restored them to me in His own good time. The ship which we had the greatest fear for, had put out to sea for safety, and reached the island of Gallega, having lost her boat and a great part of her provisions, which latter loss indeed all the ships suffered. The vessel in which I was, though dreadfully buffeted, was saved by our Lord's mercy from any injury whatever; my brother went in the ship that was unsound, and he under God was the cause of its being saved. With this tempest I struggled on till I reached Jamaica, and there the sea became calm, but there was a strong current which carried me as far as the Queen's Garden without seeing land. Hence as opportunity afforded I pushed on for terra firma, in spite of the wind and a fearful contrary current, against which I contended for sixty days, and during that time

---

riera desesperado? que por mi salvacion y de mi fijo, hermano y amigos me fuese en tal tiempo defendida la tierra y los puertos que yo, por la voluntad de Dios, gané á España sudando sangre? E torno á los navíos que así me habia llevado la tormenta y dejado á mí solo. Deparómelos nuestro Señor cuando le plugo. El navío Sospechoso habia echado á la mar, por escapar, fasta la isola la Gallega; perdió la barca, y todas gran parte de los bastimentos: en el que yo iba, abalumado á maravilla, nuestro Señor le salvó que no hubo daño de una paja. En el Sospechoso iba mi hermano; y él, despues de Dios, fue su remedio. E con esta tormenta, así á gatas, me llegué á Jamaica: allí se mudó de mar alta en calmería y grande corriente, y me llevó fasta el Jardin de la Reina sin ver tierra. De allí, cuando pude, navegué á la tierra firme; adonde me salió el viento y corriente terrible al opósito: combatí con ellos sesenta dias, y en fin no le pude ganar mas de setenta leguas. En only made seventy leagues. All this time I was unable to get into harbour, nor was there any cessation of the tempest, which was one continuation of rain, thunder and lightning; indeed it seemed as if it were the end of the world. I at length reached the Cape of Gracias a Dios, and after that the Lord granted me fair wind and tide; this was on the twelfth of September. Eighty-eight days did this fearful tempest continue, during which I was at sea, and saw neither sun nor stars; my ships lay exposed, with sails torn, and anchors, rigging, cables, boats and a great quantity of provisions lost; my people were very weak and humbled in spirit, many of them promising to lead a religious life, and all making vows and promising to perform pilgrimages, while some of them would frequently go to their messmates to make confession. Other tempests have been experienced, but never of so long a duration or so fearful as this: many whom we looked upon as brave men, on several occasions showed considerable trepidation; but the distress of my son who was with me grieved me to the soul, and the more when I considered his tender age, for he was but thirteen years old, and he enduring so much toil for so long a time. Our Lord, however, gave him

---

todo este tiempo no entré puerto, ni pude, ni me dejó tormenta del cielo, agua y trombones y relámpagos de continuo, que parecia el fin del mundo. Llegué al cabo de Gracias á Dios, y de allí me dió nuestro Señor próspero el viento y corriente. Esto fue á doce de Setiembre. Ochenta y ocho dias habia que no me habia dejado espantable tormenta, á tanto que no vide el sol ni estrellas por mar; que á los navíos tenia yo abiertos, á las velas rotas, y perdidas anclas y jarcia, cables, con las barcas y muchos bastimentos, la gente muy enferma, y todos contritos, y muchos con promesa de religion, y no ninguno sin otros votos y romerías. Muchas veces habian llegado á se confesar los unos á los otros. Otras tormentas se han visto, mas no durar tanto ni con tanto espanto. Muchos esmorecieron, harto y hartas veces, que teniamos por esforzados. El dolor del fijo que yo tenia allí me arrancaba el ánima, y mas por verle de tan nueva edad de trece años en tanta fatiga, y durar en ello tanto: nuestro Señor le dió tal strength even to enable him to encourage the rest, and he worked as if he had been eighty years at sea, and all this was a consolation to me. I myself had fallen sick, and was many times at the point of death, but from a little cabin that I had caused to be constructed on deck, I directed our course. My brother was in the ship that was in the worst condition and the most exposed to danger; and my grief on this account was the greater that I brought him with me against his will.

Such is my fate, that the twenty years of service through which I have passed with so much toil and danger, have profited me nothing, and at this very day I do not possess a roof in Spain that I can call my own; if I wish to eat or sleep, I have nowhere to go but to the inn or tavern, and most times lack wherewith to pay the bill. Another anxiety wrung my very heartstrings, which was the thought of my son Diego, whom I had left an orphan in Spain, and stripped of the honour and property which were due to him on my account, although I had looked upon it as a certainty, that your Majesties, as just and grateful Princes, would restore it to him in all respects with increase. I reached the land of Cariay, where I stopped to repair my vessels and take in pro-

---

esfuerzo que él avivaba á los otros, y en las obras hacia él como si hubiera navegado ochenta años, y él me consolaba. Yo habia adolescido y llegado fartas veces á la muerte. De una camarilla, que yo mandé facer sobre cubierta, mandaba la via. Mi hermano estaba en el peor navío y mas peligroso. Gran dolor era mio, y mayor porque lo truje contra su grado ; porque por mi dicha, poco me han aprovechado veinte años de servicio que yo he servido con tantos trabajos y peligros, que hoy dia no tengo en Castilla una teja ; si quiero comer ó dormir no tengo, salvo al meson ó taberna, y las mas de las veces falta parar pagar el escote. Otra lastima me arrancaba el corazon por las espaldas, y era de D. Diego mi hijo, que yo dejé en España tan huérfano y desposesionado de mi honra é hacienda ; bien que tenia por cierto que allá como justos y agradecidos Principes le restituirian con acrescentamiento en todo. Llegué á tierra visions, as well as to afford relaxation to the men, who had become very weak. I myself (who, as I said before, had been several times at the point of death) gained information respecting the gold mines of which I was in search, in the province of Ciamba; and two Indians conducted me to Carambaru, where the people (who go naked) wear golden mirrors round their necks, which they will neither sell, give, nor part with for any consideration. They named to me many places on the sea-coast where there were both gold and mines. The last that they mentioned was Veragua, which was five-and-twenty leagues distant from the place where we then were. I started with the intention of visiting all of them, but when I had reached the middle of my journey I learned that there were other mines at so short a distance that they might be reached in two days. I determined on sending to see them. It was on the eve of St. Simon and St. Jude, which was the day fixed for our departure; but that night there arose so violent a storm, that we were forced to go wherever it drove us, and the Indian who was to conduct us to the mines was with us all the time. As I had found every thing true that had been told me in the different places which I had visited,

---

de Cariay, adonde me detuve á remediar los navíos y bastimentos, y dar aliento á la gente, que venia muy enferma. Yo que, como dije, habia llegado muchas veces á la muerte, allí supe de las minas del oro de la provincia de Ciamba, que yo buscaba. Dos indios me llevaron á Carambaru, adonde la gente anda desnuda y al cuello un espejo de oro, mas no le querian vender ni dar á trueque. Nombraronme muchos lugares en la costa de la mar, adonde decian que habia oro y minas ; el postrero era Veragua, y lejos de allí obra de veinte y cinco leguas : partí con intencion de los tentar á todos, y llegado ya el medio supe que habia minas á dos jornadas de andadura : acorde de inviarlas á ver vispera de San Simon y Judas, que habia de ser la partida : en esa noche se levantó tanta mar y viento, que fue necesario de correr hácia adonde él quiso ; é el indio adalid de las minas siempre conmigo. En todos estos lugares, adonde yo habia estado, fallé verdad todo ly que yo habia oido : esto me

I felt satisfied it would be the same with respect to Ciguare, which according to their account, is nine days journey across the country westward: they tell me there is a great quantity of gold there, and that the inhabitants wear coral ornaments on their heads, and very large coral bracelets and anklets, with which article also they adorn and inlay their seats, boxes and tables.   They also said that the women there wore necklaces hanging down to their shoulders.   All the people agree in the report I now repeat, and their account is so favourable that I should be content with the tithe of the advantages that their description holds out.   They are all likewise acquainted with the pepper-plant; according to the account of these people, the inhabitants of Ciguare are accustomed to hold fairs and markets for carrying on their commerce, and they showed me also the mode and form in which they transact their various exchanges; others assert that their ships carry guns, and that the men go clothed and use bows and arrows, swords and cuirasses, and that on shore they have horses which they use in battle, and that they wear rich clothes and have most excellent houses.[1]   They also say that the sea sur-

certifico que es así de la provincia de Ciguare, que segun ellos, es descrita nueve jornadas de andadura por tierra al Poniente: allí dicen que hay infinito oro, y que traen corales en las cabezas, manillas á los pies y á los brazos dello, y bien gordas; y dél sillas, arcas, y mesas las guarnecen y enforran.   Tambien dijeron que las mugeres de allí traian collares colgados de la cabeza á las espaldas. En esto que yo digo, la gente toda de estos lugares conciertan en ello, y dicen tanto que yo seria contento con el diezmo.   Tambien todos conocieron la pimienta.   En Ciguare usan tratar en ferias y mercaderías: esta gente así lo cuentan, y me amostraban el modo y forma que tienen en la barata.   Otrosi dicen que las naos traen bombardas, arcos y flechas, espadas y corazas, y andan vestidos, y en la tierra hay caballos, y usan la guerra, y traen ricas vestiduras, y tienen buenas cosas.   Tambien dicen que la mar boxa á Ci-

[1] The word " cosas" has been replaced on conjecture by " casas," such being the idea entertained in the Italian translation, republished by Morelli.

rounds Ciguare, and that at ten days' journey from thence is
the river Ganges; these lands appear to hold the same relation
to Veragua, as Tortosa to Fontarabia, or Pisa to Venice.
When I left Carambaru and reached the places in its neighbourhood, which I have above-mentioned as being spoken of
by the Indians, I found the customs of the people correspond
with the accounts that had been given of them, except as regarded the golden mirrors: any man who had one of them
would willingly part with it for three hawk's-bells, although
they were equivalent in weight to ten or fifteen ducats. These
people resemble the natives of Española in all their habits.
They have various modes of collecting the gold, none of which
will bear comparison with the plans adopted by the Christians.

All that I have here stated is from hearsay. This, however, I know, that in the year ninety-four I sailed twenty-
four degrees to the westward in nine hours, and there can be
no mistake upon the subject, because there was an eclipse;
the sun was in Libra and the moon in Aries. What I had
learned by the mouth of these people I already knew in detail
from books. Ptolemy thought that he had satisfactorily cor-
rected Marinus, and yet this latter appears to have come very

---

guare, y de allí á diez jornadas es el rio de Gangues. Parece que
estas tierras estan con Veragua, como Tortosa con Fuenterabía, ó
Pisa con Venecia. Cuando yo partí de Carambaru y llegué á esos
lugares que dije, fallé la gente en aquel mismo uso, salvo que los
espejos del oro: quien los tenia los daba por tres cascabeles de
gabilan por el uno, bien que pesasen diez ó quince ducados de peso.
En todos sus usos son como los de la Española. El oro cogen con
otras artes, bien que todos son nada con los de los Cristianos. Esto
que yo he dicho es lo que oyo. Lo que yo sé es que el año de
noventa y cuatro navegué en veinte y cuatro grados al Poniente
en término de nueve horas, y no pudo haber yerro porque hubo
eclipses: el sol estaba en Libra y la luna en Ariete. Tambien
esto que yo supe por palabra habialo yo sabido largo por escrito.
Tolomeo creyó de haber bien remedado á Marino, y ahora se falla
su escritura bien propincua al cierto. Tolomeo asienta Catigara á

near to the truth.　Ptolemy places Catigara at a distance of twelve lines to the west of his meridian,[2] which he fixes at two degrees and a third above Cape St. Vincent, in Portugal. Marinus comprises the earth and its limits in fifteen lines, and the same author describes the Indus in Ethiopia as being more than four-and-twenty degrees from the equinoctial line, and now that the Portuguese have sailed there they find it correct.　Ptolemy says also that the most southern land is the first boundary, and that it does not go lower down than fifteen degrees and a third.　The world is but small; out of seven divisions of it the dry part occupies six, and the seventh is entirely covered by water.[3]　Experience has shown it, and I have written it with quotations from the Holy Scripture, in other letters, where I have treated of the situation of the terrestrial paradise, as approved by the Holy Church; and I say that the world is not so large as vulgar opinion makes it, and that one degree from the equinoctial line measures fifty-six

---

doce lineas lejos de su Occidente, que él asentró sobre el cabo de San Vicente en Portugal dos grados y un tercio.　Marino en quince líneas constituyó la tierra é términos.　Marino en Etiopia escribe al Indo la línea equinocial mas de veinte y cuatro grados, y ahora que los Portugueses le navegan le fallan cierto.　Tolomeo diz que la tierra mas austral es el plazo primero, y que no abaja mas de quince grados y un tercio.　E el mundo es poco : el enjuto de ello es seis partes, la séptima solamente cubierta de agua : la experiencia ya está vista, y la escribí por otras letras y con adornamiento de la Sacra Escriptura, con el sitio del Paraiso terrenal, que la santa Iglesia aprueba : digo que el mundo no es tan grande como dice el vulgo, y que un grado de la equinoccial está cincuenta

---

[2] The "line" of Columbus implies fifty degrees, or one hour of longitude ; and the twelve lines which describe the distance of Catigara from the meridian of Ptolemy, equal one hundred and eighty degrees. Marinus of Tyre, reckoned two hundred and twenty-five degrees to the same space, which is equivalent to the fifteen degrees of Columbus.

[3] Every one will immediately see the incorrectness of this notion ; as instead of the land bearing a proportion of six-sevenths to the water, the water bears a proportion of about two-thirds to the land.

miles and two-thirds; and this may be proved to a nicety. But I leave this subject, which it is not my intention now to treat upon, but simply to give a narrative of my laborious and painful voyage, although of all my voyages it is the most honourable and advantageous. I have said that on the eve of St. Simon and St. Jude I ran before the wind wherever it took me, without power to resist it; at length I found shelter for ten days from the roughness of the sea and the tempest overhead, and resolved not to attempt to go back to the mines, which I regarded as already in our possession. When I started in pursuance of my voyage it was under a heavy rain, and reaching the harbour of Bastimentos I put in, though much against my will. The storm and a rapid current kept me in for fourteen days, when I again set sail, but not with favourable weather. After I had made fifteen leagues with great exertions, the wind and the current drove me back again with great fury, but in again making for the port which I had quitted, I found on the way another port, which I named Retrete, where I put in for shelter with as much risk as regret, the ships being in sad condition, and my crews and myself exceedingly fatigued. I remained there fifteen days, kept in

---

y seis millas y dos tercios : pero esto se tocará con el dedo. Dejo esto, por cuanto no es mi propósito de fablar en aquella materia, salvo de dar cuenta de mi duro y trabajoso viage, bien que él sea el mas noble y provechoso. Digo que víspera de San Simon y Judas corrí donde el viento me llevaba, sin poder resistirle. En un puerto excusé diez dias de gran fortuna de la mar y del cielo : allí acordé de no volver atras á las minas, y dejelas ya por ganadas. Partí, por seguir mi viage, lloviendo : llegué á puerto de Basti- mentos, adonde entré y no de grado : la tormenta y gran corriente me entró allí catorce dias ; y despues partí, y no con buen tiempo. Cuando yo hube andado quince leguas forzosamente, me reposó atras el viento y corriente con furia : volviendo yo al puerto de donde habia salido fallé en el camino al Retrete, adonde me retruje con harto peligro y enojo y bien fatigado yo y los navíos y la gente : detúveme allí quince dias, que así lo quiso el cruel tiempo ; y

by stress of weather, and when I fancied my troubles were at
an end, I found them only begun. It was then that I changed
my resolution with respect to proceeding to the mines, and
proposed doing something in the interim, until the weather
should prove more favourable for my voyage. I had already
made four leagues when the storm recommenced, and wearied
me to such a degree that I absolutely knew not what to do;
my wound reopened, and for nine days my life was despaired
of; never was the sea so high, so terrific, and so covered
with foam; not only did the wind oppose our proceeding on-
ward, but it also rendered it highly dangerous to run in for
any headland, and kept me in that sea which seemed to me
as a sea of blood, seething like a cauldron on a mighty fire.
Never did the sky look more fearful; during one day and one
night it burned like a furnace, and every instant I looked to
see if my masts and my sails were not destroyed; for the
lightnings flashed with such alarming fury that we all thought
the ships must have been consumed. All this time the waters
from heaven never ceased descending, not to say that it rained,
for it was like a repetition of the deluge. The men were at
this time so crushed in spirit that they longed for death as a

---

cuando creí de haber acabado me fallé de comienzo : allí mudé de
sentencia de volver á las minas, y hacer algo fasta que me viniese
tiempo para mi viage y marear; y llegado con cuatro leguas revino
la tormenta, y me fatigó tanto á tanto que ya no sabia de mi parte.
Allí se me refrescó del mal la llaga ; nueve dias anduve perdido sin
esperanza de vida : ojos nunca vieron la mar tan alta, fea y hecha
espuma. El viento no era para ir adelante, ni daba lugar para
correr hácia algun cabo. Allí me detenia en aquella mar fecha
sangre, herbiendo como caldera por gran fuego. El cielo jamas
fue visto tan espantoso : un dia con la noche ardió como forno ; y
así echaba la llama con los rayos, que cada vez miraba yo si me
habia llevado los masteles y velas ; venian con tanta furia espantables que todos creiamos que me habian de fundir los navíos. En
todo este tiempo jamas cesó agua del cielo, y no para decir que
llovia, salvo que resegundaba otro diluvio. La gente estaba ya tan

deliverance from so many martyrdoms. Twice already had the
ships suffered loss in boats, anchors, and rigging, and were
now lying bare without sails.

When it pleased our Lord, I returned to Puerto Gordo,
where I recruited my condition as well as I could. I then
once more attempted the voyage towards Veragua, although
I was by no means in a fit state to undertake it. The wind
and currents were still contrary. I arrived at nearly the same
spot as before, and there again the wind and currents still opposed my progress; and once again I was compelled to put into
port, not daring to encounter the opposition of Saturn[4] with
such a boisterous sea, and on so formidable a coast; for it
almost always brings on a tempest or severe weather. This
was on Christmas-day, about the hour of mass. Thus, after all
these fatigues, I had once more to return to the spot from
whence I started; and when the new year had set in, I returned again to my task : but although I had fine weather for
my voyage, the ships were no longer in a sailing condition, and
my people were either dying or very sick. On the day of the

---

molida que deseaban la muerte para salir de tantos martirios. Los
navíos ya habian perdido dos veces las barcas, anclas, cuerdas, y
estaban abiertos, sin velas.

Cuando plugo á nuestro Señor volví á Puerto Gordo, adonde re-
paré lo mejor que pude. Volví otra vez hácia Veragua para mi
viage, aunque yo no estuviera para ello. Todavía era el viento y
corrientes contrarios. Llegué casi adonde antes, y allí me salió
otra vez el viento y corrientes al encuentro, y volví otra vez al puerto, que no osé esperar la oposicion de Saturno con mares tan desbaratados en costa brava, porque las mas de las veces trae tempestad
ó fuerte tiempo. Esto fue dia de Navidad en horas de misa. Volví
otra vez adonde yo habia salido con harta fatiga ; y pasado año
nuevo torné á la porfia, que aunque me hiciera buen tiempo para mi
viage, ya tenia los navíos innavegables, y la gente muerta y enferma.

[4] Morelli has given this passage thus : " la opposizion de Saturno con
Marte." The adjective " desbaratados," however, sufficiently proves this
reading to be incorrect. The sentence is here literally translated without
any random guessing at the author's meaning.

Epiphany, I reached Veragua in a state of exhaustion; there, by our Lord's goodness, I found a river and a safe harbour, although at the entrance there were only ten spans of water. I succeeded in making an entry, but with great difficulty; and on the following day the storm recommenced, and had I been still on the outside at that time, I should have been unable to enter on account of the reef. It rained without ceasing until the fourteenth of February, so that I could find no opportunity of penetrating into the interior, nor of recruiting my condition in any respect whatever; and on the twenty-fourth of January, when I considered myself in perfect safety, the river suddenly rose with great violence to a considerable height, breaking my cables and the supports[5] to which they were fastened, and nearly carrying away my ships altogether, which certainly appeared to me to be in greater danger than ever. Our Lord, however, brought a remedy as He has always done. I do not know if any one else ever suffered greater trials.

On the sixth of February, while it was still raining, I sent seventy men on shore to go into the interior, and, at five leagues' distance they found several mines. The Indians who

---

Dia de la Epifania llegué á Veragua, ya sin aliento : allí me deparó nuestro Señor un rio y seguro puerto, bien que á la entrada no tenia salvo diez palmos de fondo : metíme en él con pena, y el dia siguiente recordó la fortuna : si me falla fuera, no pudiera entrar á causa del banco. Llovió sin cesar fasta catorce de Febrero, que nunca hubo lugar de entrar en la tierra, ni de me remediar en nada: y estando ya seguro á veinte y cuatro de Enero, de improviso vino el rio muy alto y fuerte ; quebróme las amarras y proeses, y hubo de llevar los navíos, y cierto los ví en mayor peligro que nunca. Remedio nuestro Señor, como siempre hizo. No sé si hubo otro con mas martirios.

A seis de Febrero, lloviendo, invié setenta hombres la tierra aden-tro ; y á las cinco leguas fallaron muchas minas : los Indios que iban con ellos los llevaron á un cerro muy alto, y de allí les mos-

---

[5] The word *proeses* or *proizes*, answers to our English word bollards— or the posts to which cables are fastened.

went with them, conducted them to a very lofty mountain,
and thence showing them the country all round, as far as the
eye could reach, told them there was gold in every part, and
that, towards the west, the mines extended twenty days' journey; they also recounted the names of the towns and villages
where there was more or less of it.   I afterwards learned that
the cacique Quibian, who had lent these Indians, had ordered
them to show the distant mines, and which belonged to an
enemy of his; but that in his own territory, one man
might, if he would, collect in ten days a great abundance of
gold.[6]   I bring with me some Indians, his servants, who
are witnesses of this fact.   The boats went up to the spot
where the dwellings of these people are situated; and, after
four hours, my brother returned with the guides, all of them
bringing back gold which they had collected at that place.
The gold must be abundant, and of good quality, for none of
these men had ever seen mines before; very many of them
had never seen pure gold, and most of them were seamen and
lads.   Having building materials in abundance, I established
a settlement, and made many presents to Quibian, which is

---

traron hácia toda parte cuanto los ojos alcanzaban, diciendo que en
toda parte habia oro, y que hácia el Poniente llegaban las minas
veinte jornadas, y nombraban las villas y lugares, y adonde habia
de ello mas ó menos.   Despues supe yo que el Quibian que habia
dado estos Indios, les habia mandado que fuesen á mostrar las minas
lejos y de otro su contrario; y que adentro de su pueblo cogian,
cuando, el queria, un hombre en diez dias una mozada de oro: los
indios sus criados y testigos de esto traigo conmigo.   Adonde él
tiene el pueblo llegan las barcas. Volvió mi hermano con esa gente,
y todos con oro que habian cogido en cuatro horas que fué allá á la
estada.   Lacalidad es grande, porque ninguno de estos jamas habia
visto minas, y los mas oro.   Los mas eran gente de la mar, y casi
todos grumetes.   Yo tenia mucho aparejo para edificar y muchos
bastimentos,   Asenté pueblo, y dí muchas dádivas al Quibian, que

---

[6] " Mozada," probably " mojada," a moistening, and hence the idea of a
" shower," or " great abundance " of gold.

the name they gave to the lord of the country. I plainly saw that harmony would not last long, for the natives are of a very rough disposition, and the Spaniards very encroaching; and, moreover, I had taken possession of land belonging to Quibian. When he saw what we did, and found the traffic increasing, he resolved upon burning the houses, and putting us all to death; but his project did not succeed, for we took him prisoner, together with his wives, his children, and his servants. His captivity, it is true, lasted but a short time, for he eluded the custody of a trustworthy man, into whose charge he had been given, with a guard of men; and his sons escaped from a ship, in which they had been placed under the special charge of the master.

In the month of January the mouth of the river was entirely closed up, and in April the vessels were so eaten with the teredo, that they could scarcely be kept above water. At this time the river forced a channel for itself, by which I managed, with great difficulty, to extricate three of them after I had unloaded them. The boats were then sent back into the river for water and salt, but the sea became so high and furious, that it afforded them no chance of exit; upon which

---

así llaman al Señor de la tierra ; y bien sabia que no habia de durar la concordia : ellos muy rústicos y nuestra gente muy importunos, y me aposesionaba en su término : despues que él vido las cosas fechas y el tráfago tan vivo acordó de las quemar y matarnos á todos : muy al reves salió su propósito : quedó preso él, mugeres y fijos y criados ; bien que su prision duró poco : el Quibian se fuyo á un hombre honrado, á quien se habia entregado con guarda de hombres ; é los hijos se fueron á un Maestre de navío, a quien se dieron en él á buen recaudo.

En Enero se habia cerrado la boca del rio. En Abril los navíos estaban todos comidos de broma, y no los podia sostener sobre agua. En este tiempo hizo el rio una canal, por donde saqué tres dellos vacios con gran pena. Las barcas volvieron adentro por la sal y agua. La mar se puso alta y fea, y no les dejó salir fuera : los Indios fueron muchos y juntos y las combatieron, y en fin los ma-the Indians collected themselves together in great numbers, and made an attack upon the boats, and at length massacred the men. My brother, and all the rest of our people, were in a ship which remained inside; I was alone, outside, upon that dangerous coast, suffering from a severe fever and worn with fatigue. All hope of escape was gone. I toiled up to the highest part of the ship, and, with a quivering voice and fast-falling tears, I called upon your Highnesses' war-captains from each point of the compass to come to my succour, but there was no reply. At length, groaning with exhaustion, I fell asleep, and heard a compassionate voice address me thus:— " O fool, and slow to believe and to serve thy God, the God of all! what did He do more for Moses, or for David his servant, than He has done for thee? From thine infancy He has kept thee under His constant and watchful care. When He saw thee arrived at an age which suited His designs respecting thee, He brought wonderful renown to thy name throughout all the land. He gave thee for thine own the Indies, which form so rich a portion of the world, and thou hast divided them as it pleased thee, for He gave thee power to do so. He gave thee also the keys of those barriers of the ocean sea

---

taron. Mi hermano y la otra gente toda estaban en un navío que quedo adentro : yo muy solo de fuera en tan brava costa, con fuerte fiebre, en tanta fatiga : la esperanza de escapar era muerta : subi así trabajando lo mas alto, llamando á voz temerosa, llorando y muy aprisa, los maestros de la guerra de vuestras Altezas, á todos cuatro los vientos, por socorro ; mas nunca me respondieron. Cansado, me dormecí gimiendo : una voz muy piadosa oí, diciendo : "¡ O estulto y tardo á creer y servir á tu Dios, Dios de todos ! ¿ Que hizo él mas por Moysés ó por David su siervo ? Desque nasciste, siempre él tuvo de tí muy grande cargo. Cuando te vido en edad de que él fue contento, maravillosamente hizo sonar tu nombre en la tierra. Las Indias, que son parte del mundo, tan ricas, te las dió por tuyas : tu las repartiste adonde te plugo, y te dió poder para ello. De los atamientos de la mar océana, que estaban cerrados con cadenas tan fuertes, te dió las llaves ; y fuiste obedescido en which were closed with such mighty chains; and thou wast obeyed through many lands, and gained an honourable fame throughout Christendom. What more did the Most High do for the people of Israel, when he brought them out of Egypt? or for David, whom from a shepherd He made to be king in Judea? Turn to Him, and acknowledge thine error—His mercy is infinite. Thine old age shall not prevent thee from accomplishing any great undertaking. He holds under His sway the greatest possessions. Abraham had exceeded a hundred years of age when he begat Isaac; nor was Sarah young. Thou criest out for uncertain help: answer, who has afflicted thee so much and so often, God or the world? The privileges promised by God, He never fails in bestowing; nor does He ever declare, after a service has been rendered Him, that such was not agreeable with His intention, or that He had regarded the matter in another light; nor does he inflict suffering, in order to give effect to the manifestation of His power. His acts answer to His words; and it is His custom to perform all his promises with interest. Thus I have told you what the Creator has done for thee, and what He does for all men. Even now He partially shows thee the reward of so many toils and dangers incurred by thee in the service of others."

---

tantas tierras, y de los cristianos cobraste tan honrada fama. ¿ Qué hizo el mas alto pueblo de Israel cuando le sacó de Egipto? ¿ Ni por David, que de pastor hizo Rey en Judea? Tórnate á él, y conoce ya tu yerro: su misericordia es infinita: tu vejez no impedirá á toda cosa grande: muchas heredades tiene él grandísimas. Abrahan pasaba de cien años cuando engendró á Isaac, ¿ni Sara era moza? Tú llamas por socorro incierto: responde, ¿ quién te ha afligido tanto y tantas veces, Dios ó el mundo? Los privilegios y promesas que dá Dios, no las quebranta, ni dice despues de haber recibido el servicio, que su intencion no era esta, y que se entiende de otra manera, ni dá martirios por dar color á la fuerza: él vá al pie de la letra: todo lo que él promete cumple con acrescentamiento: ¿ esto es uso? Dicho tengo lo que tu Criador ha fecho por tí y

I heard all this, as it were, in a trance; but I had no answer to give in definite words, and could but weep for my errors. He who spoke to me, whoever it was, concluded by saying,—"Fear not, but trust; all these tribulations are recorded on marble, and not without cause." I arose as soon as I could; and at the end of nine days there came fine weather, but not sufficiently so to allow of drawing the vessels out of the river. I collected the men who were on land, and, in fact, all of them that I could, because there were not enongh to admit of one party remaining on shore while another stayed on board to work the vessel. I myself should have remained with my men to defend the buildings I had constructed, had your Highnesses been cognizant of all the facts; but the doubt whether any ships would ever reach the spot where we were, as well as the thought, that while I was asking for succour I might bring succour to myself, made me decide upon leaving. I departed, in the name of the Holy Trinity, on Easter night, with the ships rotten, worn out, and eaten into holes. One of them I left at Belen, with a supply of necessaries; I did the same at Belpuerto. I then had only two left, and they in

---

hace con todos. Ahora medio muestra el galardon de estos afanes y peligros que has pasado sirviendo á otros."

Yo así amortecido oí todo ; mas no tuve yo respuesta á palabras tan ciertas, salvo llorar por mis yerros. Acabó él de fablar, quien quiera que fuese, diciendo : "No temas, confia: todas estas tribulaciones estan escritas en piedra mármol, y no sin causa."

Levantéme cuando pude : y al cabo de nueve dias hizo bonanza, mas no para sacar navíos del rio. Recogí la gente que estaba en tierra, y todo el resto que puede, porque no bastaban para quedar y para navegar los navíos. Puedara yo á sostener el pueblo con todos, si vuestras Altezas supieran de ello. El temor que nunca aportarian allí navíos me determinó á esto, y la cuenta que cuando se haya de proveer de socorro se proveerá de todo. Partí en nombre de la Santísima Trinidad, la noche de Pascua, con los navíos podridos, abrumados, todos fechos agujeros. Allí en Belen dejé uno, y hartas cosas. En Belpuerto hice otro tanto. No me que-the same state as the others. I was without boats or provisions, and in this condition I had to cross seven thousand miles of sea; or, as an alternative, to die on the passage with my son, my brother, and so many of my people. Let those who are accustomed to slander and aspersion, ask, while they sit in security at home, "Why didst thou not do so and so under such circumstances?" I wish that they were now embarked in this voyage. I verily believe that another journey of another kind awaits them, if there is any reliance to be placed upon our holy faith.

On the thirteenth of May I reached the province of Mago, which is contiguous to that of Cathay, and thence I started for the island of Española. I sailed two days with a good wind, after which it became contrary. The route that I followed called forth all my care to avoid the numerous islands, that I might not be stranded on the shoals that lie in their neighbourhood. The sea was very tempestuous, and I was driven backward under bare poles. I anchored at an island, where I lost, at one stroke, three anchors; and, at midnight, when the weather was such that the world appeared to be coming to an end, the cables of the other ship broke, and

---

daron salvo dos en el estado de los otros, y sin barcas y bastimentos, por haber de pasar siete mil millas de mar y de agua, ó morir en la via con figo y hermano y tanta gente. Respondan ahora los que suelen tachar y reprender, diciendo allá de en salvo : ¿ por qué no haciades esto allí ? Los quisiera yo en esta jornada. Yo bien creo que otra de otro saber los aguarda : á nuestra fe es ninguna. Llegué á trece de Mayo en la provincia de Mago, que parte con aquella del Catayo, y de allí partí para la Española : navegué dos dias con buen tiempo, y despues fue contrario. El camino que yo llevaba era para desechar tanto número de islas, por no me embarazar en los bajos de ellas. La mar brava me hizo fuerza, y hube volver atras sin velas : surgí á una isla adonde de golpe perdí tres anclas, y á la media noche, que parecia que el mundo se ensolvia, se rompieron las amarras al otro navío, y vino sobre mí, que fue maravilla como no nos acabamos de se hacer rajas : el ancla, de it came down upon my vessel with such force that it was a wonder we were not dashed to pieces; the single anchor that remained to me, was, next to the Lord, our only preservation. After six days, when the weather became calm, I resumed my journey, having already lost all my tackle; my ships were pierced with worm-holes, like a bee-hive, and the crew entirely dispersed and down-hearted. I reached the island a little beyond the point at which I first arrived at it, and there I stayed to recover myself from the effects of the storm; but I afterwards put into a much safer port in the same island. After eight days I put to sea again, and reached Jamaica by the end of June; but always beating against contrary winds, and with the ships in the worst possible condition. With three pumps, and the use of pots and kettles, we could scarcely clear the water that came into the ship, there being no remedy but this for the mischief done by the ship-worm. I steered in such a manner as to come as near as possible to Española, from which we were twenty-eight leagues distant, but I afterwards wished I had not done so, for the other ship which was half under water was obliged to run in for a port. I determined on keeping the sea in spite of the weather, and

---

forma que me quedó, fue ella despues de nuestro Señor, quien me sostuvo. Al cabo de seis dias, que ya era bonanza, volví á mi camino : asi ya perdido del todo de aparejos y con los navíos horadados de gusanos mas que un panal de abejas, y la gente tan acobardada y perdida, pasé algo adelante de donde yo habia llegado denantes : allí me torné á reposar atras la fortuna : paré en la misma isla en mas seguro puerto : al cabo de ocho dias torné á la via y llegué á Jamaica en fin de Junio, siempre con vientos punteros, y los navíos en peor estado : con tres bombas, tinas y calderas no podian con toda la gente vencer el agua que entraba en el navío, ni para este mal de broma hay otra cura. Cometí el camino para me acercar á lo mas cercar de la Española, que son veinte y ocho leguas, y no quisiera haber comenzado. El otro navío corrió á buscar puerto casi anegado. Yo porfié la vuelta de la mar con tormenta. El navio se me anegó, que milagrosamente my vessel was on the very point of sinking when our Lord miraculously brought us upon land. Who will believe what I now write? I assert that in this letter I have not related one hundredth part of the wonderful events that occurred in this voyage; those who were with the Admiral[7] can bear witness to it. If your Highnesses would be graciously pleased to send to my help a ship of above sixty-four tons, with two hundred quintals of biscuits and other provisions, there would then be sufficient to carry me and my crew from Española to Spain. I have already said that there are not twenty-eight leagues between Jamaica and Española; and I should not have gone there, even if the ships had been in a fit condition for so doing, because your Highnesses ordered me not to land there. God knows if this command has proved of any service. I send this letter by means of and by the hands of Indians; it will be a miracle if it reaches its destination.

This is the account I have to give of my voyage. The men who accompanied me were a hundred and fifty in number, among whom were many calculated for pilots and good sailors, but none of them can explain whither I went nor whence I

---

me trujo nuestro Señor á tierra. ¿ Quién creyera lo que yo aquí escribo? Digo que de cien partes no he dicho la una en esta letra. Los que fueron con el Almirante lo atestigüen. Si place á vuestras Altezas de me hacer merced de socorro un navío que pase de sesenta y cuatro, con ducientos quintales de bizcocho y algun otro bastimento, abastará para me llevar á mí y á esta gente á España de la Española. En Jamaica ya dije que no hay veinte y ocho leguas á la Española. No fuera yo, bien que los navíos estuvieran para ello. Ya dije que me fue mandado de parte de vuestras Altezas que no llegase á alla. Si este mandar ha aprovechado, Dios lo sabe. Esta carta invio por via y mano de Indios: grande maravilla será si allá llega. De mi viage digo: que fueron ciento y cincuenta personas conmigo, en que hay hartos suficientes para pilotos y grandes marineros: ninguno puede dar razon cierta por donde fuí yo ni vine: la razon es muy presta. Yo partí de sobre

[7] Of course he here speaks of himself.

came; the reason is very simple: I started from a point above the port of Brazil, and while I was in Española, the storm prevented me from following my intended route, for I was obliged to go wherever the wind drove me; at the same time I fell very sick, and there was no one who had navigated in these parts before. However, after some days, the wind and sea became tranquil, and the storm was succeeded by a calm, but accompanied with rapid currents. I put into harbour at an island called Isla de las Bocas, and then steered for terra firma; but it is impossible to give a correct account of all our movements, because I was carried away by the current so many days without seeing land. I ascertained, however, by the compass and by observation, that I moved parallel with the coast of terra firma. No one could tell under what part of the heavens we were, nor at what period I bent my course for the island of Española. The pilots thought we had come to the island of St. John, whereas it was the land of Mango, four hundred leagues to the westward of where they said. Let them answer and say if they know where Veragua is situated. I assert that they can give no other account than that they went to lands, where there was an abundance of gold, and this they

---

el puerto del Brasil: en la Española no me dejó la tormenta ir al camino que yo queria: fue por fuerza correr adonde el veinto quiso. En ese dia caí yo muy enfermo: ninguno habia navegado hácia aquella parte: cesó el viento y mar dende á ciertos dias, y se mudó la tormenta en calmería y grandes corrientes. Fuí á aportar á una isla que se dijo de las Bocas, y de allí a Tierra firme. Ninguno puede dar cuenta verdadera de esto, porque no hay razon que abaste; porque fue ir con corriente sin ver tierra tanto número de dias. Seguí la costa de la Tierra firme: esta se asentó con compás y arte. Ninguno hay que diga debajo cuál parte del cielo ó cuándo yo partí de ella para venir á la Española. Los pilotos creian venir á parar á la isla de Sanct-Joan; y fue en tierra de Mango, cuatrocientas leguas mas al Poniente de adonde decian. Respondan, si saben, adónde es el sitio de Veragua. Digo que no pueden dar otra razon ni cuenta, salvo que fueron á unas tierras

can certify surely enough; but they do not know the way to
return thither for such a purpose; they would be obliged to
go on a voyage of discovery as much as if they had never
been there before. There is a mode of reckoning derived
from astronomy which is sure and safe, and a sufficient guide
to any one who understands it. This resembles a prophetic
vision. The Indian vessels do not sail except with the wind
abaft, but this is not because they are badly built or clumsy,
but because the strong currents in those parts, together with
the wind, render it impossible to sail with the bowline,[8] for in
one day they would lose as much way as they might have
made in seven; for the same reason I could make no use of
caravels, even though they were Portuguese latteens. This
is the cause that they do not sail unless with a regular
breeze, and they will sometimes stay in harbour waiting for
this seven or eight months at a time; nor is this anything
wonderful, for the same very often occurs in Spain. The
nation of which Pope Pius writes has now been found, judging
at least by the situation and other evidences, excepting the
horses with the saddles and poitrels and bridles of gold; but

adonde hay mucho oro, y certificarle; mas para volver á ella el
camino tienen ignoto: seria necesario para ir á ella descubrirla
como de primero. Una cuenta hay y razon de astrología, y cierta:
quien la entiende esto le abasta. A vision profética se asemeja
esto. Las naos de las Indias, sino navegan, salvo á popa, no es
por la mala fechura, ni por ser fuertes; las grandes corrientes que
allí vienen; juntamente con el viento hacen que nadie porfie con
bolina, porque en un dia perderian lo que hubiesen ganado en
siete; ni saco carabela aunque sea latina portuguesa. Esta razon
hace que no naveguen, salvo con colla, y por esperarle se detienen
á las veces seis y ocho meses en puerto; ni es maravilla, pues, que
en España muchas veces acaece otro tanto. La gente de que
escribe Papa Pio, segun el sitio y señas, se ha hallado, mas no los

8 Bow-lines are ropes employed to keep the windward edges of the principal sails steady, and are only used when the wind is so unfavourable that
the sails must be all braced sideways, or close hauled to the wind.

this is not to be wondered at, for the lands on the sea-coast
are only inhabited by fishermen, and moreover I made no
stay there, because I was in haste to proceed on my voyage.
In Cariay and the neighbouring country there are great en-
chanters of a very fearful character. They would have given
the world to prevent my remaining there an hour. When I
arrived they sent me immediately two girls very showily
dressed; the eldest could not be more than eleven years of age
and the other seven, and both exhibited so much immodesty,
that more could not be expected from public women; they
carried concealed about them a magic powder; when they
came I gave them some articles to dress themselves out with,
and directly sent them back to the shore. I saw here, built on
a mountain, a sepulchre as large as a house, and elaborately
sculptured, the body lay uncovered and with the face down-
wards; they also spoke to me of other very excellent works
of art. There are many species of animals both small and
large, and very different from those of our country. I had
at the time two pigs, and an Irish dog who was always in
great dread of them. An archer had wounded an animal like
an ape, except that it was larger, and had a face like a

---

caballos, pretales y frenos de oro, ni es maravilla, porque allí las
tierras de la costa de la mar no requieren, salvo pescadores, ni yo
me detuve porque andaba á prisa. En Cariay, y en esas tierras de
su comarca, son grandes fechiceros y muy medrosos. Dieran el
mundo porque no me detuviera allí una hora. Cuando llegué allí
luego me inviaron dos muchachas muy ataviadas : la mas vieja no
seria de once años y la otra de siete ; ambas con tanta desenvoltura
que no serian mas unas putas : traian polvos de hechizos escondi-
dos : en llegando las mandé adornar de nuestras cosas y las invié
luego á tierra : allí vide una sepultura en el monte, grande como
una casa y labrada, y el cuerpo descubierto y mirando en ella. De
otras artes me dijeron y mas excelentes. Animalias menudas y
grandes hay hartas y muy diversas de las nuestras. Dos puercos
hube yo en presente, y un perro de Irlanda no osaba esperarlos.
Un ballestero habia herido una animalia, que se parece á gato paul,

man's; the arrow had pierced it from the neck to the tail, which made it so fierce that they were obliged to disable it by cutting off one of its arms and a leg; one of the pigs grew wild on seeing this and fled; upon which I ordered the *begare* (as the inhabitants called him) to be thrown to the pig, and though the animal was nearly dead, and the arrow had passed quite through his body, yet he threw his tail round the snout of the pig, and then holding him firmly, seized him by the nape of the neck with his remaining hand, as if he were engaged with an enemy. This action was so novel and so extraordinary, that I have thought it worth while to describe it here. There is a great variety of animals here, but they all die of the barra.[9] I saw some very large fowls (the feathers of which resemble wool), lions, stags, fallow-deer and birds.

When we were so harassed with our troubles at sea, some of our men imagined that we were under the influence of sorcery, and even to this day entertain the same notion. Some of the people whom I discovered were cannibals, as was evidenced by the brutality of their countenances. They

---

salvo que es mucho mas grande, y el rostro de hombre : teniale atravesado con una saeta desde los pechos á la cola, y porque era feroz le hubo de cortar un brazo y una pierna : el puerco en viéndole se le encrespó y se fue huyendo : yo cuando esto ví mandé echarle *begare*, que así se llama adonde estaba : en llegando á él, así estando á la muerte y la saeta siempre en el cuerpo, le echó la cola por el hocico y se la amarró muy fuerte, y con la mano que le quedaba le arrebató por el copete como á enemigo. El auto tan nuevo y hermosa montería me hizo escribir esto. De muchas maneras de animalias se hubo, mas todas mueren de barra. Gallinas muy grandes y la pluma como lana vide hartas. Leones, ciervos, corzos, otro tanto, y así aves.

Cuando yo andaba por aquella mar en fatiga en algunos se puso heregía que estabamos enfechizados, que hoy dia estan en ello. Otra gente fallé que comian hombres : la desformidad de su gesto lo dice.

[9] This is a malady undefined in any dictionary.

say that there are great mines of copper in the country, of which they make hatchets and other elaborate articles both cast and soldered; they also make of it forges, with all the apparatus of the goldsmith, and crucibles. The inhabitants go clothed; and in that province I saw some large sheets of cotton very elaborately and cleverly worked, and others very delicately pencilled in colours. They tell me that more inland towards Cathay they have them interwoven with gold. For want of an interpreter we were able to learn but very little respecting these countries, or what they contain. Although the country is very thickly peopled, yet each nation has a very different language; indeed so much so, that they can no more understand each other than we understand the Arabs. I think, however, that this applies to the barbarians on the sea-coast, and not to the people who live more inland. When I discovered the Indies, I said that they composed the richest lordship in the world; I spoke of gold and pearls and precious stones, of spices and the traffic that might be carried on in them; and because all these things were not forthcoming at once I was abused. This punishment causes me to refrain from relating anything but what the natives tell me. One

---

Allí dicen qué hay grandes mineros de cobre : hachas de ello, otras cosas labradas, fundidas, soldadas hube, y fraguas con todo su aparejo de platero y los crisoles. Allí van vestidos ; y en aquella provincia vide sábanas grandes de algodon, labradas de muy sotiles labores ; otras pintadas muy sútilmente á colores con pinceles. Dicen que en la tierra adentro hácia el Catayo las hay tejidas de oro. De todas estas tierras y de lo que hay en ellas, faila de lengua, no se saben tan presto. Los pueblos, bien que sean espesos, cada uno tiene diferenciada lengua, y es en tanto que no se entienden los unos con los otros, mas que nos con los de Arabia. Yo creo que esto sea en esta gente salvage de la costa de lar mar, mas no en la tierra dentro. Cuando yo descubrí las Indias dije que eran el mayor señorío rico que hay en el mundo. Yo dije del oro, perlas, piedras preciosas, especerías, con los tratos y ferias, y porque no pareció todo tan presto fuí escandalizado. Este castigo me hace agora que no diga salvo lo que yo oigo de los naturales de la tierra.

thing I can venture upon stating, because there are so many witnesses of it, viz., that in this land of Veragua I saw more signs of gold in the two first days than I saw in Española during four years, and that there is not a more fertile or better cultivated country in all the world, nor one whose inhabitants are more timid; added to which there is a good harbour, a beautiful river, and the whole place is capable of being easily put into a state of defence. All this tends to the security of the Christians and the permanency of their sovereignty, while it affords the hope of great increase and honour to the Christian religion; moreover the road hither will be as short as that to Española, because there is a certainty of a fair wind for the passage. Your Highnesses are as much lords of this country as of Xerez or Toledo, and your ships that may come here will do so with the same freedom as if they were going to your own royal palace. From hence they will obtain gold, and whereas if they should wish to become masters of the products of other lands, they will have to take them by force or retire empty-handed; in this country they will simply have to trust their persons in the hands of a savage.

I have already explained my reason for refraining to treat

De una oso decir, porque hay tantos testigos, y es que yo vide en esta tierra de Veragua mayor señal de oro en dos dias primeros que en la Española en cuatro años, y que las tierras de la comarca no pueden ser mas fermosas, ni mas labradas, ni la gente mas cobarde, y buen puerto, y fermoso rio, y defensible al mundo. Todo esto es seguridad de los cristianos y certeza de señorío, con grande esperanza de la honra y acrescentamiento de la religion cristiana ; y el camino allí será tan breve como á la Española, porque ha de ser con viento. Tan señores son vuestras Altezas de esto como de Jerez ó Toledo : sus navíos que fueren allí van á su casa. De allí sacarán oro : en otras tierras, para haber de lo que hay en ellas, conviene que se lo lleven, ó se volverán vacíos ; y en la tierra es necesario que fien sus personas de un salvage. Del otro que yo dejo de decir, ya dije por qué me encerré : no digo así, ni que yo of other subjects respecting which I might speak. I do not state as certain, nor do I confirm even the sixth part of all that I have said or written, nor do I pretend to be at the fountain-head of the information. The Genoese, Venetians, and all other nations that possess pearls, precious stones, and other articles of value, take them to the ends of the world to exchange them for gold. Gold is the most precious of all commodities ; gold constitutes treasure, and he who possesses it has all he needs in this world, as also the means of rescuing souls from purgatory, and restoring them to the enjoyment of paradise. They say that when one of the lords of the country of Veragua dies, they bury all the gold he possessed with his body. There were brought to Solomon at one journey six hundred and sixty-six quintals of gold, besides what the merchants and sailors brought, and that which was paid in Arabia. Of this gold he made two hundred lances and three hundred shields, and the entablature which was above them was also of gold, and ornamented with precious stones : many other things he made likewise of gold, and a great number of vessels of great size, which he enriched with precious stones. This is related by Josephus in his Chronicle de " Antiquita-

---

me afime en el tres doble en todo lo que yo haya jamas dicho ni escrito, y que yo estó á la fuente. Genoveses, Venecianos y toda gente que tenga perlas, piedras preciosas y otras cosas de valor, todos las llevan hasta el cabo del mundo para las trocar, convertir en oro : el oro es excelentísimo : del oro se hace, tesoro, y con él, quien lo tiene, hace cuanto quiere en el mundo, y llega á que echa las animas al paraiso. Los señores de aquellas tierras de la comarca Veragua cuando mueren entierran el oro que tienen con el cuerpo, así lo dicen : á Salomon llevaron de un camino seiscientos y sesenta y seis quintales de oro, allende lo que llevaron los mercaderes y marineros, y allende lo que se pagó en Arabia. De este oro fizo doscientas lanzas y trescientos escudos, y fizo el tablado que habia de estar arriba dellas de oro y adornado de piedras preciosas, y fizo otras muchas cosas de oro, y vasos muchas y muy grandes y ricos de piedras preciosas. Josefo en su corónica de Antiquitatibus

tibus"; mention is also made of it in the Chronicles and in the Book of Kings. Josephus thinks that this gold was found in the Aurea; if it were so, I contend that these mines of the Aurea are identical with those of Veragua, which, as I have said before, extends westward twenty days' journey, at an equal distance from the Pole and the Line. Solomon bought all of it,—gold, precious stones, and silver,—but your Majesties need only send to seek them to have them at your pleasure. David, in his will, left three thousand quintals of Indian gold to Solomon, to assist in building the Temple; and, according to Josephus, it came from these lands. Jerusalem and Mount Sion are to be rebuilt by the hands of Christians, as God has declared by the mouth of His prophet in the fourteenth Psalm. The Abbé Joaquim said that he who should do this was to come from Spain; Saint Jerome showed the holy woman the way to accomplish it; and the emperor of China has, some time since, sent for wise men to instruct him in the faith of Christ. Who will offer himself for this work? Should any one do so, I pledge myself, in the name of God, to convey him safely thither, provided the

---

lo escribe. En el Paralipomenon y en el libro de los Reyes se cuenta de esto. Josefo quiere que este oro se hobiese en la Aurea: si así fuese digo que aquellas minas de la Aurea son unas y se convienen con estas de Veragua, que como yo dije arriba se alarga al Poniente veinte jornadas, y son en una distancia lejos del polo y de la línea. Salomon compró todo aquello, oro, piedras y plata, é allí le pueden mandar á coger si les aplace. David en su testamento dejó tres mil quintales de oro de las Indías á Salomon para ayuda de edificar el templo, y segun Josefo era el destas mismas tierras. Hierusalem y el monte Sion ha de ser reedificado por mano de cristianos : quien ha de ser, Dios por boca del Profeta en el décimo cuarto salmo lo dice. El Abad Joaquin dijo que este habia de salir de España. San Gerónimo á la santa muger le mostró el camino para ello. El Emperador del Catayo ha dias que mandó sabios que le enseñen en la fé de Cristo. ¿ Quién será que se ofrezca á esto ? Si nuestro Señor me lleva á España, yo me

Lord permits me to return to Spain. The people who have sailed with me have passed through incredible toil and danger, and I beseech your Highnesses, since they are poor, to pay them promptly, and to be gracious to each of them according to their respective merits; for I can safely assert, that to my belief they are the bearers of the best news that ever were carried to Spain. With respect to the gold which belongs to Quibian, the cacique of Veragua, and other chiefs in the neighbouring country, although it appears by the accounts we have received of it to be very abundant, I do not think it would be well or desirable, on the part of your Highnesses, to take possession of it in the way of plunder; by fair dealing, scandal and disrepute will be avoided, and all the gold will thus reach your Highnesses' treasury without the loss of a grain. With one month of fair weather I shall complete my voyage. As I was deficient in ships, I did not persist in delaying my course; but in everything that concerns your Highnesses' service, I trust in Him who made me, and I hope also that my health will be re-established. I think your Highnesses will remember that I had intended to build some ships in a new manner, but the shortness of the time did not

---

obligo de llevarle, con el nombre de Dios, en salvo. Esta gente que vino conmigo han pasado increibles peligros y trabajos. Suplico á V. A., porque son pobres, que les mande pagar luego, y les haga mercedes á cada uno segun la calidad de la persona, que les certifico que á mi creer les traen las mejores nuevas que nunca fueron á España. El oro que tiene el Quibian de Veragua y los otros de la comarca, bien que segun informacion él sea mucho, no me paresció bien ni servicio de vuestras Altezas de se le tomar por via de robo : la buena orden evitará escándalo y mala fama, y hará que todo ello venga al tesoro, que no quede un grano. Con un mes de buen tiempo yo acabára todo mi viage : por falta de los navíos no porfié á esperarle para tornar á ello, y para toda cosa de su servicio espero en aquel que me hizo, y estaré bueno. Yo creo que V. A. se acordará que yo queria mandar hacer los navíos de nueva manera : la brevedad del tiempo no dió lugar á ello, y cierto permit it. I had certainly foreseen how things would be. I think more of this opening for commerce, and of the lordship over such extensive mines, than of all that has been done in the Indies. This is not a child to be left to the care of a step-mother.

I never think of Española, and Paria, and the other countries, without shedding tears. I thought that what had occurred there would have been an example for others; on the contrary, these settlements are now in a languid state, although not dead, and the malady is incurable, or at least very extensive: let him who brought the evil come now and cure it, if he knows the remedy, or how to apply it; but when a disturbance is on foot, every one is ready to take the lead. It used to be the custom to give thanks and promotion to him who placed his person in jeopardy; but there is no justice in allowing the man who opposed this undertaking, to enjoy the fruits of it with his children. Those who left the Indies, avoiding the toils consequent upon the enterprise, and speaking evil of it and me, have since returned with official appointments,—such is the case now in Veragua: it is an evil example, and profitless both as regards the business in which we

---

yo habia caido en lo que cumplia. Yo tengo en mas esta negociacion y minas con esta escala y señorio, que todo lo otro que está hecho en las Indias. No es este hijo para dar á criar á madrastra. De la Española, de Paria y de las otras tierras no me acuerdo de ellas, que yo no llore : creia yo que el ejemplo dellas hobiese de ser por estotras al contrario : ellas estan boca á yuso, bien que no mueren : la enfermedad es incurable, ó muy larga : quien las llegó á esto venga agora con el remedio si puede ó sabe : al descomponer cada uno es maestro. Las gracias y acrescentamiento siempre fue uso de las dar á quien puso su cuerpo á peligro. No es razon que quien ha sido tan contrario á esta negociacion le goce ni sus fijos. Los que se fueron de las Indias fuyendo los trabajos y diciendo mal dellas y de mí, volvieron con cargos : así se ordenaba agora en Veragua : malo ejemplo, y sin provecho del negocio y para la justicia del mundo : este temor con otros casos hartos que yo veia are embarked, and as respects the general maintenance of justice. The fear of this, with other sufficient considerations, which I clearly foresaw, caused me to beg your Highnesses, previously to my coming to discover these islands and terra firma, to grant me permission to govern in your royal name. Your Highnesses granted my request; and it was a privilege and treaty granted under the royal seal and oath, by which I was nominated viceroy, and admiral, and governor-general of all: and your Highnesses limited the extent of my government to a hundred leagues beyond the Azores and Cape Verde islands, by a line passing from one pole to the other, and gave me ample power over all that I might discover beyond this line; all which is more fully described in the official document.

But the most important affair of all, and that which cries most loudly for redress, remains inexplicable to this moment. For seven years was I at your royal court, where every one to whom the enterprise was mentioned, treated it as ridiculous; but now there is not a man, down to the very tailors, who does not beg to be allowed to become a discoverer. There is reason to believe, that they make the voyage only for plunder, and

---

claro, me hizo suplicar á V. A. antes que yo viniese á descubrir esas islas y tierra firme, que las dejasen gobernar en su Real nombre: plúgoles y fue por privilegio y asiento, y con sello y juramento, y me intitularon de Viso-Rey y Almirante y Gobernador general de todo; y aseñalaron el término sobre las islas de los Azores cien leguas, y aquellas del Cabo Verde por línea que pasa de polo á polo, y desto y de todo que mas se descubriese, y me dieron poder largo: la escritura á mas largamente lo dice. El otro negocio famosísimo está con los brazos abiertos llamando: extrangero ha sido fasta ahora. Siete años estuve yo en su Real corte, que á cuantos se fabló de esta empresa todos á una dijeron que era burla: agora fasta los sastres suplican por descubrir. Es de creer que van á saltear, y se les otorga, que cobran con mucho perjuicio de mi honra y tanto daño del negocio. Bueno es de dar á Dios lo suyo y acetar lo que le pertenece. Esta es justa sentencia, y de

that they are permitted to do so, to the great disparagement
of my honour, and the detriment of the undertaking itself.
It is right to give God His due,—and to receive that which
belongs to one's self. This is a just sentiment, and proceeds
from just feelings. The lands in this part of the world, which
are now under your Highnesses' sway, are richer and more extensive than those of any other Christian power, and yet, after
that I had, by the Divine will, placed them under your high
and royal sovereignty, and was on the point of bringing your
majesties into the receipt of a very great and unexpected
revenue; and while I was waiting for ships, to convey me in
safety, and with a heart full of joy, to your royal presence,
victoriously to announce the news of the gold that I had discovered, I was arrested and thrown, with my two brothers,
loaded with irons, into a ship, stripped, and very ill-treated,
without being allowed any appeal to justice. Who could
believe, that a poor foreigner would have risen against your
Highnesses, in such a place, without any motive or argument
on his side; without even the assistance of any other prince
upon which to rely; but on the contrary, amongst your own
vassals and natural subjects, and with my sons staying at your
royal court? I was twenty-eight years old when I came into
your Highnesses' service, and now I have not a hair upon me

---

justo. Las tierras que acá obedecen á V. A. son mas que todas las
otras de cristianos y ricas. Despues que yo, por voluntad divina,
las hube puestas debajo de su Real y alto señorío, y en filo para
haber grandísima renta, de improviso, esperando navíos para venir
á su alto conspecto con victoria y grandes nuevas del oro, muy seguro y alegre, fuí preso y echado con dos hermanos en un navío,
cargados de fierros, desnudo en cuerpo, con muy mal tratamiento,
sin ser llamado ni vencido por justicia : ¿ quién creerá que un pobre extrangero se hobiese de alzar en tal lugar contra V. A. sin
causa, ni sin brazo de otro Príncipe, y estando solo entre sus vasallos y naturales, y teniendo todos mis fijos en su Real corte ? Yo
vine á servir de veinte y ocho años, y agora no tengo cabello en mi
persona que no sea cano y el cuerpo enfermo, y gastado cuanto me

that is not grey; my body is infirm, and all that was left to me, as well as to my brothers, has been taken away and sold, even to the frock that I wore, to my great dishonour. I cannot but believe that this was done without your royal permission. The restitution of my honour, the reparation of my losses, and the punishment of those who have inflicted them, will redound to the honour of your royal character; a similar punishment also is due to those who plundered me of my pearls, and who have brought a disparagement upon the privileges of my admiralty. Great and unexampled will be the glory and fame of your Highnesses, if you do this; and the memory of your Highnesses, as just and grateful sovereigns, will survive as a bright example to Spain in future ages. The honest devotedness I have always shown to your majesties' service, and the so unmerited outrage with which it has been repaid, will not allow my soul to keep silence, however much I may wish it : I implore your Highnesses to forgive my complaints. I am indeed in as ruined a condition as I have related; hitherto I have wept over others ;—may Heaven now have mercy upon me, and may the earth weep for me. With regard to temporal things, I have not even a blanca for an offering; and in spiritual things, I have ceased here in the

---

quedó de aquellos, y me fue tomado y vendido, y á mis hermanos fasta el sayo, sin ser oido ni visto, con gran deshonor mio. Es de creer que esto no se hizo por su Real mandado. La restitucion de mi honra y daños, y el castigo en quien lo fizo, fará sonar su Real nobleza ; y otro tanto en quien me robó las perlas, y de quien ha fecho daño en ese almirantado. Grandísima virtud, fama con ejemplo será si hacen esto, y quedará á la España gloriosa memoria con la de vuestras Altezas de agradecidos y justos Príncipes. La intencion tan sana que yo siempre tuve al servicio de vuestras Altezas, y la afrenta tan desigual, no da lugar al anima que calle, bíen que yo quiera : suplico á vuestras Altezas me perdonen. Yo estoy tan perdido como dije : yo he llorado fasta aquí á otros : haya misericordia agora el Cielo, y llore por mi la tierra. En el temporal no tengo solamente una blanca para el oferta : en el

Indies from observing the prescribed forms of religion. Solitary in my trouble, sick, and in daily expectation of death, surrounded by millions of hostile savages full of cruelty, and thus separated from the blessed sacraments of our holy Church, how will my soul be forgotten if it be separated from the body in this foreign land? Weep for me, whoever has charity, truth, and justice! I did not come out on this voyage to gain to myself honour or wealth; this is a certain fact, for at that time all hope of such a thing was dead. I do not lie when I say, that I went to your Highnesses with honest purpose of heart, and sincere zeal in your cause. I humbly beseech your Highnesses, that if it please God to rescue me from this place, you will gracionsly sanction my pilgrimage to Rome and other holy places. May the Holy Trinity protect your Highnesses' lives, and add to the prosperity of your exalted position.

Done in the Indies, in the island of Jamaica, on the seventh of July, in the year one thousand five hundred and three.

---

espiritual he parado aquí en las Indias de la forma que está dicho : aislado en esta pena, enfermo, aguardando cada dia por la muerte, y cercado de un cuento de salvages y llenos de crueldad y enemigos nuestros, y tan apartado de los Santos Sacramentos de la Santa Iglesia, que se olvidará desta anima si se aparta acá del cuerpo. Llore por mí quien tiene caridad, verdad y justicia. Yo no vine este viage á navegar por ganar honra ni hacienda : esto es cierto, porque estaba ya la esperanza de todo en ella muerta. Yo vine á V. A. con sana intencion y buen zelo, y no miento. Suplico humildemente á V. A. que si á Dios place de me sacar de aquí, que haya por bien mi ida á Roma y otros romerías. Cuya vida y alto estado la Santa Trinidad guarde y acresciente. Fecha en las Indias en la Isla de Jamaica á siete de Julio de mil quinientos y tres años.

AN ACCOUNT

Given by Diego Mendez in his will of some events that occurred in the last voyage of the Admiral Don Christopher Columbus.

DIEGO MENDEZ, citizen of St. Domingo, in the island of Española, being in the city of Valladolid, where the Court of their most sacred Majesties was at the time staying, made his will on the sixth day of June, of the year one thousand five hundred and thirty-six, before Fernando Perez, their Majesties' scrivener, and notary public in that their Court, and in all their Kingdoms and Lordships, the witnesses to the same being Diego de Arana, Juan Diez Miranda de la Cuadra, Martin de Orduña, Lucas Fernandez, Alonzo de Angulo, Francisco de Hinojosa and Diego de Aguilar, all servants of my Lady the Vicequeen of the Indies.[10] And among other chapters of the said will there is one which runs literally as follows :—

RELACION

Hecha por Diego Mendez, de algunos acontecimientos del último viage del Almirante Don Cristóbal Colon.

DIEGO Mendez, vecino de la ciudad de Santo Domingo de la Isla Española, hallándose en la villa de Valladolid, donde á la sazon estaba la Corte de SS. MM., otorgó testamento en seis dias del mes de Junio del año de mil quinientos treinta y seis, por testimonio de Fernan Perez, escribano de SS. MM., y su notario público en la su Corte y en todos los sus Reinos y Señoríos ; siendo testigos al otorgamiento Diego de Arana, Juan Diez Miranda de la Cuadra, Martin de Orduña, Lucas Fernandez, Alonso de Angulo, Francísco de Hinojosa y Diego de Aguilar, todos criados de la Señora Vireina de las Indias.   Y entre otros capítulos del mencionado testamento hay uno que á la letra dice así.

10 Donna Maria de Toledo, widow of Diego Columbus.

Clause of the will, Item: The very illustrious gentlemen, the admiral Don Christopher Columbus, of glorious memory, and his son the admiral Don Diego Columbus, and his grandson the admiral Don Louis, (whom may God long preserve), and through them my Lady, the Vicequeen, as tutress and guardian of the latter, are in debt to me, for many and great services that I have rendered them, in as much as I have spent and worn out the best part of my life even to its close in their service; especially did I serve the admiral Don Christopher, going with his Lordship to the discovery of the islands and terra firma, and often putting myself in danger of death in order to save his life and the lives of those who were with him, more particularly when we were shut in at the mouth of the river Belen or Yebra, through the violence of the sea and the winds which drove up the sand, and raised such a mountain of it as to close up the entrance of the port. His Lordship being there greatly afflicted, a multitude of Indians collected together on shore to burn the ships, and kill us all, pretending that they were going to make war against other Indians of the province of Cabrara Aurira,

---

Cláusula del testamento. Item: Los muy ilustres Señores, el Almirante D. Cristobal Colon, de gloriosa memoria, y su hijo el Almirante D. Diego Colon, y su nieto el Almirante D. Luis, á quien Dios dé largos dias de vida, y por ellos la Vireina mi Señora, como su tutriz y curadora, me son en cargo de muchos y grandes servicios que yo les hice, en que consumí y gasté todo lo mejor de mi vida hasta acaballa en su servicio; especialmente serví al gran Almirante D. Cristóbal andando con su Señoria descubriendo Islas y Tierra firme, en que puse muchas veces mi persona á peligro de muerte por salvar su vida y de los que con él iban y estaban; mayormente cuando se nos cerró el puerto del rio de Belen ó Yebra donde estábamos con la fuerza de las tempestades de la mar y de los vientos que acarrearon y amontonaron la arena en cantidad con que cegaron la entrada del puerto. Y estando su Señoria allí muy congojado, juntóse gran multitud de Indios de la tierra para venir á quemarnos los navios y matarnos á todos, con color que decian que

with whom they were at enmity. Though many of them
passed by that port where our ships were lying, none of the
fleet took notice of the matter except myself, who went to
the admiral and said to him, "Sir, these people who have
passed by in order of battle, say that they go to unite themselves with the people of Veragua, to attack the people
of Cobrara Aurira: I do not believe it, but, on the contrary, I think that they are collected together to burn our
ships and kill all of us,"—as in fact was the case. The
admiral then asked me what were the best means of pre-
venting this, and I proposed to his Lordship that I should
go with a boat along the coast towards Veragua, to see where
the royal court sat. I had not proceeded on my errand half
a league when I found nearly a thousand men of war with
great stores of provisions of all kinds, and I went on shore
alone amongst them, leaving my boat at sea; I then spoke
with them, making them understand me as well as I could,
and offered to go with them to the battle with that armed
boat; but this they strongly refused, saying there was no
need of such a thing. After that I returned to the boat, and

---

iban á hacer guerra a otros Indios de las provincias de Cobrava
Aurira, con quien tenian guerra: y como pasaron muchos dellos
por aquel puerto en que teniamos nosotros las naos, ninguno de la
armada caia en el negocio sino yo, que fuí al Almirante y le dije:
"Señor, estas gentes que por aquí han pasado en orden de guerra
dicen que se han de juntar con los de Veragoa para ir contra los de
Cobrava Aurira: yo no lo creo sino el contrario, y es que se jun-
tan para quemarnos los navíos y matarnos á todos," como de hecho
lo era. Y diciéndome el Almirante cómo se remediaria, yo dije á
su Señoría que saldria con una barca é iria por la costa hácia Veragoa, para ver donde asentaban el real. Y no hube andado media
legua cuando halle al pie de mil hombres de guerra con muchas vituallas y brevages, y salté en tierra solo entre ellos, dejando mi
barca puesta en flota: y hablé con ellos segun pude entender, y
ofrecíme que queria ir con ellos á la guerra con aquella barca armada, y ellos se escusaron reciamente diciendo que no le habian

remained there in sight of them all that night, so that they could not go to the ships to burn or destroy them, according to their previous arrangements, without my seeing them, upon which they changed their plan, and on that same night they all returned to Veragua. I then went back to the ships, and related all this to his Lordship, who thought no little of what I had done, and upon his consulting me as to the best manner of proceeding so as clearly to ascertain what was the intention of the people, I offered to go to them with one single companion; and this task I undertook, though more certain of death than of life in the result.

After journeying along the beach up to the river of Veragua, I found two canoes of strange Indians, who related to me more in detail, that these people were indeed collected together to burn our ships and kill us all, and that they had forsaken their purpose in consequence of the boat which had come up to the spot, but that they intended to return after two days to make the attempt once more. I then asked them to carry me in their canoes to the upper part of the river, offering to remunerate them if they would do so; but they

---

menester : y como yo me volviese á la barca y estuviese allí á vista dellos toda la noche, vieron que no podian ir á las naos para quemallas y destruillas, segun tenian acordado, sin que yo lo viese, y mudaron propósito ; y aquella noche se volvieron todos á Veragoa, y yo me volví á las naos y hice relacion de todo á su Señoría, é no lo tuvo en poco. Y platicando conmigo sobrello sobre que manera se ternia para saber claramente el intento de aquella gente, yo me ofrecí de ir allá con un solo compañero, y lo puse por obra, yendo mas cierto de la muerte que de la vida : y habiendo caminado por la playa hasta el rio de Veragoa hallé dos canoas de Indios extrangeros que me contaron muy á la clara como aquellas gentes iban para quemar las naos y matarnos á todos, y que lo dejaron de hacer por la barca que allí sobrevino, y questaban todavia de propósito de volver á hacello dende á dos dias, é yo les rogué que me llevasen en sus canoas el rio arriba, y que gelo pagaria ; y ellos se escusaban aconsejándome que en ninguna manera excused themselves, and advised me by no means to go, for that both myself and my companion would certainly be killed. At length, in spite of their advice, I prevailed upon them to take me in their canoes to the upper part of the river, until I reached the villages of the Indians, whom I had found in order of battle. They, however, would not, at first, allow me to go to the principal residence of the cacique, till I pretended that I was come as a surgeon to cure him of a wound that he had in his leg; then, after making them some presents, they suffered me to proceed to the seat of royalty, which was situated on the top of a hillock, surmounted by a plain, with a large square surrounded by three hundred heads of the enemies he had slain in battle. When I had passed through the square, and reached the royal house, there was a great clamour of women and children at the gate, who ran into the palace screaming. Upon this, one of the chief's sons came out in a high passion, uttering angry words in his own language; and, laying hands upon me, with one push he thrust me far away from him. In order to appease him, I told him that I was come to cure the wound in

---

fuese, porque fuese cierto que en llegando me matarian á mí y al compañero que llevaba. E sin embargo de sus consejos hice que me llevasen en sus canaos el rio arriba hasta llegar á los pueblos de los Indios, los cuales hallé todos puestos en orden de guerra, que no me querian dejar ir al asiento principal del Cacique ; y yo fingiendo que le iba á curar como cirujano de una llaga que tenia en una pierna, y con dádivas que les dí me dejaron ir hasta el asiento Real, que estaba encima de un cerro llano con una plaza grande, rodeada de trescientas cabezas de muertos que habian ellos muerto en una batalla : y como yo hubiese pasado toda la plaza y llegado á la Casa Real hubo grande alboroto de mugeres y muchachos que estaban á la puerta, que entraron gritando dentro en el palacio. Y salió de él un hijo del Señor muy enojado diciendo palabras recias en su lenguage, é puso las manos en mí y de un empellon me desvió muy lejos de sí : diciéndole yo por amansarle como iba á curar á su padre de la pierna, y mostrándole cierto unguento que his father's leg, and showed him an ointment that I had brought for that purpose; but he replied, that on no account whatever should I go in to the place where his father was. When I saw that I had no chance of appeasing him in that way, I took out a comb, a pair of scissors, and a mirror, and caused Escobar, my companion, to comb my hair and then cut it off.   When the Indian, and those who were with him, saw this, they stood in astonishment; upon which I prevailed on him to suffer his own hair to be combed and cut by Escobar; I then made him a present of the scissors, with the comb and the mirror, and thus he became appeased.   After this, I begged him to allow some food to be brought, which was soon done, and we ate and drank in love and good fellowship, like very good friends. I then left him and returned to the ships, and related all this to my lord the Admiral, who was not a little pleased when he heard all these circumstances, and the things that had happened to me.   He ordered a large stock of provisions to be put into the ships, and into certain straw houses that we had built there, with a view that I should remain, with some of the men, to examine and ascertain the secrets of the country.   The next morning his lordship called me to ask my

---

para ello llevaba, dijo que en ninguna manera habia de entrar donde estaba su padre.   Y visto por mí que por aquella via no podia amansarle, saqué un peine y unas tijeras y un espejo, y hice que Escobar mi compañero me peinase y cortase el cabello.   Lo cual visto por él y por los que allí estaban quedaban espantados ; y yo entonces hice que Escobar le peinase á él y le cortase el cabello con las tijeras, y díselas y el peine y el espejo, y con esto se amansó ; y yo pedí que trajesen algo de comer, y luego lo trajeron, y comimos y bebimos en amor y compaña, y quedamos amigos ; y despedime dél y vine á las naos, y hice relacion de todo esto al Almirante mi Señor, el cual no poco holgó en saber todas estas circunstancias y cosas acaecidas por mi ; y mandó poner gran recabdo en las naos y en ciertas casas de paja, que teniamos hechas allí en la playa con intencion que habia yo de quedar allí con cierta gente para calar y saber los secretos de la tierra.

E E

advice as to what ought to be done : my opinion was that we
ought to seize that chief and all his captains; because, when
they were taken, great numbers of the people would submit.
His lordship was of the same opinion.   I then submitted the
stratagem and plan by which this might be accomplished; and
his lordship ordered that the Adelantado, his brother, and I,
accompanied by eighty men, should go to put it into execution.   We went, and our Lord gave us such good fortune,
that we took the cacique and most of his captains, his wives,
sons, and grandsons, with all the princes of his race; but in
sending them to the ships, thus captured, the cacique extri-
cated himself from the too slight grasp of the man who held
him, a circumstance which afterwards caused us much injury.
At this moment it pleased God to cause it to rain very heavily,
occasioning a great flood, by which the mouth of the harbour
was opened and the Admiral enabled to draw out the ships to
sea, in order to proceed to Spain; I, meanwhile, remaining
on land as Accountant of his Highness, with seventy men, and
the greater part of the provisions of biscuit, wine, oil, and
vinegar being left with me.

———

Otro dia de mañana su Señoría me llamó para tomar parecer conmigo de lo que sobre ello se debia hacer, y fue mi parecer que de-
biamos prender aquel Señor y todos sus Capitanes, porque presos
aquellos se sojuzgaria la gente menuda ; y su Señoria fue del mismo parecer : é yo di el ardid y la manera con que se debia hacer,
y su Señoría mandó que el Señor Adelantado, su hermano, y yo
con él fuesemos á poner en efecto lo sobredicho con ochenta hombres.
Y fuimos, y diónos Nuestro Señor tan buena dicha que prendimos
el Cacique y los mas de sus Capitanes y mugeres y hijos y nietos
con todos los principales de su generacion ; y enviándolos á las
naos ansí presos, soltóse el Cacique al que le llevaba por su mal
recabdo, el cual despues nos hizo mucho daño.   En este instante
plugó á Dios que llovió mucho, y con la gran avenida abriósenos
el puerto, y el Almirante sacó los navíos á la mar para venirse á
Castilla, quedando yo en tierra para haber de quedar en ella por
Contador de su Alteza con setenta hombres, y quedábame allí la

The Admiral had scarcely got to sea (while I stayed on shore with about twenty men, for the others had gone to assist the Admiral), when suddenly more than four hundred natives, armed with cross-bows and arrows, came down upon me, extending themselves along the face of the mountain; they then gave a shriek, then another, and another, and these repeated cries, by the goodness of God, gave me opportunity to prepare for the engagement. While I was on the shore among the huts which we had built, and they were collected on the mountain at about the distance of an arrow's flight, they began to shoot their arrows and hurl their darts, as if they had been attacking a bull. The arrows and cross-bow shots came down thick as hail, and some of the Indians then separated themselves from the rest, for the purpose of attacking us with clubs; none of them, however, returned, for with our swords we cut off their arms and legs, and killed them on the spot; upon which the rest took such fright, that they fled, after having killed in the contest seven out of twenty of our men; while, on their side, they lost nine or ten of those who advanced the most boldly towards us. This contest lasted three long

---

mayor parte de los mantenimientos de bizcocho y vino y aceite y vinagre.

Acabado de salir el Almirante á la mar, y quedando yo en tierra con obra de veinte hombres porque los otros se habian salido con el Almirante á despedir, subitamente sobrevino sobre mi mucha gente de la tierra, que serian mas de cuatrocientos hombres armados con sus varas y flechas y tiraderos, y tendiéronse por el monte en haz y dieron una grita y otra y luego otra, con las cuales plugo á Dios me apercibieron á la pelea y defensa de ellos : y estando yo en la playa entre los bohios que tenia hechos, y ellos en el monte á trecho de tiro de dardo, comenzaron á flechar y á garrochar como quien agarrocha toro, y eran las flechas y tiraderas tantas y tan continuas como granizo ; y algunos dellos se desmandaban para venirnos á dar con las machadasnas ; pero ninguno dellos volvian porque quedaban allí cortados brazos y piernas y muertos á espada : de lo cual cobraron tanto miedo que se retiraron atras, habiéndonos muerto siete hours, and our Lord gave us the victory in a marvellous manner, we being so few and they so numerous. After this fight was over, the captain, Diego Tristan, came with the boats from the ships to ascend the river, in order to take in water for the voyage; and, notwithstanding I advised and warned him not to go, he would not trust me, but, against my wish, went up the river with two boats and twelve men; upon which the natives attacked him, and killed him and all the men that he took with him, except one who escaped by swimming, and from whom we heard the news. The Indians then took the boats and broke them to pieces, which caused us great vexation; for the Admiral was at sea with his ships without boats, while we were on shore deprived of the means of going to him. Besides this, the Indians came continually to assail us; every instant playing trumpets and kettle-drums, and uttering loud cries in the belief that they had conquered us. The only means of defending ourselves against these people, were two very good brass falconets and plenty of powder and ball, with

---

hombres en la pelea de veinte que eramos, y de ellos murieron diez ó nueve de los que se venian á nosotros mas arriscados. Duró esta pelea tres horas grandes, y Nuestro Señor nos dió la vitoria milagrosamente, siendo nosotros tan poquitos y ellos tanta muchedumbre.

Acabada esta pelea vino de las naos el Capitan Diego Tristan con las barcas para subir el rio arriba á tomar agua para su viage; y no embargante que yo le aconsejé y amonesté que no subiese el rio arriba no me quiso creer, y contra mi grado subió con las dos barcas y doce hombres el rio arriba, donde le toparon aquella gente y pelearon con él, y le mataron á él y todos los que llevaba, que no escapó sino uno á nado que trujo la nueva; y tomaron las barcas y hiciéronlas pedazos, de que quedamos en gran fatiga, ansí el Almirante en la mar con sus naos sin barcas como nosotros en tierra sin tener con que poder ir á él. Y á todo esto no cesaban los Indios de venirnos á cometer cada rato tañiendo bocinas y atabales, y dando alaridos pensando que nos tenian vencidos. El remedio contra esta gente que teniamos eran dos tiros falconetes which we frightened them so that they did not dare approach us. This lasted for the space of four days, during which time I caused several bags to be made out of the sails of one of the vessels which we had remaining on shore, and into them I put all our biscuit. I then took two canoes, and secured them together with sticks across the tops, and, after loading them with the biscuit, the pipes of wine, and the oil and vinegar, I fastened them together with a rope, and had them towed along the sea while it was calm, so that in seven trips we contrived to get all of it to the ships, and the people were also carried over by few at a time. Meanwhile I remained with five men to the last, and at night I put to sea with the last boatful. The Admiral thought very highly of this conduct of mine, and did not content himself with embracing me and kissing me on the cheeks for having performed so great a service, but asked me take the captaincy of the ship *Capitana*, with the government of all the crew, and, in fact, of the entire voyage; which I accepted in order to oblige him, as it was a service of great responsibility.

---

de fruslera, muy buenos, y mucha pólvora y pelotas con que los ojeábamos que no osaban llegar á nosotros. Y esto duró por espacio de cuatro dias, en los cuales yo hice cosar muchos costales de las velas de una nao que nos quedaba, y en aquellos puse todo el bizcocho que teniamos, y tomé dos canoas y até la una con la otra parejas, con unos palos atravesados por encima, y en estos cargué el bizcocho todo en viages, y las pipas de vino y azeite y vinagre atadas en una guindaleja y á jorno por la mar, tirando por ellas las canoas, abonanzando la mar, en siete caminos que hicieron lo llevaron todo á las naos, y la gente que conmigo estaba poco á poco la llevaron, é yo quedé con cinco hombres á la postre siendo de noche, y en la postrera barcada me embarqué : lo cual el Almirante tuvo á mucho, y no se hartaba de me abrazar y besar en los carrillos por tan gran servicio como allí le hice, y me rogó tomase la capitanía de la nao Capitana y el regimiento de toda la gente y del viage, lo cual yo acepté por le hacer servicio en ello por ser, como era, cosa de gran trabajo.

On the last day of April, in the year fifteen hundred and three we left Veragua, with three ships, intending to make our passage homeward to Spain, but as the ships were all pierced and eaten by the teredo, we could not keep them above water; we abandoned one of them after we had proceeded thirty leagues; the two which remained were even in a worse condition than that,[11] so that all the hands were not sufficient with the use of pumps and kettles and pans to draw off the water that came through the holes made by the worms.   In this state with the utmost toil and danger we sailed for thirty-five days, thinking to reach Spain, and at the end of this time we arrived at the lowest point of the island of Cuba, at the province of Homo, where the city of Trinidad now stands, so that we were three hundred leagues further from Spain than when we left Veragua for the purpose of proceeding thither; and this, as I have said, with the vessels in very bad condition, unfit to encounter the sea, and our provisions nearly gone.   It pleased God that we were enabled to reach the island of Jamaica, where we drove the two ships on shore, and

---

Postrero de Abril de mil quinientos y tres partimos de Veragoa con tres navíos, pensando venir la vuelta de Castilla : y como los navíos estaban todos abujerados y comidos de gusanos no los podiamos tener sobre agua ; y andadas treinta leguas dejamos el uno, quedándonos otros dos peor acondicionados que aquel, que toda la gente no bastaba con las bombas y calderas y vasijas á sacar el agua que se nos entraba por los abujeros de la broma : y de esta manera, no sin grandísimo trabajo y peligro, pensando venir á Castilla navegamos treinta y cinco dias, y en cabo dellos llegamos á la isla de Cuba á lo mas bajo della, á la provincia de Homo, allá donde agora está el pueblo de la Trinidad ; de manera que estábamos mas lejos de Castilla trescientas leguas que cuando partimos de Veragoa para ir á ella ; y como digo los navíos mal acondicionados, innavegables, y las vituallas que se nos acababan.   Plugo á Dios Nuestro Señor que pudimos llegar á la isla de Jamaica, donde zabordamos

[11] Possibly the ship they abandoned was inferior in size, or in some other respect.

made of them two cabins thatched with straw, in which we took up our dwelling, not however without considerable danger from the natives, who were not yet subdued, and who might easily set fire to our habitation in the night, in spite of the greatest watchfulness. It was there that I gave out the last ration of biscuit and wine; I then took a sword in my hand, three men only accompanying me, and advanced into the island; for no one else dared go to seek food for the admiral and those who were with him. It pleased God that I found some people who were very gentle and did us no harm, but received us cheerfully, and gave us food with hearty good will. I then made a stipulation with the Indians who lived in a village called Aguacadiba, and with their cacique, that they should make cassava bread, and that they should hunt and fish to supply the admiral every day with a sufficient quantity of provisions, which they were to bring to the ships, where I promised there should be a person ready to pay them in blue beads, combs and knives, hawks-bells and fish-hooks, and other such articles which we had with us for that purpose. With this understanding I despatched one of the

---

los dos navíos en tierra, y hicimos de ellos dos casas pajizas, en que estabamos no sin gran peligro de la gente de aquella isla, que no estaba domada ni conquistada, nos pusiesen fuego de noche, que fácilmente lo podian hacer por mas que nosotros velabamos.

Aquí acabé de dar la postrera racion de bizcocho y vino, y tomé una espada en la mano y tres hombres conmigo, y fuíme por esa isla adelante, porque ninguno osaba ir á buscar de comer para el Almirante y los que con él estaban : y plugo á Dios que hallaba la gente tan mansa que no me hacian mal, antes se holgaban conmigo y me daban de comer de buena voluntad. Y en un pueblo que se llama Aguacadiba, concerté con los Indios y Cacique que harian pan cazabe, y que cazarian y pescarian, y que darian de todas las vituallas al Almirante cierta cuantía cada dia, y lo llevarian á las naos, con que estuviese allí persona que ge lo pagase en cuentas azules y peines y cuchillos y cascabeles y anzuelos y otros rescates que para ello llevabamos : y con este concierto despaché uno de los

Spaniards whom I had brought with me to the admiral, in order that he might send a person to pay for the provisions, and secure their being sent. From thence I went to another village, at three leagues distance from the former, and made a similar agreement with the natives and their cacique, and then despatched another Spaniard to the admiral, begging him to send another person with a similar object to this village. After this I went further on, and came to a great cacique named Huareo, living in a place which is now called Melilla, thirteen leagues from where the ships lay. I was very well received by him; he gave me plenty to eat, and ordered all his subjects to bring together in the course of three days a great quantity of provisions, which they did, and laid them before him, whereupon I paid him for them to his full satisfaction. I stipulated with him that they should furnish a constant supply, and engaged that there should be a person appointed to pay them; having made this arrangement I sent the other Spaniard to the admiral with the provisions they had given me, and then begged the cacique to allow me two Indians to go with me to the extremity of the island, one to

---

dos cristianos que conmigo traía al Almirante, para que enviase persona que tuviese cargo de pagar aquellas vituallas y enviarlas.

Y de allí fuí á otro pueblo que estaba tres leguas de este y hice el mismo concierto con el Cacique y Indios de él, y envié otro cristiano al Almirante para que enviase allí otra persona al mismo cargo.

Y de allí pasé adelante y llegué á un gran Cacique que se llamaba Huareo, donde agora dicen Melilla, que es trece leguas de las naos, del cual fuí muy bien recebido, que me dió muy bien de comer, y mandó que todos sus vasallos trajiesen dende á tres dias muchas vituallas, que le presentaron, é yo ge las pagué de manera que fueron contentos : y concerté que ordinariamente las traerian, habiendo allí persona que ge las pagase, y con este concierto envié el otro cristiano con los mantenimientos que allá me dieron al Almirante, y pedí al Cacique que me diese dos Indios que fuesen conmigo fasta el cabo de la isla, que el uno me llevaba la hamaca carry the hammock in which I slept, and the other carrying the food.

In this manner I journeyed eastward to the end of the island, and came to a cacique who was named Ameyro, with whom I entered into close friendship. I gave him my name and took his, which amongst these people is regarded as an evidence of brotherly attachment. I bought of him a very good canoe, and gave him in exchange an excellent brass helmet that I carried in a bag, a frock, and one of the two shirts that I had with me; I then put out to sea in this canoe, in search of the place that I had left, the cacique having given me six Indians to assist in guiding the canoe. When I reached the spot to which I had dispatched the provisions, I found there the Spaniards whom the admiral had sent, and I loaded them with the victuals that I had brought with me, and went myself to the admiral, who gave me a very cordial reception. He was not satisfied with seeing and embracing me, but asked me respecting everything that had occurred in the voyage, and offered up thanks to God for having delivered me in safety from so barbarous a people. The men rejoiced

---

en que dormia é el otro la comida. Y desta manera camine hasta el cabo de la isla, á la parte del Oriente, y llegué á un Cacique que se llamaba Ameyro, é hice con él amistades de hermandad, y díle mi nombre y tomé el suyo, que entre ellos se tiene por grande hermandad. Y compréle una canoa muy buena que él tenia, y díle por ella una bacineta de laton muy buena que llevaba en la manga y el sayo y una camisa de dos que llevaba, y embarquéme en aquella canoa, y vine por la mar requiriendo las estancias que habia dejado con séis Indios que el Cacique me dió para que me la ayudasen á navegar, y venido á los lugares donde yo habia proveido, hallé en ellos los cristianos que el Almirante habia enviado, y cargué de todas las vituallas que les hallé, y fuime al Almirante, del cual fuí muy bien recebido, que no se hartaba de verme y abrazarme, y preguntar lo que me habia sucedido en el viage, dando gracias á Dios que me habia llevado y traido á salvamiento libre de tanta gente salvage. Y como el tiempo que yo llegué á las naos no greatly at my arrival, for there was not a loaf left in the ships when I returned to them with the means of allaying their hunger; this, and every day after that, the Indians came to the ships loaded with provisions from the places where I had made the agreements; so that there was enough for the two hundred and thirty people who were with the admiral. Ten days after this, the admiral called me aside, and spoke to me of the great peril he was in, addressing me as follows :— " Diego Mendez, my son, not one of those whom I have here with me, has any idea of the great danger in which we stand, except myself and you; for we are but few in number, and these wild Indians are numerous and very fickle and capricious: and whenever they may take it into their heads to come and burn us in our two ships, which we have made into straw-thatched cabins, they may easily do so by setting fire to them on the land side, and so destroy us all. The arrangement that you have made with them for the supply of food, to which they agreed with such good-will, may soon prove disagreeable to them; and it would not be surprising if, on the morrow, they were not to bring us anything at all : in such case

---

habia en ellas un pan que comer, fueron todos muy alegres con mi venida, porque les maté la hambre en tiempo de tanta necesidad, y de allí adelante cada dia venian los Indios cargados de vituallas á las naos de aquellos lugares que yo habia concertado, que bastaban para doscientas y treinta personas que estaban con el Almirante. Dende á diez dias el Almirante me llamó á parte y me dijo el gran peligro en que estaba, deciéndome ansi : " Diego Mendez, hijo : ninguno de cuantos aquí yo tengo siente el gran peligro en que estamos sino yo y vos, porque somos muy poquitos, y estos indios salvages son muchos y muy mudables y antojadizos, y en la hora que se les antojare de venir y quemarnos aquí donde estamos en estos dos navioa hechos casas pajizas, fácilmente pueden echar fuego dende tierra y abrasarnos aquí á todos : y el concierto que vos habeis hecho con ellos del traer los mantenimientos que traen de tan buena gana, mañana se les antojará otra cosa y no nos traerán nada, y nosotros no somos parte para tomargelo por fuerza si no we are not in a position to take it by main force, but shall be compelled to accede to their terms. I have thought of a remedy, if you consider it advisable; which is, that some one should go out in the canoe that you have purchased, and make his way in it to Española, to purchase a vessel with which we may escape from the extremely dangerous position in which we now are. Tell me your opinion." To which I answered:—"My lord, I distinctly see the danger in which we stand, which is much greater than would be readily imagined. With respect to the passage from this island to Española in so small a vessel as a canoe, I look upon it not merely as difficult, but impossible; for I know not who would venture to encounter so terrific a danger as to cross a gulf of forty leagues of sea, and amongst islands where the sea is most impetuous, and scarcely ever at rest." His lordship did not agree with the opinion that I expressed, but adduced strong arguments to show that I was the person to undertake the enterprise. To which I replied:—"My lord, I have many times put my life in danger to save yours, and the lives of all those who are with you, and God has marvellously preserved me: in consequence of this, there have not been wanting murmur-

---

estar á lo que ellos quisieren. Yo he pensado un remedio si á vos os parece : que en esta canoa que comprastes se aventurase alguno á pasar á la Isla Española á comprar una nao en que pudiesen salir de tan gran peligro como este en que estamos. Decidme vuestro parecer." Yo le respondí : "Señor : el peligro en que estamos bien lo veo, que es muy mayor de lo que se puede pensar. El pasar desta Isla á la Isla Española en tan poca vasija como es la canoa, no solamente lo tengo por dificultoso, sino por imposible : porque haber de atravesar un golfo de cuarenta leguas de mar y entre islas donde la mar es mas impetuosa y de menos reposo, no sé quien se ose aventurar á peligro tan notorio. Su Señoría no me replicó, persuadiendome reciamente que yo era el que lo habia de hacer, á lo cual yo respondí : "Señor : muchas veces he puesto mi vida á peligro de muerte por salvar la vuestra y de todos estos que aqui estan, y nuestro Señor milagrosamente me ha guardado y ers who have said that your lordship entrusts every honourable undertaking to me, while there are others amongst them who would perform them as well as I. My opinion is, therefore, that your lordship would do well to summon all the men, and lay this business before them, to see if, amongst them all, there is one who will volunteer to undertake it, which I certainly doubt; and if all refuse, I will risk my life in your service, as I have done many times already."

On the following day his lordship caused all the men to appear together before him, and then opened the matter to them in the same manner as he had done to me. When they heard it they were all silent, until some said that it was out of the question to speak of such a thing; for it was impossible, in so small a craft, to cross a boisterous and perilous gulf of forty leagues' breadth, and to pass between those two islands, where very strong vessels had been lost in going to make discoveries, not being able to encounter the force and fury of the currents. I then arose, and said:—" My lord, I have but one life, and I am willing to hazard it in the service

---

la vida; y con todo no han faltado murmuradores que dicen que vuestra Señoría me acomete á mí todas las cosas de honra, habiendo en la compañía otros que las harian tan bien como yo : y por tanto paréceme á mí que vuestra Señoría los haga llamar á todos y los proponga este negocio, para ver si entre todos ellos habrá alguno que lo quiera emprender, lo cual yo dudo; y cuando todos se echen de fuera, yo pondré mi vida á muerte por vuestro servicio, como muchas veces lo he hecho.

Luego el dia siguiente su Señoría los hizo juntar á todos delante sí, y les propuso el negocio de la manera que á mí : é oido, todos enmudecieron, y algunos dijeron que era por demas platicarse en semejante cosa, porque era imposible en tan pequeña vasija pasar tan impetuoso y peligroso golfo de cuarenta leguas como este, entre estas dos islas donde muy recias naos se habian perdido andando á descubrir, sin poder romper ni forzar el ímpetu y furia de las corrientes. Entonces yo me levanté y dije : " Señor : una vida tengo no mas, yo la quiero aventurar por servicio de vuestra of your lordship, and for the welfare of all those who are here with us; for I trust in God, that in consideration of the motive which actuates me, he will give me deliverance, as he has already done on many other occasions." When the admiral heard my determination, he arose and embraced me, and, kissing me on the cheek, said,—"Well did I know that there was no one here but yourself, who would dare to undertake this enterprise: I trust in God, our Lord, that you will come out of it victoriously, as you have done in the others which you have undertaken." On the following day I drew my canoe on to the shore, fixed a false keel on it, and pitched and greased it; I then nailed some boards upon the poop and prow, to prevent the sea from coming in, as it was liable to do from the lowness of the gunwales; I also fixed a mast in it, set up a sail, and laid in the necessary provisions for myself, one Spaniard, and six Indians, making eight in all, which was as many as the canoe would hold. I then bade farewell to his lordship, and all the others, and proceeded along the coast of Jamaica, up to the extremity of the island,[12] which was

---

Señoría y por el bien de todos los que aquí estan, porque tengo esperanza en Dios nuestro Señor que vista la intencion con que yo lo hago me librará, como otras muchas veces lo ha hecho." Oida por el Almirante mi determinacion levantóse y abrazóme y besóme en el carrillo, diciendo: "Bien sabia yo que no habia aquí ninguno que osase tomar esta empresa sino vos: esperanza tengo en Dios nuestro Señor saldreis della con vitoria como de las otras que habeis emprendido."

El dia siguiente yo puse mi canoa á monte, y le eché una quilla postiza, y le dí su brea y sebo, y en la popa y proa clavéle algunas tablas para defensa de la mar que no se me entrase como hiciera siendo rasa; y púsele un mástil y su vela, y metí los mantenimientos que pude para mí y para un cristiano y para seis indios, que éramos ocho personas, y no cabian mas en la canoa: y despedíme de su Señoría y de todos, y fuime la costa arriba de la Isla de

[12] Ferdinand Columbus says that the Indians called this eastern point of the island Aramaquique, and that it was thirty-four leagues from Maima, where the admiral was.

thirty-five leagues from the point whence we started. Even this distance was not traversed without considerable toil and danger; for on the passage I was taken prisoner by some Indian pirates, from whom God delivered me in a marvellous manner. When we had reached the end of the island, and were remaining there in the hope of the sea becoming sufficiently calm to allow us to continue our voyage across it, many of the natives collected together with the determination of killing me, and seizing the canoe with its contents, and they cast lots for my life, to see which of them should carry their design into execution.

As soon as I became aware of their project, I betook myself secretly to my canoe, which I had left at three leagues distance from where I then was, and set sail for the spot where the admiral was staying, and reached it after an interval of fifteen days from my departure. I related to him all that had happened, and how God had miraculously rescued me from the hands of those savages. His lordship was very joyful at my arrival, and asked me if I would recommence my voyage; I replied that I would, if I might be allowed to take some men, to be with me at the extremity of the island

---

Jamaica, donde estábamos, que hay dende las naos hasta el cabo della treinta y cinco leguas, las cuales yo navegué con gran peligro y trabajo, porque fuí preso en el camino de Indios salteadores en la mar, de que Dios me libró milagrosamente. Y llegado al cabo de la isla, estando esperando que la mar se amansase para acometer mi viage, juntáronse muchos Indios y determinaron de matarme y tomar la canoa y lo que en ella llevaba; y así juntos jugaron mi vida á la pelota para ver á cual dellos cabria la ejecucion del negocio. Lo cual sentido por mí víneme ascondidamente á mi canoa, que tenia tres leguas de allí, y hícime á la vela y víneme donde estaba el Almirante, habiendo quince dias que de allí habia partido: y contele todo lo sucedido, y cómo Dios milagrosamente me habia librado de las manos de aquellos salvages. Su Señoría fue muy alegre de mi venida, y preguntóme si volveria al viage. Yo dije que sí, llevando gente que estuviese conmigo en el cabo de until I should find a fair opportunity of putting to sea to prosecute my voyage. The admiral gave me seventy men, and with them his brother the Adelantado, to stay with me until I put to sea, and to remain there for three days after my departure; with this arrangement I returned to the extremity of the island and waited there four days. Finding the sea become calm I parted from the rest of the men with much mutual sorrow; I then commended myself to God and our Lady of Antigua, and was at sea five days and four nights without laying down the oar from my hand, but continued steering the canoe while my companions rowed. It pleased God that at the end of five days I reached the island of Española at Cape San Miguel,[13] having been two days without eating or drinking, for our provisions were exhausted. I brought my canoe up to a very beautiful part of the coast, to which many of the natives soon came, and brought with them many articles of food, so that I remained there two days to take rest. I took six Indians from this place, and leaving those that I had brought with me, I put off to sea again, moving

---

la isla hasta que yo entrase en la mar á proseguir mi viage. Su Señoría me dió setenta hombres y con ellos á su hermano le Adelantado, que fuesen y estuviesen conmigo hasta embarcarme, y tres dias despues. Y desta manera volví al cabo de la isla donde estuve cuatro dias. Viendo que la mar se amansaba me despedí dellos y ellos de mí, con hartas lágrimas; y encomendéme á Dios y á nuestra Señora del Antigua, y navegué cinco dias y cuatro noches que jamas perdí el remo de la mano gobernando la canoa y los compañeros remando. Plugo á Dios nuestro Señor que en cabo de cinco dias yo arribé á la Isla Española, al Cabo de S. Miguel, habiendo dos dias que no comiamos ni bebiamos por no tenello; y entré con mi canoa en una ribera muy hermosa, donde luego vino mucha gente de la tierra y trajeron muchas cosas de comer, y estuve allí dos dias descansando. Yo tomé seis Indios de allí, dejados los

[13] This cape is since called Cape Tiburon. Mendez does not speak of his arrival at the little island of Naraza, and other places spoken of by Ferdinand Columbus and Herrera.

along the coast of Española, for it was a hundred and thirty leagues from the spot where I landed to the city of St. Domingo, where the Governor dwelt, who was the commander of Lares.   When I had proceeded eighty leagues along the coast of the island (not without great toil and danger, for that part of the island was not yet brought into subjugation), I reached the province of Azoa, which is twenty-four leagues from San Domingo, and there I learned from the commander Gallego, that the governor was gone out to subdue the province of Xuragoa, which was at fifty leagues distance. When I heard this I left my canoe and took the road for Xuragoa,[14] where I found the governor, who kept me with him seven months, until he had burned and hanged eighty-four caciques, lords of vassals, and with them Nacaona, the sovereign mistress of the island, to whom all rendered service and obedience.   When that expedition was finished I went on foot to San Domingo, a distance of seventy leagues, and waited in expectation of the arrival of ships from Spain, it being now more than a year since any had come.   In this interval it

---

que llevaba, y comencé á navegar por la costa de la Isla Española, que hay dende allí hasta la Cibdad de Santo Domingo ciento y treinta leguas que yo habia de andar, porque estaba allí el Gobernador, que era el Comendador de Lares ; y habiendo andado por la costa de la isla ochenta leguas, no sin grandes peligros y trabajos, porque la isla no estaba conquistada ni allanada, llegué á la Provincia de Azoa, que es veinte y cuatro leguas antes de Santo Domingo, y allí supe del Comendador Gallego como el Gobernador era partido á la Provincia de Xuragoa á allanarla ; la cual estaba cincuenta leguas de allí.   Y esto sabido dejé mi canoa y tomé el camino por tierra de Xuragoa, donde hallé el Gobernador, el cual me detuvo allí siete meses hasta que hizo quemar y ahorcar ochenta y cuatro Caciques, señores de vasallos, ycon ellos á Nacaona la mayor señora de la isla, á quien todos ellos obedecian y servian. Y esto acabado vine de pie á tierra de Santo Domingo, que era setenta leguas de allí, y estuve esperando que viniesen naos de

[14] This should be Xaragua.

pleased God that three ships arrived, one of which I bought, and loaded it with provisions, bread, wine, meat, hogs, sheep, and fruit, and despatched it to the place where the admiral was staying, in order that he might come over in it with all his people to San Domingo, and from thence sail for Spain. I myself went on in advance with the two other ships, in order to give an account to the king and queen of all that had occurred in this voyage.

I think I should now do well to say somewhat of the events which occurred to the admiral and to his family during the year that they were left on the island. A few days after my departure the Indians became refractory, and refused to bring food as they had hitherto done; the admiral therefore caused all the caciques to be summoned, and expressed to them his surprise that they should not send food as they were wont to do, knowing as they did, and as he had already told them, that he had come there by the command of God. He said that he perceived that God was angry with them, and that He would that very night give tokens of His displeasure by signs that He would cause to appear in the

---

Castilla, que habia mas de un año que no habian venido. Y en este comedio plugo á Dios que vinieron tres naos, de las cuales yo compré la una y la cargué de vituallas, de pan y vino y carne y puercos y carneros y frutas, y la envié adonde estaba el Almirante para en que viniesen él y toda la gente como vinieron allí á Santo Domingo y de allí á Castilla E yo me vine delante en las otras dos naos á hacer relacion al Rey y á la Reina de todo lo sucedido en aquel viage.

Pareceme que será bien que se diga algo de lo acaecido al Almirante y á su familiar en un año que estuvieron perdidos en aquesta isla : y es que dende á pocos dias que yo me partí los Indios se amotinaron y no le querian traer de comer como antes ; y él los hizo llamar á todos los Caciques y les digo que se maravillaba dellos en no traerle la comida como solian, sabiendo como él les habia dicho, que habia venido allí por mandado de Dios,y que Dios estaba enojado dellos, y que él ge lo mostraria aquella noche por heavens; and as on that night there was to be an almost total eclipse of the moon, he told them that God caused that appearance, to signify His anger against them for not bringing the food. The Indians, believing him, were very frightened, and promised that they would always bring him food in future; and so in fact they did, until the arrival of the ship which I had sent loaded with provisions. The Admiral, and those who were with him, felt no small joy at the arrival of this ship; and his lordship afterwards informed me in Spain, that in no part of his life did he ever experience so joyful a day, for he had never hoped to have left that place alive: and in that same ship he set sail,[15] and went to San Domingo, and thence to Spain.

I have wished thus to give a succinct account of my troubles, and of my great and important services; which are such as no man in the world ever rendered to a master, or ever will again; and I do so in order that my sons may know these facts, and be encouraged to serve faithfully, and that, at the same time, his lordship may see that he is bound to make them a handsome return for such services. When his lord-

---

señales que haria en el cielo; y como aquella noche era el eclipse de la luna que casi toda se escureció, díjoles que Dios hacia aquello por enojo que tenia dellos porque no le traian de comer, y ellos lo creyeron y fueron muy espantados, y prometieron que le traerian siempre de comer, como de hecho lo hicieron, hasta que llegó la nao con los mantenimientos que yo envié, de que no pequeño gozo fue en el Almirante y en todos los que con él estaban: que despues en Castilla me dijo su Señoría que en toda su vida [nunca?] habia visto tan alegre dia, y que nunca pensó salir de allí vivo: y en esta nao se embarcó y vino á Santo Domingo y de alli á Castilla.

He querido poner aqui esta breve suma de mis trabajos y grandes y señalados servicios, cuales nunca hizo hombre á Señor, ni los hará de aquí adelante del mundo; y esto á fin que mis hijos lo

[15] On the twenty-eighth of June 1504; he entered the harbour of St. Domingo on the thirteenth of August, started for Spain on the twelfth of September, and arrived at San Lucar on Thursday, the seventh of November.

ship came to the court, and while he was at Salamanca, confined to his bed with the gout, and I was left in sole charge of his affairs, endeavouring to obtain the restitution of his estate and government for his son Diego, I addressed him thus: "My lord, your lordship knows how much I have done in your service, and what trouble I am still taking, night and day, in the management of your affairs; I beseech your lordship to grant me some recompense for what I have done." He cheerfully replied that he would do for me whatever I asked, adding, that there was very great reason for his so doing. I then specified my wish, and begged his lordship to do me the favour to grant me the office of principal Alguazil of the island of Española for life; to which his lordship assented most cordially, saying, that it was but a trifling remuneration for the great services I had rendered. He also desired me to communicate his wish to his son Diego, who was very glad to hear of the favour his father had shown me in appointing me to the said office; and said, that if his father gave it me with one hand, he, for his part, gave it me with both hands. This promise

---

sepan y se animen á servir, é su Señoria sepa que es obligado á hacerles muchas mercedes.

Venido su Señoría á la Corte, y estando en Salamanca en la cama enfermo de gota, andando yo solo entendiendo en sus negocios y en la restitucion de su estado y de la gobernacion para su hijo D. Diego, yo le dije ansi: "Señor: ya vuestra Señoría sabe lo mucho que os he servido y lo mas que trabajo de noche y de dia en vuestros negocios: suplico á vuestra Señoría me señale algun galardon para en pago dello": y él me respondió alegremente que yo lo señalase y él lo cumpliria, porque era mucha razon. Y entonces yo le señalé y suplique á su Señoría me hiciese merced del oficio del Alguacilazgo mayor de la Isla Española para en toda mi vida: y su Señoría dijo que de muy buena voluntad, y que era poco para lo mucho que yo habia servido; y mandóme que lo dijese ansi al Sr. D. Diego, su hijo, el cual fue muy alegre de la merced á mí hecha de dicho oficio, y dijo que si su padre me lo daba con una mano, él con dos. Y esto es ansi la verdad para el siglo que á ellos tiene y á mi espera.

holds good as much now as it did then; but when, after I had succeeded, with considerable difficulty, in securing the restitution of the government of the Indies to my lord the Admiral Don Diego, (his father being then dead), I asked him for the provision of the said office, his lordship replied that he had given it to his uncle, the Adelantado, saying, however, that he would give me another post equivalent to it. I told him that he ought to make such a proposition to his uncle, and that he ought to give me that which his father, and he himself, had promised to me. But he did not do so; and thus I remained without any recompense for all my services: while my lord, the Adelantado, without having rendered any service at all, continued in the enjoyment of the dignity which belonged to me, and reaped the reward of all my exertions.

When his lordship arrived at the city of San Domingo, he assumed the reins as governor, and gave the post which he had promised to me, to Francisco de Garay, a servant of the Adelantado, to hold it for him. This took place on the tenth day of July of the year fifteen hundred and ten, and the office was then worth at least a million per annum. My lady, the Vicequeen, as tutress and guardian of my lord the

---

Habiendo yo acabado, no sin grandes trabajos mios, de negociar la restitucion de la gobernacion de las Indias al Almirante D. Diego, mi Señor, siendo su padre fallecido, le pedí la provision del dicho oficio. Su Señoria me respondió que lo tenia dado al Adelantado su tio; pero que él me daria otra cosa equivalente á aquella. Yo dije que aquella diese él á su tio, y á mi me diese lo que su padre y él me habian prometido, lo cual no se hizo; y yo quedé cargado de servicios sin ningun galardon, y el Sr. Adelantado, sin haberlo servido, quedó con mi oficio y con el galardon de todos mis afanes.

Llegado su Señoría á la Cibdad de Santo Domingo por Gobernador tomó las varas y dió este oficio á Francisco de Garay, criado del Sr. Adelantado, que lo sirviese por él. Esto fue en diez dias del mes de Julio de mil quinientos diez años. Valia entonces el oficio á lo menos un cuento de renta, del cual la Vireina, mi Se-

viceroy, and my lord the viceroy himself, are really charge-
able to me for this loss, and are debtors to me for it in justice
and on the score of conscience. The post had been given to
me by way of recompense, and nothing has been done in my
favour towards the accomplishment of the Admiral's promise,
since the day in which it was given, to this, the close of my
life; if it had been given to me, I should have been the richest
and most honoured man in the island; whereas, I am now the
poorest, and have not even a house of my own to live in, but
am obliged to pay rent for the roof over my head. As it would
be very difficult to refund the revenues which this office has
produced, I will suggest an alternative, which is this: that
his lordship grant the rank of principal Alguazil of the city
of San Domingo, to one of my sons, for his life, and bestow
upon the other the rank of Vice-Admiral in the same city:
by the grant of these two offices to my sons in the manner I
have said, and by appointing some one to hold them on their
behalf until they come of age, his lordship will discharge the
conscience of the Admiral his father, and I shall hold myself
satisfied, as duly paid for my services. I shall say nothing

ñora, como tutriz y curadora del Virey, mi Señor y él me son en
cargo realmente y me lo deben de justicia y de foro conscientiæ,
porque me fue hecha la merced de él, y no se cumplió conmigo
dende el dia que se dió al Adelantado hasta el postrero de mis dias,
porque si se me diera yo fuera el mas rico hombre de la isla y mas
honrado; y por no se me dar soy el mas pobre della, tanto que no
tengo una casa en que more sin alquiler.

Y porque haberseme de pagar lo que el oficio ha rentado seria
muy dificultoso, yo quiero dar un medio y será este: que su Señoría haga merced del Alguacilazgo mayor de la Cibdad de Santo
Domingo á uno de mis hijos para en toda su vida, y al otro le haga
merced de su Teniente de Almirante en la dicha Cibdad: y con
hacer merced destos dos oficios á mis hijos de la manera que he
aquí dicho, y poniéndolos en cabeza de quien los serva por ellos
hasta que sean de edad, su Señoría descargará la conciencia del
Almirante su padre, y yo me satisfaré de la paga que se me debe

further upon the subject, but leave it to the consciences of their lordships, and let them do whatever they think proper.

Item.   I leave as executors and administrators of my will here at the court, the bachelor Estrada and Diego de Arana, together with my lady the Vicequeen; and I beg his lordship to undertake this charge, and to direct the others to undertake it likewise.

Another clause.   Item.   I order that my executors purchase a large stone, the best that they can find, and place it upon my grave, and that they write round the edge of it these words: " Here lies the honourable Chevalier Diego Mendez, who rendered great services to the royal crown of Spain, in the discovery and conquest of the Indies, in company with the discoverer of them, the Admiral Don Christopher Columbus, of glorious memory, and afterwards rendered other great services by himself, with his own ships, and at his own cost.   He died, etc.   He asks of your charity a Paternoster and an Ave Maria."

Item.   In the middle of the said stone let there be the representation of a canoe, which is a hollowed tree, such as the

---

de mis servicios ; y en esto no diré mas de dejallo en sus conciencias de sus Señorías, y hagan en ello lo que mejor les pareciere.

Item : Dejo por mis albaceas y ejecutores deste mi testamento, aquí en la corte, al Bachiller Estrada y á Diego de Arana, juntamente con la Vireina, mi Señora, y suplico yo á su Señoría lo acepte y les mande á ellos lo mismo.

Otra cláusula.   Item : Mando que mis albaceas compren una piedra grande, la mejor que hallaren, y se ponga sobre mi sepultura, y se escriba en derredor della estas letras : " Aquí yace el honrado caballero Diego Mendez que sirvió mucho á la Corona Real de España en el descubrimiento y conquista de las Indias con el Almirante D. Cristobal Colon, de gloriosa memoria, que las descubrió, y despues por sí con naos suyas á su costa : falleció, &c.   Pido de limosna un Pater noster y una Ave María.

Item : En medio de la dicha piedra se haga una canoa, que es un madero cavado en que los Indios navegan, porque en otra tal

Indians use for navigation; for in such a vessel did I cross three hundred leagues of sea; and let them engrave above it this word : " Canoe."

My dear and beloved sons, children of my very dear and beloved wife Doña Francisca de Ribera,—may the blessing of God Almighty, Father, Son, and Holy Ghost, descend upon you, together with my blessing, and protect you, and make you Catholic Christians, and give you grace always to love and fear Him. I earnestly recommend you to cultivate peace and concord amongst yourselves, and that you be meek, and not haughty, but, on the contrary, be very humble and courteous towards those with whom you have to do, so that all may love you. Serve loyally my lord the Admiral, and may his lordship grant you large recompense, considering who he is himself, and by what great services I have deserved his favours. Above all I charge you, my sons, to be very pious, and to attend devoutly to your religious duties, and in so doing, may the Lord grant you long life. May it please Him of His infinite goodness, to make you as good as I wish you to be, and guide you always with His hand. Amen.

---

navegó trescientas leguas, y encima pongan unas letras que digan : " Canoa."

Caros y amados hijos mios, y de mi muy cara y amada muger Doña Francisca de Ribera, la bendicion de Dios Todopoderoso, Padre y Hijo y Espíritu Santo y la mia descienda sobre vos y vos cubra y os haga catolicos cristianos, y os dé gracia que siempre le ameis y temais. Hijos : encomiendoos mucho la paz y concordia, y que seais muy conformes y no soberbios, sino muy humildes y muy amigables á todos los que contratáredes, porque todos os tengan amor : servid lealmente al Almirante mi Señor, y su Señoría os hará muchas mercedes por quien él es, y porque mis grandes servicios lo merecen ; y sobre todo os mando, hijos mios, seais muy devotos y oyais muy devotamente los Oficios Divinos, y haciéndolo ansi Dios nuestro Señor os dará largos dias de vida. A él plega por su infinita bondad haceros tan buenos como yo deseo que seais, y os tenga siempre de su mano. Amen.

The books which I send you are as follows :

The Art of Well-living, by Erasmus ; a *Sermon*, of Erasmus, in Spanish ; *Josephus de Bello Judaico* ; the *Moral Philosophy*, of Aristotle ; the books called *Lingua Erasmi* ; the book of *The Holy Land* ; *The conversations of Erasmus* ; *A treatise on the Complaints of Peace* ; *A book of Contemplation of the Passion of our Redeemer* ; *A treatise on the Revenging of the Death of Agamemnon* ; and other small tracts.

I have already told you, my sons, that I leave you these books under the conditions described above in my will, and I wish them to be put together with my other documents, which will be found in the cedar box, at Seville, as I have already said ; I wish also the marble mortar should be placed in it, which is now in the possession of Don Ferdinand, or of his major-domo.

I, Diego Mendez, affirm that this document, contained in thirteen sheets, is my last will and testament, for I have dictated it and caused it to be written, and have signed it with my name ; and by it I revoke and annul any other

---

Los libros que de acá os envio son los siguientes :

Arte de bien morir de Erasmo. Un sermon de Erasmo en romance. Josefo de Bello Judaico. La Filosofía moral de Aristóteles. Los libros que se dicen Lingua Erasmi. El libro de la Tierra santa. Los coloquios de Erasmo. Un tratado de las querellas de la Paz. Un libro de Contemplaciones de la Pasion de nuestro Redentor. Un tratado de la venganza de la muerte de Agamemnon, y otros tratadillos.

Ya dije, hijos mios, que estos libros os dejo por mayorazgo, con las condiciones que estan dichas de suso en el testamento, y quiero que vayan todos con algunas Escrituras mias, que se hallarán en el arca que está en Sevilla, que es de cedro, como ya está dicho : pongan tambien en esta el mortero de mármol que está en poder del Sr. D. Hernando, ó de su mayordomo.

Digo yo Diego Mendez que esta Escritura contenida en trece hojas es mi testamento y postrimera voluntad, porque yo lo ordené é hice escribir, y lo firmé de mi nombre, y por él revoco y doy por will or wills whatever made by me at any other time or place, and I desire that this only be considered valid. Made in the city of Valladolid, the nineteenth day of June, in the year of our Redeemer one thousand five hundred and thirty-six.— DIEGO MENDEZ. And I, the said Garcia de Vera, scrivener and notary public, was present at all which has been herein said; and it has all been set down by me by order of the said lord-lieutenant, and by request of the said Bachelor Estrada, forming the testament in these twenty-six leaves of folio paper, as is here seen. I caused it to be written as it was presented and laid before me, and have kept the original in my possession. And to this effect I have here placed this my seal *(here was placed the seal)*, in testimony of the truth.— *(Signed)* GARCIA DE VERA.

This agrees literally with the clauses copied from a will sealed and signed by the said scrivener, Garcia de Vera, the original of which is in the archives of the most excellent the Admiral Duke of Veraguas, from which I copied it in Madrid on the twenty-eighth day of March, in the year eighteen hundred and twenty-five.—Tomas Gonzalez.

ningunos otros cualesquier testamentos hechos en cualesquier otros tiempos ó lugar ; y solo este quiero que valga, que es hecho en la villa de Valladolid en diez y nueve dias del mes de Junio, año de nuestro Redentor de mil quinientos treinta y seis años. Diego Mendez. E yo el dicho García de Vera, Escribano Notario público, presente fui á todo lo que dicho es, que de mi se hace mencion, é por mandado del dicho Sr. Teniente é pedimento del dicho Bachiller Estrada, este testamento en estas veinte é seis hojas de papel, pliego entero, como aquí parece, fice escrebir como ante mí se presentó é abrió, é ansi queda originalmente en mi poder. E por ende fice aquí este mi signo tal en *(está signado)* testimonio de verdad. García de Vera. *(Está firmado.)*

Concuerda literalmente con las cláusulas copiadas de un testimonio signado y firmado por el expresado Escribano García de Vera, que obra originalmente en el Archivo del Excmo. Sr. Almirante Duque de Veraguas, de donde lo copié en Madrid á veinte y cinco dias del mes de Marzo de mil ochocientos veinte y cinco años. — Tomas Gonzalez.

Note.—*The other clauses of this will of Diego Mendez, refer to his funeral arrangements, and the declaration of debts, due both to him and by him, in Spain and in the island of Hispaniola, as well as other matters purely personal, and relating to his family ; but they bear no reference or allusion to the Admiral Columbus, or to his voyages and discoveries, and therefore have not been copied.*

FINIS.

INDEX.

www.ingramcontent.com/pod-product-compliance
Lightning Source LLC
Chambersburg PA
CBHW062034090426
42740CB00016B/2901